Management on Wall Street:
Making Securities Firms Work

Management on Wall Street:
Making Securities Firms Work

By
Stephen P. Rappaport

DOW JONES-IRWIN
Homewood, Illinois 60430

Certain information contained in this volume is based on data and sources believed to be reliable. However, such information has not been verified by the publisher or the author, and they do not make any representations as to its accuracy or completeness. Any statements nonfactual in nature constitute only current opinions, which are subject to change without notice. The opinions expressed herein do not necessarily represent those of any institution with which the author has been, is now, or will be affiliated, nor do they represent the views of any firm or individual named in this book. The examples used herein are hypothetical, employed for illustrative purposes only, and do not represent the views, activities, or organizational arrangements of any particular firm, division, or department or any employee or former or prospective one. Any similarity discerned is a matter of coincidence. Neither the publisher nor the author is responsible for errors or omissions in this book or for actions taken based on information provided herein. In addition, neither the publisher nor the author is engaged in rendering investment, tax, legal, accounting, management, or other advice. If such advice is sought, firms, individuals, and others should obtain the services of their own competent professional.

Acquisitions editor: Richard A. Luecke
Project editor: Jane Lightell
Production manager: Stephen K. Emry
Jacket Designer: Mark Swimmer
Compositor: Caliber Design Planning, Inc.
Typeface: 11/13 Century Schoolbook
Printer: Arcata Graphics/Kingsport

ISBN 1-55623-031-1

Library of Congress Catalog Card No. 87–72841

Printed in the United States of America

1 2 3 4 5 6 7 8 9 0 K 5 4 3 2 1 0 9 8

To my father, Dr. Bernard Francis Rappaport, for, among other things, teaching me to read, reason, reflect, and write, fortunately, in that order.

ACKNOWLEDGMENTS

More than anyone else, professionals with whom authors work daily and others with whom they interact, exert a tremendous, though unusually unrecognized, impact on them. This volume is no exception, but time and space do not allow one to mention all who have had some hand, however ephemeral, in this process.

Nevertheless, it is important to recognize those who have provided unfailing encouragement and support for this and other related projects. These individuals include: Edward I. O'Brien, President, Securities Industry Association; George Ball, James Barton, James Gahan, Peter Costiglio, Thomas Monti, and Richard Poirier, all of Prudential-Bache Securities Inc.; Demetrios Caraley and Charles Hamilton of Columbia University; Richard West, Robert Lamb, and Robert Kuhn of the New York University Graduate School of Business Administration; William Sharwell, George Parks, Clarke Johnson, Verne Atwater, George Matson, and Kenneth Halcott of the Lubin Graduate School of Business, Pace University. While none of these professionals, their institutions, or any others bear responsibility for the material and opinions expressed herein, their continuing countenance in this effort has been particularly gratifying and is appreciated.

Stephen P. Rappaport
January 1, 1988

CONTENTS

Smorgasbord. Assets Under Management: A Special
Case. Product Differentiation to Match Market
Segmentation. The Account Executive as Product
Exhibitor. Marketing Beyond the Firm's Confines.
Marketing Financial Products: The First Customer
Is the Employee. The Product Management
Structure. Managerial Hotlines. The Product
Delivery Systems of Tomorrow. Notes.

The Meaning of Success. The Underwriting
Rankings. Developing an Investment Banking
Department. Banking at Midsize Firms. Preventing
Client Base Deterioration. Quality Professionals and
Management. Notes.

The New Issue Business in Perspective. Some Major
Product Areas. The Institutional Sales Manager as
Catalyst for Action. Structural Reporting
Relationships. Account Management.

The Research Menu. The Point of It All. The
External Audience. The Internal Audience. The
Problem of Access. All Things to All People?

The Numbers Game. The Analytical Perspective.
The Capital Crunch. Risk Management: Problems of
Employing the Firm's Capital. Management
Concerns in Risk Management. Risk Management
at a Minimum. Notes.

From a Profit Center to Firmwide Accounting
Mentality. Illusory Revenues and Expenses.
Management's Explanation. Contemporary
Accounting-related Issues.

Life on the Mainframe: It Began with Operations.
Where Did They Go from Here? From Mainframes
to Micros: On-line Information for Account
Executives. The Next Wave: Investment Analysis.
Technology-inspired Management Concerns. The
Computer Management Structure. The
Internationalization of the Securities Markets.
Notes.

The Gatekeepers and Motivation. The "We're Going
to Win" Philosophy. Some Answers to Motivation
Issues. Motivation and Compensation. Motivating
the Motivated. Notes.

Markets. The Products Division and Support Areas.
Management and Reorganization.

Analysts, Summer Associates, and Associates. The
Three Jobs and Their Purposes. The Requisite
Capabilities of an Investment Banker. The Levels of
Development. The Investment Banking Training
Programs.

Stability of Personnel. Expanding and Contracting
Firm Operations. Setting Goals and Objectives. The
Bottom Line: Small Business Unit Management.
Horizontal and Vertical Integration. Insider
Trading. Tomorrow's Manager. Notes.

Where Are We Now? Why Has This Occurred? The
Pragmatic Issues. The Conceptual Issues. What Will

the Foreseeable Future Bring? The Securities
Industry at the Crossroads. Notes.

CHAPTER 1

INTRODUCTION: SECURITIES FIRMS AS ORGANIZATIONS

THE SECURITIES FIRM IN THE CORPORATE ARENA

By any measure, securities firms are markedly different from the modern corporation. In terms of what they do, how they do it, and the nature of the management challenges they face, securities firms are unique among both industrial and service-based companies. They are also in one of the important lanes of U.S. economic life: the broad-based financial services industry.

Unfortunately, management scholars have paid little attention to this industry; instead, they have focused their research predominantly on manufacturing companies. Although some studies have included service-oriented businesses, few have focused totally on the management of financial services firms. Indeed, there has been no comprehensive review of securities firm management to date. Consequently, management theories, practices, and principles derived from other corporate sectors have been grafted onto the business of running securities organizations, whether or not they fit. Coming from "incompatible donors," many of these grafted applications have failed to take hold.

Business is business, and securities firms naturally share many forms and practices with other corporations, for example, the types of organizational structures through which their operations are managed. Like many corporations, securities firms have divisions, departments, profit centers, product development areas, salespeople, distribution outlets, and research departments. Managers become involved in planning and budgeting, they set goals and objectives, and senior officers engage in strategic decision making. However, apart from these most basic characteristics, securities firms of today depart from other corporations.

Simply stated, securities firms provide securities products and services of all types to all kinds of customers. They also trade, originate, and underwrite them against a backdrop of different and rapidly changing financial markets. These tasks confront managers with an unusual set of challenges. Securities firms differ from their corporate counterparts in strategy and structure; even more importantly, they diverge dramatically in substance and style. Not surprisingly, then, management's response to the problems and potential of securities firms cannot be cloned from the textbooks that guided managers of other industries. Rather, they must be tailor-made to what is, and is likely to remain, the world of Wall Street. A brief comparison of the attributes of most corporations to those of securities firms should be sufficient to make this point.

Most corporations are involved in some way with the product process; they develop, manufacture, and sell their own creations. Securities firms, however, sell products of their own, products of their competitors, and even products of their own clients. In fact, many securities firms also market identical products. Moreover, the prices of products made by most corporations are fixed and do not move without the approval of the seller, but the prices of the securities products fluctuate with changes in the securities markets, over which the participants have no control.

From a marketing standpoint, tangible products and certain services provided by more typical corporations are easily identifiable. In these instances, the customer's tastes can be measured through studies of past buying patterns. Customer response to quality, price, and other product-related characteristics can be quantified to some extent. Feedback from customers is easily garnered, and competing products of other firms can be compared. Yet, it is most difficult for marketing analysts to measure with any real accuracy the reasons for the purchase or rejection of the myriad of products sold by securities firms.

Characteristics of securities products are not easily compared, and receiving adequate feedback about specific securities for marketing analytical purposes is difficult. It is simply not common practice to survey clients about why they did or did not buy a stock or a bond. In the product delivery area, most corporations can somewhat easily target a particular market and segment it in terms of a buyer/product matrix, but most securities products do not necessarily fit within defined customer markets. Indeed, the firms could sell the vast majority of their securities to any individual or institution presently in the market.

Once the products of most corporations are purchased, little can change the direction of the transaction—it goes from seller to buyer—except when some product deficiency or service failure occurs. Also, in this traditional product sales process, usually only a very small percentage of a customer's assets are used to purchase any given product. Securities firm customers not only purchase the firm's products, but also they can, and do, sell them back to the firm, sometimes very shortly after purchasing them; they often trade them for other similar products. In many cases, customers may purchase securities with all the money they have. Furthermore, the products of most corporations are sold by many distributors; service is important here, but the identifiable and tangible products can often speak for themselves. At a securities firm, personnel, more than anything else, are responsible for product sales. Client relationships to the firm's sales force are vital. In short, the less tangible the product, the more important is this human element.

A strikingly unusual aspect of the securities industry is the way employees and managers view career advancement. On this point, migrants from manufacturing companies to Wall Street would think they had come to an alien planet. In most corporations, employees and managers generally perceive, realistically or not, a career path to the higher levels of the organization. They believe that their opportunities for promotion are based on some mix of the quality and quantity of their work, and that as they successfully move up the corporate ladder, they learn more about the firm's operations under their jurisdiction. The successful accumulation of this knowledge is translated into expertise that provides the thrust, and in part the reason, for their corporate climb. This entire process is an important part of on-line management training in most corporations.

The vast majority of securities firm employees, however, do not perceive that they could have, or even should have, a career path carrying them to the upper reaches of the firm. More importantly, most do not want it, and some clearly shun opportunities in securities firm management. At best, desire for and ability to move up the securities firm corporate ladder end with the management of an individual's specialized area, so that the finale of management training is often the time when professionals become experts and overseers of their small business units. Also, the high degree of job specialization that typifies securities firms in many cases limits the ability of senior managers to be totally knowledgeable about every complex area under their jurisdiction.

Finally, in most modern corporations, professional ascendancy goes hand in hand with increased remuneration; managers and professionals earn more as they move up in the corporate hierarchy. In securities firms, however, this custom is regularly turned on its head. Managers may earn far less than some employees under their supervision; increased compensation is often unrelated to the individual's position in the organization.

From a larger perspective, the organizational units of most corporations are usually very much dependent on one another to complete the whole product cycle that runs from product design to product sales. In securities firms, however, not all organizational units are truly dependent on one another. Even where interdependence is a fact, many employees see themselves and their departments as semiautonomous and independent profit centers, whether realistically or not.

Perhaps what sets the modern securities firm apart from other corporations is that the securities market greatly impacts securities firms, their professionals, their products and services, and their profitability. The market prices of most securities products fluctuate on a moment-to-moment basis, and constant changes in market conditions are a two-edged sword in the product delivery process. These movements often present tremendous opportunities but carry with them the possibility of great risk for the firm and its clients, which is virtually out of human control. Finally, even if a securities firm is successful through most of the year based on net income numbers (or any other measure), the securities market fluctuations can result in losses of such magnitude that they can wipe out a firm's profits.

A SNAPSHOT PICTURE OF THE SECURITIES FIRM STRUCTURE

Industry analysts usually view the securities firm as an organization with five separate parts. The typical firm has a branch office system for retail account executives or some institutional salespeople or, in many firms, some combination of both; a capital markets division, which includes the trading, underwriting, and institutional sales departments for most securities; an investment banking area, which, depending on the degree to which it is developed, usually has a corporate and a public finance department; an administrative services division, which is responsible for legal and compliance work, accounting and auditing, and a host of other support-type services; and a products division, which is usually well developed in a firm with a large number of branch offices. This outline is simplistic at best but provides a conceptual view of a securities firm in terms of its basic functions. Despite the myriad departments, profit centers, and the variety of specialized tasks that form the basic fabric of the firms, almost all securities firm professionals can be placed within three general categories, based on the type of job that they perform. The three areas are discussed below.

A Tripartite View of the Securities Firm

1. *Securities Sales.* This group of professionals covers all those engaged in the selling of securities of any type. It includes both institutional salespeople and account executives in the firm's retail branch offices. These professionals sell the firm's products, such as stocks and bonds, commodities, as well as mutual funds, among many others, and also its various services.

2. *Competitive Product Creation Areas.* The next major group of professionals consists of those who create new issue banking products. These include individuals who are in the investment banking areas of corporate and public finance. They also encompass any small business unit or department within the firm that engages in the product process through the trading or underwriting of securities.

3. *All Types of Support Areas.* There are essentially three subcategories within the support area group. (In many cases this concept of "support" goes far beyond the common meaning of the term.) The first subgroup might be called "active" or "direct" support departments. These include the products division, which is an umbrella grouping for product origination, marketing, service, and support departments. Another division that is actively involved in providing direct support is the research area of the firm, and it includes such departments as equity, fixed income, municipal research, economics, and commodity research areas, among others. The second subgroup encompasses the administrative services division, the accounting and auditing departments, the legal and compliance departments, the information processing department, the communications department, and the operations division. These are often thought of as "passive" units of support, but in some firms are anything but passive. The third group includes the more traditional type of support employees who provide secretarial and administrative assistance. These individuals are located throughout the organization and are generally considered to provide support-type functions even though they may at times, and to a limited extent, engage in other activities.

INSTITUTIONAL VERSUS RETAIL FIRMS

There are generally two types of securities firms. One is defined as institutional and exists primarily for originating new issue securities and the trading, sales, and underwriting of new products and work in the secondary markets. Its natural clients are institutional investors. The other type of firm is retail oriented, with branch offices that may be located around the country and the world that may number into the hundreds. Its account executives deal primarily with individual investors. To be sure, there are hybrid firms that have tremendous institutional capabilities as well as large retail sales networks and firms best described as institutional that also cater to a particular individual clientele.

These are the basic kinds of securities firms. There are others that are similar, but also offer specialized or "boutique"-type services, such as financial advisory work. These are usually smaller firms that may have proportionately sized trading and sales operations and that may deal with retail or institutional accounts or both.

WHO ARE THE MANAGERS?

Since this book is about management, it is important that who the managers are in the securities firm be defined. Indeed, managers in most companies are easily identifiable in number and kind. In a securities firm, however, managers can populate the hundreds of small business units scattered throughout the firm. Within this context, a manager may be an individual who supervises an over-the-counter stock desk, a municipal trading unit, a fixed-income research operation, a government agency bond area, a municipal institutional sales department, a corporate syndicate department, a product development area, an operations division, an order processing department, a branch office, a regional branch office system, a nationwide branch operation, a public finance department, an infrastructure group within a public finance department, a municipal bond department, a municipal note-trading desk, a communications development department, or a firmwide communications system. Managers, in short, can be located all over the securities firm, and there are many who supervise powerful small business units with the capacity to generate enormous revenue streams.

A CONCEPTUAL APPROACH TO THE MANAGEMENT MILIEU

Specialization

There is an intense degree of job-related specialization within each division of a securities firm, within departments, and even within departments' small business units. For instance, the investment banking division may have a corporate finance department and a public finance department. While all the professionals in both departments are investment bankers, they travel in very different circles. The corporate finance people may be calling on large companies to provide financial advice or to underwrite their securities; they may deal directly with corporate chieftains. Public finance professionals, on the other hand, may be soliciting water districts or states and cities, becoming involved with civil servants, local politicians, and citizen board members. Even within a corporate finance department, some investment bankers may be soliciting new business from financial institutions, while others may be calling on high-technology companies; some investment bankers may be providing financial advice to corporate utilities, and others may be working with worldwide conglomerates on mergers, acquisitions, or divestitures. In public finance, one group of investment bankers may be working closely with state officials on a major debt-restructuring situation, while others may be providing financial advice to a public authority for a new airport addition. These examples are all within the organizational structure of an investment banking division, and even within these specific job descriptions, certain investment bankers may be more adept at getting new business, while others may have developed an expertise in computer-related work. Some may be proficient with legal documents, and others may be experts at providing arguments about a government's or corporation's credit rating.

Specialization extends to the trading area as well. One group of traders might be trading corporate high-yield bonds, while other traders may be dealing exclusively in large blocks of securities guaranteed by the U.S. government. In the municipal bond trading area, some professionals may specialize in long-term bonds of particular states or localities or revenue authorities, while some may trade in short-term municipal note issues of all types. Other traders at a securities firm may specialize in commodities such as gold, cotton, sugar, or copper. The clients of traders could range from individual investors to commercial banks to other financial institutions to the largest corporations located around the globe. Each of these trading environments has its own complex relationships resulting from the way particular securities or commodities are traded or from the various cultural barriers that must often be traversed in the trading business.

In the research area, there is also great specialization. One equity analyst may specialize in evaluating retail stores. Others may have developed expertise in analyzing cosmetic companies, oil corporations, banks and insurance companies, high-technology firms, or corporate utilities. Within the municipal research area, some analysts evaluate only public power agencies, housing authorities, projects that convert refuse to salable energy, municipal hospitals, mass transit facilities, local governments, or states. All of these research specialties mirror the different groups within a corporate and public finance department, and investment bankers and research analysts often spend their entire careers specializing in work with, for, or on any one of these types of corporate or government issuers.

Similarly, in the securities sales area, some account executives at securities firms may specialize in selling a large number of different products and securities to individual investors, while others, who are selling to institutional accounts, devote their energies to selling a particular type of security, such as long-term, high-quality municipal bonds to a small number of different institutional purchasers or clients. Other salespeople may specialize in mutual funds or unit trusts, and some may market financial advice or financial-planning services. The list is endless.

Additionally, the securities industry operates under a tremendous number of federal, state, and regulatory agency rules, procedures, and laws. Many of these govern the selling, underwriting, and trading of securities, and from a legal and regulatory standpoint, require an incredible amount of specialized knowledge simply to work within the industry in a particular area on a daily basis.

Specialization is indeed the way of the world, but it is especially so in the securities industry. Many professionals specialize in areas that their colleagues, even within the same department or division, only vaguely understand. It is this highly developed individual expertise that has tremendous impact on the management of securities firms.

Decentralization and Autonomy

Specialization in the securities firm has given rise to a decentralized structure and autonomous decision-making process, in which specialists in particular departments and small business units have tremendous latitude for making decisions about the firm's activities, the use of its capital, the development of its client base, and its relationships to clients. This type of autonomy is exemplified in the decentralized branch office system within major retail-oriented firms, where the branch office is tantamount to a small business unit. A large degree of autonomy extends into the trading and sales departments of the securities firms, where professionals, almost unilaterally, can commit the firm's capital in large amounts. It also extends into the investment banking division, where many professionals have great opportunities to deal with clients and develop the department's client base. Research analysts operate in a virtual hands-off atmosphere in providing opinions on securities and issuers. Decentralized decision making and autonomy of professionals and their business units in securities firms are also part of the product service departments, the information and communications areas, and the administrative service division, among others. This serves up to the management menu all kinds of potential difficulties and opportunities, most of which are almost unheard of in the modern corporation but are actually a way of life in securities firms.

The Changing Nature of the Profit Center Orientation

A logical outgrowth of specialization and the resultant decentralization is the ability to generate revenues both on an individual basis and within small business units. From this has stemmed a profit center atmosphere and, in some cases, an individually oriented revenue generation and compensation structure that is pervasive throughout the vast majority of securities firms' professional personnel, from the individual account executive to the institutional salesperson to the trader to the investment banker. It has also been subsumed in the many small business units. This concept has come to be regarded as both a blessing and a curse to securities firm managers, and is being altered at many firms. Also, both enterprising small business units and "superstar" individuals could bring in huge revenues to the firm on the one hand, but it is their meteoric rises that engender conditions that may expose the firm to personnel problems and potentially devastating trading losses, on the other.

THE IMPACT OF THE FINANCIAL MARKETS

All professional and managerial activity within a securities firm takes place in the context of the financial markets, which are not only unpredictable, but also often extremely volatile. Markets are to the securities firm what water is to a fish. Even budgeting, accounting, control procedures, and strategic decision making all evolve within the context of the fluctuating financial markets. Major market movements in securities prices can occur all the time. Keeping track of them, monitoring their impact, and developing financial recommendations for the purchase, sale, or holding of securities is certainly more than a full-time job. In this context, management is a difficult job.

Finally, it is within the world's financial markets that activity takes place at securities firms around the globe on a 24-hour basis. There is much at stake, the circumstances of the markets are uncontrollable, the competition in the industry is fierce, the intellectual capacity of professionals is tremendous, and the management problems presented, while not totally unique to organizations, are clearly unusual in scope, dimension, and complexity. In an increasingly competitive financial service world, however, one which stands at the threshold of the capital-raising process for corporations and governments, these problems are exceedingly important to explore, understand, and attempt to solve.

PART 1

THE RETAIL AND INSTITUTIONAL SECURITIES BUSINESS

CHAPTER 2

THE BRANCH OFFICE SYSTEM: COMPETITIVE STRATEGY IN A MARKET SHARE ENVIRONMENT

When individuals think of the brokerage industry, what usually comes to mind are the branch offices located in cities and towns throughout the United States and around the world. Most people realize that they are staffed with account executives who sell securities to individuals and to institutions. Individuals with a more in-depth knowledge of the industry know that some of these branch offices have underwriting and trading capabilities and others are satellite offices of those in nearby cities with much smaller staffs who sometimes specialize in selling particular types of securities or services. Nonetheless, most people envision the branch office as one with account executives who ply their trade on behalf of the firm and their clients.

Much has happened in the industry since its inception. Structural changes have occurred over the last few years that have resulted in numerous combinations of securities firms and other corporations through mergers or takeovers and in the burgeoning of different kinds of products. The basic element of the securities firm, however—the branch office staffed with account executives—has not changed in the drastic ways that the industry has. Indeed, branches have been, are now, and seem likely to be, run by branch managers, and staffed by account executives who operate much like independent contractors.

THREE CONCEPTUAL VIEWS
OF A BRANCH OFFICE

There are perhaps three conceptual ways to view a branch office. Each assumes something slightly different about what the branch means to the overall firm and the way its operations should be structured to provide the firm with a sound business. Usually when industry professionals view a branch or branch office system, they conceptualize it as a combination of these three perspectives, and in many ways, a branch office should be best portrayed in this fashion. From a management standpoint, however, there is really only one important way to conceptualize how a branch should be viewed and the way it should operate within the corporate body of the securities firm. When seen in this way, certain other managerial principles cascade from this perspective, forming the basis of the way a firm should develop a branch office, handle the proliferation of securities products available for its account executives to sell, and manage itself, both from the standpoint of the branch office manager and also its surrounding community.

The first way a branch office is seen within a firm is from what might be called a "microperspective." This focuses on account executives as the branch's heartbeat and views their entrepreneurial activities as all-important to the branch and thus to the servicing of customers and the development of a revenue stream for the firm. The individual account executive must be provided with the support necessary to build a business through the development of a franchise with any group of products or clients. In this microcosmic view, the account executive is seated on top of the branch office corporate pyramid. The better the account executive does, the better clients are serviced, the more clients are developed, the better off the firm is, and so on. The better the account executives an office has in whatever product areas they specialize and by whatever resourceful means are available, the better the office is, the better it services the community, and the more important it is from a revenue standpoint to the firm.

Another way to view a branch office is from a "macroperspective," as part of a larger organizational structure. The branch office, when looked at from this view, is a customer-oriented, revenue-generating machine at a different stage of development than other branch offices in the system. When taken together with the other branch offices, it provides (from a divisional or corporate standpoint) a revenue stream to the firm through the sales of its products and the servicing of its customers as well as the development of other clients. The macroview of the branch system is that of a corporate behemoth with a broad bottom-line orientation based on the total number of account executives in the entire system and their average across-the-board production when compared to other firms. This revenue stream flushes through the securities firm, becomes a part of revenues generated from other areas within the firm, and is one major portion of the overall corporate income pie. When viewed in this way, a branch office is also another outlet for a firm's products and for the servicing of customers located strategically in areas where management believes the firm could make a client-servicing impact. Thus, the view of a branch office from this macroorganizational standpoint is one that meshes the goings on within the office and the work of the individual account executive with a broader perspective of a corporatewide mission to provide products and service customers. In doing so, a branch office is part of a larger branch revenue production system as an important area for firmwide profitability.

The third, and perhaps more realistic, way of looking at a branch office in a securities firm is through a view that might be called the "franchise" or "market share" approach. This perspective views each branch office as an ongoing sales, product delivery, and customer service operation located geographically in a given market with a definable customer base and a group of competitors. The goal of the office, as seen through the development of its account executives, is to compete for and gain market share and develop the client base within that geographic location to the greatest extent possible. The market or potential customer base within this franchise approach can be segmented economically, socially, and financially. Within these categories are points of access to important clients or leaders within the community, both informal and formal, who are, in many cases, identifiable. As a result, in the franchise or market share approach to viewing the branch office, the customer base defines not only the sales activities of the office and its account executives but also the products sold in varying quantities across the different customer segments. Under this approach, the development of a diversified account executive team is a critical function of the branch manager, who assumes management responsibilities not unlike those of a ship's captain who must strategically orient a vessel towards a definable, chartable, and doable objective. In many ways, the franchise or market share approach is a cross between the macro and micro orientations. It also makes the branch manager a key figure in moving the branch's development towards its goals through the penetration of the client market.

A BRANCH OFFICE MARKET TYPOLOGY

Geographic Diversity

One need not look far to find tremendous population diversity in the towns and cities across the United States where securities firm offices are situated. These locations give rise to widely varying clients of different financial, economic, cultural, demographic, and social groups. For instance, one geographically definable population segment may be small towns such as those located in the New England states of Vermont, New Hampshire, and Maine. Another type might be the suburban towns and small cities that, by virtue of their transportation networks, are linked closely with one another and are often contiguous. Some examples of these communities include those located near the southwestern coast of Connecticut and those which dot the Florida and California coasts, as well as the outlying areas near major midwestern and southern cities. A third type of client base that is somewhat more populated and diverse consists of midsize cities. Some examples of these include Amarillo, Texas; Berkeley, California; Orlando, Florida; and Savannah, Georgia. A fourth type of locality and one still larger and more demographically complex are other cities such as Louisville, Kentucky; Portland, Oregon; Richmond, Virginia; and St. Paul, Minnesota. By virtue of their larger size, this group and other cities like them presents securities firms with a more complex market to penetrate. A fifth type are large cities and for which it is somewhat difficult for a branch office to develop a market share concept. This client base includes financially and economically diverse cities of large size such as Chicago, Dallas, Los Angeles, and New York City.

These are just some examples of the geographic areas that serve up to securities firms client markets of great diversity having different appetites for a vast array of securities products because of their own cultural makeups, financial needs, likes and dislikes, and risk perspectives. To be sure, there is much overlap among the different client segments within each city and across different groups, but unless the environments in which a securities firm branch office is located are understood and defined, it is unlikely that products can be marketed effectively.

Market Segmentation

A potential client market base within a given geographic area can be segmented along the lines of employment and relative wealth. Each geographic milieu has different proportions of job types, and others can be devoid of certain kinds of employment. Some general employment groups are: government service, heavy industry or manufacturing, service, agriculture, retirement, financial services, or any combination thereof. In addition, and depending on concentrations of employment within these categories, relative wealth on a per-capita basis can be determined. Segmenting a community along these lines is a critical determinant of the kinds and relative amounts of products that a firm's branch office can ultimately sell and is also important in determining the way in which a branch's account executives could and should go about developing their client bases. There are other ways to segment the market.

Community Points of Access

For the account executives in a branch office who are servicing a client base within their given community, it is important to isolate the points of access to the different community segments as they relate to relative wealth and different employment sectors. This is important to understand and operationalize, not only from the standpoint of the individual account executive, but also from the broader perspective of the entire branch office. It is rarely ever perceived as a dual function and developed accordingly. Each community has points of access, and the leaders of different formal and informal groups can be isolated and contacted for any number of reasons. More than that, the groups they represent provide opportunities if account executives desire to, and perhaps should, become involved in helping them succeed in their missions and also in aiding the community. In any event, groups exist within the community that provide others formal points of access to individuals and that do not necessarily run parallel to the community's segmentation along the lines of employment or wealth. These formal access points include: political parties, industry and company associations, small business councils, charitable organizations, unions, and parent-teacher associations. Informal points of access to community groups include: private and public clubs, hobby-related associations, such as fishing and skiing groups, ad hoc committees, and special interest associations.

DEVELOPING A BRANCHWIDE MARKETING STRATEGY

When a branch office's potential client market is viewed along these typological lines, the client thus defines the market and the account executive's approach to it, rather than the other way around. As a result, the focus is more on a branch's development of the market and its potential client base to the widest extent possible rather than on account executives pursuing their own business strategies in a unilateral way. In this sense, then, it is unlikely that having a group of account executives pursuing their own individual missions is likely to be as effective as a branch office totally understanding what the market and customer base is all about and proceeding to penetrate the various market segments of that customer base. This is done through appropriate formal and informal points of access on a regulated basis to supply that target market with the best possible financial service and thus to increase the branch office's market share relative to other competitors within that geographic area.

There are perhaps as many strategies to develop market share as there are branch offices or, better yet, potential customer segments and overall client bases. Those markets that have not been covered or are not receiving adequate coverage should be addressed based on an appropriate allocation of branch office resources. This is one way, albeit a conceptual one, to have the efforts of account executives within a branch result in value-added benefits to the account executives, to the branch as a whole, and to the community. This directed approach must be staffed, ordered, maintained, and monitored, providing strategy on an ongoing basis, feedback, and reasons for reallocation of resources, including personnel and time. In the purest sense, this overall franchise type or market share approach to the branch office business may be complicated to put into practice, but it is a worthy conceptual model of what may very well be an optimum situation and one avenue that will be pursued by firms in the future.

PRODUCT DIFFERENTIATION IN THE BRANCH OFFICE

Perhaps one of the most important issues facing management in securities firms today is how to deal effectively with the process of product knowledge and understanding in the branch office. This problem comes as a result of a large number of products being developed and marketed by securities firms nationwide. Indeed, most account executives today at many of the large securities firms have between 50 and 150 products that they can offer on any day. Some of these products are securities related and others have service elements to them. Most are either stocks, bonds, or other types of securities or commodities, while others may be related to financial planning, retirement services, real estate, or even insurance. In addition to these products, there are what might be called "packaged products." These include many different mutual funds and unit trusts with different quality variations and different securities. Most of these will be discussed in the following chapter; but it should be remembered that there are professionals in the securities firms who may spend their careers working with and trading or selling any one of these investment vehicles.

Every day, account executives are only going to sell those products on which they have information, they understand, and about which they or an analyst at their firm can answer questions. Many account executives today, however, are not conversant with every one of these products. In many of these cases, most of the products they know are related because many are similar in nature from a generic standpoint, such as all of them can be classified as fixed-income type of securities, are different types of stocks and stock funds, or might even be certain kinds of tax-advantaged investments. They may also be related to the kind of investor group to which they are directed; some products may be more appropriate for risk adverse investors, while others may be securities investors seek who are interested in earning a greater return on their money in the face of a higher risk.

In any event, the understanding by an account executive of a certain group of products is often the result of client development activity, time available to understand the product, and ability to market particular products. As a result, the entire process of account executive development is dependent on the amount and number of products an account executive can successfully understand and market. Another related consequence of this activity is the fact that an account executive's client list may have a large percentage of customers who purchase similar types of products. For periods when these products are not appropriate investment vehicles, most branch managers suggest that the account executive develop some expertise in other product areas. Many individuals, however, agree that an account executive can develop an expertise in a given number of products; we are all only human.

An obvious outgrowth of this apparent fact of life is that, in any branch office, there are account executives who have developed understanding of different types of products. Some may know fixed-income products very well, and others may have a keen interest and ability to work with stocks. Some account executives may be particularly conversant with commodities, options, or futures, or may have developed specialties in other investment vehicles or securities. In a similar way, when a community's client base is appropriately segmented, certain clients could ultimately use particular types of products to a greater or lesser degree than others, depending on their needs.

The critical management prescription to understand here, however, is that although there is an ongoing need to develop the individual account executive's understanding of a broader range of products and therefore to be able to service the customers better, there is still an opportunity of coordination in product work within the office and cross-fertilizing of product knowledge in the customer base. More simply, there are certain account executives in a branch office who may work better with specific products and services because of their knowledge about them than others could. This is not to say that account executives should begin learning about everything. This concept, however, does suggest the need for account executives within the office not only to develop better understanding of more products but also to use the account executives within the office who have developed expertise in particular product areas for the benefit of others within the office and their customers. This all rebounds to the advantage of the branch office in achieving a deeper penetration of the client market, an increase in market share, but most important, providing better service to clients.

PRODUCT LEADERSHIP

One answer to the plethora of products problem has been the development of product leaders within the branch office. There are many different ways to develop a product leadership system, but the concept is similar in all cases. In the most general form, a product leader is assigned to monitor a particular product and educates other account executives in the branch about it. The entire concept of product leadership within a branch office, moreover, dovetails with the need of the office to educate its account executives about all types of products, to be aware of their marketability as investment vehicles, and to structure the branch's product mix according to the client base within the community. This concept has much broader implications for the management of a branch office, and it begins to develop a branchwide mentality for teamwork and the development of all the branch's account executives to their potential. More importantly, it helps the account executives view the client base as an entity critical to all of them, rather than the more common perception that it is important for an account executive to develop and penetrate the largest client base possible.

THE BRANCH MANAGER'S TRADITIONAL ROLE IN TRANSITION

The branch manager has always had a role that vacillates between two job descriptions: branch administrator and sales manager. The area of branch administration has usually involved the general operations of the branch, including trades processing, personnel administration, operations-related activities, and relations with the home office. Some of this work is delegated to assistant branch managers with compliance-related backgrounds; but as every branch manager knows, it is the manager who ultimately bears the overall responsibility for these matters. The sales manager job or function has been largely a soft-peddled role involving a number of sales-related activities but usually conceived of as a passive function. In this role, the manager is a conduit from the firm to the account executives for research-related communications and has very often pointed out newsworthy items about stocks and new products being developed at the firm. Here, the manager is sometimes the source for product-related sales suggestions and also has a general potpourri of knowledge about different products that account executives may not totally understand. The branch manager also sets standards for account executive production and monitors the development of account executives. Often the branch manager chairs sales meetings in the morning and, in the afternoon, supervises presentations by account executives at conferences and seminars in the community or for selected clients.

All of these sales-related roles are performed by branch

managers today, and some have developed more responsibility in these matters. Yet, the traditional view of a branch manager's role has been more that of a supervisor or administrator than of an active sales manager.

Years ago, few great account executives thought it worth their while professionally, intellectually, or remuneratively to apply for the job as branch manager; the best account executives shunned branch managerships. Even today many professionals agree that it is somewhat difficult to entice account executives and others to become branch managers. Most of the best account executives would rather have a better entrepreneurial opportunity as an account executive and forgo the headaches that come with the branch manager's position. They also view the role of branch manager as potentially fraught with operational difficulties and personnel problems. Most branch managers agree that the job is a 24-hour one and that it is incredibly complex and exhausting. Most professionals believe that branch managers are still more involved in the administrative and day-to-day operations of a branch than they are in the kinds of activities prescribed in the following analysis. To be sure, many are involved in a wider variety of different job functions than they were just a few years ago.

THE ACTIVE ROLE OF
THE BRANCH MANAGER

The development of a branch office along the lines suggested by the market share approach is not going to happen by itself, nor is it likely to be the result of memos from the home office or account executives' self-propulsion. The segmentation of a community for client identification purposes, the tapping into the formal and informal points of access within the community along the lines of a strategic game plan, the wholesale education of a branch office's account executives about all products, and the hiring of new account executives to fill existing client and product voids in the branch office game plan are not likely to occur in a managerial vacuum. Although most industry professionals and analysts have focused on the successful account executive as the strategic unit in the branch office system, few have accorded the branch manager the kind of full-blown managerial respect and freedom necessary to pilot the branch office into a position of competitive and strategic importance within the community.

As noted above, the position of branch manager has not been enthusiastically sought by the firm's top professionals, who are either on-line producers or general managers. Yet, if a branch office is to approach the kind of successful development conceptually outlined in the previous sections, the branch manager is the only individual in the system who can activate the branch toward appropriate goals and objectives. Indeed, to take the argument to its logical managerial conclusion, the better the branch manager is, the better the branch is; and it is likely that a branch office can only develop to its fullest extent if the branch manager is a superior professional. The branch manager is the key cog in the branch wheel and, without strong management, it is unlikely that the account executives, either individually or collectively, could develop the branch in the ways previously described.

Indeed, an active branch manager helps to strategically develop the branch's market share to compete with other firms in the geographic client base area. The branch manager designs the product mix in relation to data about the community's market segments and makes sure that the account executives have knowledge of as many products as possible. It is also within the purview of the branch manager to create an effective product leadership marketing system for all account executives in the office and to make certain that the account executives are developing according to their potential. Finally, the branch manager is responsible for developing a team effort within the branch so that high office spirit helps propel the account executives toward optimum individual achievement.

A truly active branch manager is actually a highly developed sales manager who, on a daily basis, provides account executives with suggestions about products, based on market conditions and the firm's in-house research. The branch manager thus functions as a information depository and dissemination system, and in this way, is often critical to the daily operations of the branch's sales system. More than any other professional in the branch, the branch manager can be an important "right arm" to all the account executives in the office. The branch manager, in this spirited type of role, has a function not unlike the sales manager role in the traditional way the branch manager's job was perceived and carried out. In a branch manager's operationalization of it today, however, the manager's enthusiasm, knowledge base, high level of energy, and involvement in the account executives' activities makes the sales management role a more active one. This is the critical difference between the traditional way the branch manager's role has been perceived, what it might be, and what it should be in today's fiercely competitive financial service environment.

In addition, the active branch manager is especially critical to the account executive hiring process. The branch manager has always been critical to it; but today, the branch manager must assume a much more active posture. The branch manager should be the key individual with the personality and leadership ability to attract account executives. Ultimately, when a top account executive joins the firm, the branch manager is often the key to that process. Other account executives can be helpful and are often the branch manager's eyes and ears to isolate the best talent available in the marketplace; but it is the branch manager who closes the deal. The new employee has to believe that the branch manager is someone to respect, who will be supportive, and who has the capacity and firmwide support to make that particular branch office develop a team effort.

All account executives, including the newly hired ones, look to the branch manager as the stabilizing element within their work milieu and as the key professional who will continue to keep their office operating successfully at an appropriately high level compared to other competitors in the client service area. The branch manager, in this active role, is the pivot around which the working lives of the account executives revolve. It is the active branch manager who has the mandate, the requisite ability, the firmwide support, and the support of all the branch's account executives in an effort to develop the kind of operation that can gain greater market share, provide first-rate client service, and develop an office and professionals to the greatest extent possible. Finally, more than anyone else, it is the branch manager to whom the community and the branch office's clients look as the single most important source of credibility, knowledge, interest, and service in any type of "what if" situations that may arise in the competitive financial services milieu in which a branch office so often operates. In the years ahead, it will be the branch managers who will occupy positions of strategic importance in the development of branch offices and thus in the success of many securities firms on Wall Street, especially those heavily oriented toward retail systems.

BRANCH MANAGEMENT IN THE FUTURE

The development of a branch office along the lines of a market share or franchise orientation is going to be critical to the success of many retail-oriented securities firms in the future, and it will be a function of the way in which a branch manager creates the appropriate professional environment and establishes the right kind of goals. The branch's success will depend on the manager's ability to develop actively the roles that have been passively assumed in the traditional view of branch management. Yet, the branch manager will have to go far beyond an enthusiastic embracing of those functions and will have to orient the branch's effort strategically along the lines of the community's market segments. The branch manager will also have to assume greater responsibility for the development of the office's account executives. This function will include developing account executives who are much more knowledgeable about a wider range of products and who can penetrate all segments within a community with the appropriately high level of service befitting the securities industry. This can only happen when a firm provides branch managers with appropriate levels of autonomy to structure their operations and dole out their incentives to achieve the branch's goals. When branch managers are provided the kinds of opportunities that are characteristic of the entrepreneurial nature of U.S. securities firms, the entire branch-building process will have the basics to be successful.

CHAPTER 3

THE PRODUCT PROCESS: CREATING A CUSTOMER IN A DECENTRALIZED WORLD

If there is one thing that can be said about Wall Street in recent years, it is that, more than ever, the name of the game is "product"—its development, marketing, and delivery. Nowhere is this more apparent than in the attention focused on these functions, the relationship of which seems to be in a perennial state of organizational flux, often requiring redirection, review, and revamping. One of the most complex management problems facing securities firms, and one that is likely either to herald their success in the twenty-first century or to sound their death knell, concerns their ability to match product and customer better. The task sounds basic enough, but for securities firms, the job is hard because of several factors: the complexity and number of products available; the fact that the main organs of product delivery in the retail environment are thousands of account executives; and the complicated task of providing new products, making product evaluations, and creating marketing ideas, for a decentralized sales force, by a department organizationally a few steps away from the customer.

THE PRODUCT EXPLOSION

"There is only one valid definition of business purpose," argues Peter Drucker, and that is "to create a customer."[1] In its purest form, Wall Street's product explosion is an unabashedly enthusiastic attempt to follow Drucker's long-established management dictum. Yet, getting an accurate handle on the vast array of these products is no easy feat. For every kind of product, there are a number of derivative ones, many with subtle differences in substance as well as packaging. The new bent of securities firms towards financial planning and consulting as an overall client service adds to the difficulty a client faces in choosing to do business with a firm and in selecting a particular product or service. Similarly, the product explosion has complicated the lives of account executives. Nevertheless, it is important to know what is available in today's financial supermarkets.

THE SECURITIES FIRM SMORGASBORD

Today's securities firm offers an enormous number and kind of products to investors, many as variations or derivatives of other products, and some as part of a service or planning function. Nobody can list all these products; indeed, nobody knows them all because they vary from firm to firm. What can be done, however, and what is more useful analytically, is to categorize the largest percentages of them with examples of each. Understanding what products are generally available and their nature is an absolute prerequisite to the ongoing task of better fitting product and client.

The Product Grid

Securities firms offer hundreds of individual products and services. For the sake of conceptualization, understanding, analysis, and most importantly, brevity, these products may be divided into five groups.

1. Origination-type Products
Origination-type products include the following: stocks or equities; preferred stocks; government bills and bonds; government agency securities; corporate bonds; municipal bonds; mortgage-backed securities; Eurobonds; commercial paper; certificates of deposit; bankers acceptances; convertible

bonds; commodities; and options and futures, as well as variable rate, put option, zero coupon, and other market-related derivative securities.

2. Packaged Products: Mutual Funds, Unit Trusts, and Cash Funds

Packaged products are product services and include a bevy of investment vehicles developed largely from the origination-type products. Many have special features of those products and run the gamut from investment risk to diversity to liquidity alternatives. For instance, there are municipal bond unit trusts. These may be insured or uninsured and have only bonds from specific states, certain credit qualities, yield levels, or maturities. Some other types may have floating rates, may be backed by letters of credit, may be collateralized, or may have market-related options. Others are also available with securities of foreign governments, corporate bonds, certificates of deposit, and government securities of all types, and each fund may have a different investment objective. These will be discussed later.

3. Financial Planning and Consultancy Services

The financial planning function has been a natural outgrowth of Wall Street's plethora of products, its efforts to better fit clients and products, and its drive to create a fee-based revenue stream that would survive even during the Street's dingiest days. These services can be broken down into a number of distinct categories; there are at least as many ways of providing financial planning as there are firms. Firms provide retirement planning, financial planning for corporate executives, investment management services, and combinations of these. The basic financial planning function, however, is a derivative of the approach to personal finance employed by specialists over a number of years. In any case, a brief digression into the world of financial planning is in order.

Simply stated, financial planning consists chiefly of helping to manage a person's or household's total finances with a view towards short-, medium-, and long-term objectives. The program takes into account risk predilections and assumes that the process is monitored on an ongoing basis over the term of the plan and also compared against the plan's objectives. To be sure, financial planning is a highly complex and individualized task and can result in a much closer relationship between planner and client than would ordinarily be the case. This is not to say that all these relationships must be either/or kinds of situations based on the type of services provided; the choices do not have to be dichotomous ones. There are no set rules; each relationship is different, but each is a dynamic process rather than a static one, which changes over time and is difficult to classify.

The financial planning process begins with a detailed analysis of the client's present financial situation. The client is not a blank slate but rather comes with a financial situation; the planner does not create it. Next comes assessing the degree to which the client is willing to assume risk in particular investments and over a specified time period. This process goes hand in hand with setting objectives and developing investment alternatives for the client. Implementation of the plan and the reevaluation of it compared against its original objectives are the final steps.

The financial planning process may involve employing a wide array of investment products, services, and strategies. It often requires income tax work and estate planning, retirement and pension services, and insurance-related advice, all of which mean that the financial planner may have to work with other competent professionals whose specialties are in these fields. Investment advice centers on securities risk, liquidity, rates of return, and appreciation—all placed within the context of the individual's financial plan. To be sure, financial planning does not mean instant wealth, but it helps many who deal in a world laden with complex financial products marketed within the context of an increasingly volatile and complicated financial marketplace.

4. Insurance, Annuities, and Related Investments

Some securities firms have begun to offer insurance and annuities on a large scale to clients. Much of this effort comes as a result of some firms merging with financial companies that sell these products and also from cross-marketing of these products by certain firms. Both avenues of product delivery have also resulted in the marketing of many other related kinds of services and products, too numerous to discuss here but important enough to create this fourth general category for investment products.

5. Tax-advantaged Participatory Investments
These investment alternatives were very popular in the days before the tax reform of 1986. They generally feature the opportunity of investing in partnership and other operations with the potential of tax deductions and also possible appreciable returns. These investments have typically been in real estate, oil and gas, equipment leases, and research and development activities, among others. Although the Internal Revenue Code of 1986 substantially impacted the viability of many of these, some are expected to be offered in the future, but in a substantially modified form.

ASSETS UNDER MANAGEMENT: A SPECIAL CASE

One of the most significant developments in the product marketing and service efforts of securities firms over recent years has been the desire by firms and clients alike to place client monies in packaged funds created by the firm and others, as briefly discussed earlier. Mutual funds have been around for a long time but were not heavily produced and marketed by securities firms, but recent years have seen a veritable avalanche of different fund types created with a dizzying array of features designed to make these investment vehicles increasingly more attractive to purchasers. The total fund assets under management by most securities firms have dwarfed original expectations, making the fund business one of the most significant on Wall Street.

From a management standpoint, the funds offer a competitive way to bring investors into the firm and provide, in most cases, diversity of securities, on-site professional management, and easy access to understandable investments. For account executives, they have been worthwhile, too, usually providing a return as long as the client remains with the firm, depending on how the firm arranged remuneration. Finally, the concept helps develop entrenched firm–client relationships.

The "assets under management" concept also provides the securities firm with answers to some of its vital questions about planning for the future. Firms have become concerned over the inherent and unpredictable cyclical nature of the securities business, owing in large part to stock market and interest rate volatility. The firms have been known to expand in personnel and businesses during boom years, and conversely, to lower the boom on personnel and services during slack periods. Under these scenarios, controlling and developing the firm's resources, both financial and human, became especially difficult tasks. Similarly, planning for corporate development in the increasingly competitive financial services environment became equally problematic. With a more stable revenue base derived from assets under management products, the securities firm at least begins to mitigate the potentially adverse environmental conditions in which it operates on a daily basis.

The aspect of the garnering assets under management that makes it an especially viable tool for developing a stable client and product base, and thus an anchor in the firm's turbulent product seas, is the fact that, as noted earlier, the fund business ties a client much closer to the firm. This has merit for both client and firm. The client can easily be exposed to a wide variety of products, while being freed from the day-to-day decision-making process of a transactions business. From the firm's standpoint, the client also becomes connected more closely to the firm by being more easily exposed to a wider variety of investment alternatives.

PRODUCT DIFFERENTIATION TO MATCH
MARKET SEGMENTATION

In the last chapter, it was noted that it was desirable to develop an in-depth knowledge of the financial, economic, and demographic makeup of a branch's target market, and thus to segment it. Yet market segmentation is rooted in the principle that a single product cannot be all things to all customers. There may be a few segments of a given market, however, that would be well served by a single product. All this is evaluated when product differentiation is accomplished and matched with the market segments to optimize the delivery of financial products and services to the client. This entire process includes the following steps:

1. Segmenting the market along employment and wealth lines, among others, as discussed in the previous chapter on the branch office system.
2. Risk analyzing the market in terms of what may be considered the appropriate risk position of each segment.
3. Segmenting the market along the lines of general product needs, including mortgage money, liquidity, investment analysis, insurance, comprehensive financial planning, or retirement planning, among others.
4. Identifying products that would generally fit each market segment according to information available from numbers 1 through 3.
5. Researching the market segments for information beyond what has been available to this point.

THE ACCOUNT EXECUTIVE AS PRODUCT EXHIBITOR

From a management perspective, the account executive stands at the threshold of the product and service delivery process by the firm to the client. The account executive is the ultimate judge and jury as to which product will be made available to clients and which will not, and which will be marketed successfully and which will not. This is not to say that the service and planning process is a one-way street from firm to client. In the new financial-planning environment, the client's financial situation receives first priority as the jigsaw puzzle frame into which the proper products must fit. This analogy, however, raises interesting questions because, with the multitude of products available, there may be many products that could ultimately fit neatly into a client's given financial situation and be effective in achieving a planner's goals for individual accounts.

There may be big mistakes made if the wrong products are employed, to be sure, but even some of the most specific goals could readily and easily be achieved by a number of financial products.

The product selector is the account executive. Seen from a marketing management standpoint, the account executive acts at once as both "product fitter" and "product exhibitor." In these dual roles, the account executive presents to management two decidedly different tasks that must be accomplished on an ongoing basis if the firm's products are to be optimally marketed, achieving the widest distribution possible together with the best fit for clients. The first task is to make sure that each account executive is giving the available products the widest possible exposure, and as a corollary, that no product or group of products is receiving short shrift for reasons beyond the obvious, such as that the products are not good fits for the clients. Boiling this discussion down to its most important conclusion, the firm's management must not allow products to fall into disuse because of a lack of understanding or knowledge of them by the account executive. The second problem or task presented to management concerns the role of the account executive as "product exhibitor." This is the traditional role of securities salespeople, financial planners, investment consultants, and so on. What should be discussed, however, is how the firm itself might help account executives in their task as "product exhibitors." This is a classic marketing function of management.

MARKETING BEYOND THE FIRM'S CONFINES

An analysis of external marketing of securities firm products and services, which is the marketing effort directed outside the securities firm, could be a book itself, largely because the marketing of financial products has become a major focus of many corporations throughout the country and the world. Indeed, when a securities firm seeks to develop business of any sort, be it investment banking, investment management, mortgage-related services, or even the traditional sales functions, marketing inevitably becomes inextricably linked to the total effort. For the purposes of analyzing the external marketing effort, a brief description should suffice.

In its narrowest sense, the product marketing effort of securities in most cases emanates from the home office. It basically entails hard-copy material sent to present and prospective clients. Advertising is also important and sometimes involves specific products advertised in all media. Hard-copy material and brochures designed for marketing purposes may include information related to the following:

1. Buy, sell, or hold recommendations for stocks and bonds.
2. Investment opportunities based on the firm's interest rate predictions.
3. Tax swapping suggestions.
4. Newsworthy information about the economy with possible investment implications.
5. Discussions of new products and services and how they might be useful to particular investors.

To be sure, much of the information provided to account executives for internal marketing purposes is not unlike that sent externally and directly to clients. The difference lies not in what is said, but rather in how it is said. Information made available to clients is more formal in style and substance, packaged differently, and usually, but not always, more intuitive. Material sent to account executives for internal marketing purposes is often more direct and concise. In the case of new or complicated products, material sent internally is explanatory and functional to maximize its applications to specific client situations, as discussed below.

MARKETING FINANCIAL PRODUCTS: THE FIRST CUSTOMER IS THE EMPLOYEE

In a securities firm, with its myriad products, the process of "internal marketing"—that is, educating the firm's salespeople about its products—assumes enormous significance.

Internal Marketing

First and foremost, the process of "internal marketing" takes as its basic assumption that the first customer, in companies like securities firms, is actually within, not outside of, the organization. Internal marketing for securities firm purposes is much more a job of educating account executives about the firm's products and services than it is the traditional and broader concept of selling, in effect, the firm's employees on the firm's products. As applied to securities firms, internal marketing of the educative variety is a management tool to maximize product potential, which many believe to be underdeveloped in the securities firm setting. The more successful the internal marketing effort, the more knowledgeable about the firm's products the account executives become, and the more likely it is that the products will be appropriately marketed and employed. It is as simple as that.

Internal marketing in a securities firm consists largely of two activities. First is the dissemination of product-related material internally, and second is the process of having account executives work with product specialists for particular products. Internally generated and distributed material for marketing purposes is diverse, but most of the material usually contains information on the following:

1. Insight into what is selling and why.
2. Material on new issues or syndicate items that the firm will soon underwrite.
3. Comparative advantages of different products with certain performance measures.
4. Investment strategies.
5. New product explanations.
6. Product or investment suggestions based on the financial outlook or tax changes.
7. Financial planning ideas, such as those relating to retirement planning.
8. A general investment outlook.
9. Model portfolios of different sizes suggesting buy-and-sell transactions.

Internal marketing is also accomplished by sending product

specialists into the branch offices to educate account executives. Much of this activity takes the form of classroom situations, and many are accomplished with the aid of handouts and real-life examples. Nevertheless, it is important to understand that marketing, like charity, begins at home, and nowhere is this more critical than in the product-laden milieu of today's securities firm.

The Customer Comes First

It is ultimately the client for whom the securities firm is providing a product or service. Yet, "what the people in the business think they know about customer and market is more likely to be wrong than right," argues Peter Drucker, adding that "there is only one person who really knows: the customer."[2] When it is a matter of investing their money, individuals usually come to the table with at least some preconceived ideas of what is important to them. The product development and marketing process then is viewed, at least theoretically, as a "bottom-up" rather than a "top-down" process, especially in a securities firm. Also, management's goal, in the competitive world of financial services, is to get closer to the customer, and this is especially applicable to securities firms. It can only be accomplished by surveying the customer and doing this from a locally oriented system. Then a product development strategy must be created as well as a marketing effort on a product-oriented basis. More "bottom-up" product management today could be the critical determinant of success tomorrow.

THE PRODUCT MANAGEMENT STRUCTURE

At the heart of any retail securities organization is a product managerial nexus, although some may not view it as such. This is a point at which products, product services, and marketing come together and then sweep out through the firm to the branch office system and to account executives. No major firm can survive without a successful effort in these related activities.

Located usually within the upper reaches of a firm's management hierarchy and most notably at the firm's headquarters, is the nerve center of the product origination, marketing, services, and support functions, all in the products division. Although an area of such wide scope could be broken down into smaller units, each lodged in a number of places at the firm, the division's functions are more often than not grouped together under a single umbrella. Within the products division and in the product origination department usually lie two functions critical to the branch office's life-support system: the product development and product implementation functions. The product development area might sound like it is the "think tank" arena, and to some extent it is. For it to function effectively, however, it must work in close concert with the departments that actually originate new issue products and underwrite and trade them, if the products are of that ilk. In some cases, the product development process can also actually be either a product refinement or a repackaging function. Even in these instances, close coordination with the originating areas is important in order to iron out potential problems such as those that are operationally related and may result in an inability to actually market the product, as well as those that could cause direct customer resistance to the product for any number of reasons. These may include market-related factors such as liquidity, the cost of the service, or the complexity of the product itself. Product development can take many forms; its genesis for any given product can come from many quarters of the firm, but it should not, and indeed cannot, exist in a vacuum of its own making.

The process of product implementation shares many of the same characteristics. This stage of the product process is often a "make it or break it" operation. Part operations-oriented and part education- and communications-directed, product implementation provides a necessary link between what occurs at the firm's headquarters subsequent to the product development process and what happens in the sales field. This is not to imply that product implementation is conceptually situated only in an a posterior position, after product development and before the ultimate marketing of the product. Product implementation provides a critical feedback function for management up and down the firm's hierarchy, both in test marketing and even after the product is sold. The department often finds itself in an information conduit role, thus becoming a reservoir of important data funneled to it about the products, their strengths and weaknesses, operational problems, usefulness, the ease with which they can be sold, and even their desirability from a client's and an account executive's viewpoint. Product implementation in a securities firm is one of the significant intervening support areas with significant potential for managerial leverage in the product-marketing and service processes.

MANAGERIAL HOTLINES

Horizontal Integration

Perhaps it goes without saying that better overall coordination could be achieved by management in the firm's product-related efforts if closer ties were established between the products division and related departments within the firm, notably within the capital markets group, which originates, underwrites, and trades many of the same products. Often the products division is either marketing or packaging the same kind of products for sale through the branch system that the product-originating departments are developing. For example, the products division may, through the mutual fund and unit trust departments, package and market municipal securities for sale through the branch system to individual investors. Similarly, municipal securities are sold by the branch system to individual clients but may have their genesis in the firm's municipal bond department, which often has a retail liaison desk staffed with professionals who are the "go betweens" for the account executives and the municipal traders and underwriters located either in the firm's main municipal bond headquarters or in the regional municipal bond offices. Much could be said to detail how better coordination could be achieved in order to avoid duplication in marketing and to profit from what has been learned by all areas about the sale of the generic municipal bond product. This knowledge could lead to more useful municipal bond marketing ideas, procedures, and also closer coordination could result in more efficient product implementation of new or related municipal bond products.

There are a great many other examples that could be presented here, such as those using stocks, government and corporate bonds, and so on. However, the specialized nature of the securities firms has sometimes resulted in isolating small business units that might otherwise derive great mutual benefit from closer coordination. Horizontal integration, when more fully developed, is an important answer to improving the product delivery process.

Vertical Integration

The entire product process of the securities firm as noted could be a "bottom-up" process beginning with the client base and rising into the firm's management ranks. It is not solely a "top-down" one, but it is often operationalized as such. Indeed, the product process begins and ends with the customer, a theory propounded long ago, repeated ad infinitum, but not taken to managerial heart often enough. For securities firms, this dictum assumes some added significance. Products are marketed through local branch offices, to local customers, and within financial, economic, and demographically localized settings. More than most would believe, it is a localized function, a very personalized one, and is likely to remain so.

Carrying this argument one logical step further in an effort to integrate the system vertically, product marketing also needs to be decentralized or at least much more so than it is now, and far beyond the development of branch office product leaders. This should be accomplished at least on a regional basis for large firms. Regions are basic units of branch systems, and they serve up to marketing personnel a specific geographic area that sometimes has threads of commonality—in economics, demography, culture, or other predispositions. Smaller regional firms could further decentralize their product-marketing efforts, thus creating an even more precise product-marketing system. To some degree, this is done today by a few major firms with large retail branch systems; but their decentralized product-marketing staffs are often too slim in human resources and must often cover large geographic areas with many branch offices.

THE PRODUCT DELIVERY SYSTEMS OF TOMORROW

In the setting of the securities firm, we are beset with two principal dilemmas today. The first is to "create a customer" in a world of intense, if not fierce, competition, one in which product delivery is ultimately completed at the local level through a personalized framework of account executive–client activity; one in which the firms, in many cases, essentially sell similar products, if not the same stocks, bonds, and the like; and one in which there needs to be a better fit between client and product. This might be called "the world of the customer."

In the "world of the account executive," there are similar constraining influences to optimizing fully the account executive's role as the securities firm's "product spokesperson" to the world. At most securities firms, the account executive is swimming in a sea of products, many of which require substantial amounts of time to understand, and some of which need long lead times for the account executive to market—a financial planning package is one noteworthy example. These are time-consuming tasks for account executives, so they tend to gravitate to certain products and services.

Simply stated, the management problems as they relate to the product process at securities firms are twofold. The first is to create customers or at least get closer to them. The second, which is related to the first, is to help the account executive to do just that. To alleviate these difficulties, both a movement to a more, but certainly not totally, decentralized product-marketing structure (a vertical integrative strategy) together with a cross-pollination of product departmental personnel and management (a horizontal integrative strategy) could present at least a basis on which to counter the incipient stages of product-related management problems within securities firms.

NOTES

1. Peter F. Drucker, *The Practice of Management* (New York: Harper & Row, 1986), p. 37.
2. Peter F. Drucker, *Managing for Results* (New York: Harper & Row, 1986), p. 94.

CHAPTER 4

INVESTMENT BANKING: KEY ELEMENTS TO SUCCESS

THE MEANING OF SUCCESS

Simply and succinctly stated, firms that are in the investment banking business want to be in it in a much bigger way, and many that are not in it in any way want very much to be there. Achieving success in investment banking, however, is as problematic as defining just what success in the business really is. Success, to be sure, can be defined in a number of ways in the investment banking field. It may be simply the development of a finance department from its present level to whatever level it may seek. It may mean bringing large amounts of newly originated products into the firm, or it may even mean the development of individual professionals to be successful investment bankers. Other indications of success might be the dollar volume of negotiated underwritings a finance department comanages or senior manages, or a department's movement up in the underwriting rankings, however this is measured. Success may also be defined in terms of a department's expertise in a specific type of financing. Success in investment banking, indeed, can be indicated by anything that the firm thinks is representative of success, but in most cases it boils down to the ability to originate new financings in which the firm is senior manager.

For some major securities firms, their main business effort and largest revenue source has traditionally been the result of work with their corporate finance and public finance departments' clients. In these relationships, the firms act as senior managers or comanagers of the client's financings, which could include stock, debt, and other securities for the companies as well as bonds and notes for governmental entities in the United States as well as around the world. Through securities underwritings, which are completed on a negotiated basis rather than being presented for competitive bidding among the securities firms, the firms not only receive a management fee for the services rendered to the client but also have access to a greater percentage of securities that provide products for the firm's sales forces.

For many years, institutional securities firms handled the bulk of the negotiated underwritings as senior managers or comanagers, while the retail firms were mainly involved in selling capacities. Over the years, there has developed a small group of so-called "bulge-bracket" firms, which have established a stronghold in underwriting the lion's share of new issue offerings. Within this group emerged some retail-oriented securities firms, either through extensive efforts to develop their investment banking areas or through mergers of retail houses with other investment banking firms. The hold of these major firms on the new issue market has become rather entrenched, so that in many ways the market may be said to have become institutionalized. It should be noted, however, that not all the firms that are the dominant players in the corporate finance underwriting market are identical to those that do a large percentage of the public finance underwriting business. There are some notable exceptions. Yet, many of the largest underwriters of both corporate and municipal obligations are the same, with a few remaining ones being in the top group in either of the two underwriting spheres.

THE UNDERWRITING RANKINGS

How did the big players actually become so dominant in the underwriting business? Indeed, this is often the question asked by those firms that would like to move up in the underwriting standings. Such standings, it should be noted, can be measured in three ways.[1] One ranking method attributes the dollar volume of each underwriting to the senior manager; this is called the "full credit to lead manager" category. The second divides the dollar volume of the issue among all the managers and is called "full credit to each manager." The third category, and the one most often used, is entitled "bonus credit to lead manager," in which the dollar volume of each underwriting is divided evenly among the comanagers, with the senior manager receiving double the amount of any of the comanagers.

What is critical to note, however, is that many firms that are senior managers have been able to develop relationships with both corporate and municipal clients and thus are more readily acceptable to new clients as senior managers because of the past experience they bring to the competition table. Years ago, the more retail-oriented firms were chosen as comanagers because of their ability to sell large amounts of securities through their retail networks. However, some retail firms now have also developed substantial investment banking, institutional sales, trading, and underwriting capabilities, many of which rival firms that are largely institutional in nature.

It is important to understand how certain firms broke into the first-tier standings of those firms that have established strongholds in the corporate and municipal underwriting business. The firms that have done so over recent years have been successful largely because they have capitalized on activities or specialties that they did well. Firms have permeated the bulge-bracket status because of their capital base, trading capabilities, ability to originate new products that have been successfully marketed to potential clients, or the use of their retail system to distribute securities. A few firms have also come close to the industry leaders in managed underwritings because they have been successfully able to transfer the expertise developed through their financial advisory activities into positions as senior managers. They have done this by presenting their financial advisory credentials to potential clients in a way that suggests such work was essentially the same as that required of a senior manager, without forming syndicates and selling securities. Nevertheless, the development of sophisticated investment banking skills that have been turned into senior managerships and comanagerships has been a long and arduous process for most firms, resulting in a small number of firms underwriting a large proportion of the dollar volume of new corporate and municipal issues.

DEVELOPING AN INVESTMENT BANKING DEPARTMENT

Securities firms that have long lists of corporate or municipal finance clients have not, in most cases, spent the largest amount of their time cultivating new ones. This stems from the interest of investment bankers in keeping their relationships with clients ongoing, the difficulty in isolating potential clients to pursue, and the time required to have those relationships long enough to make the potential client an actual one. From the banker's standpoint, it is a much more precarious position to be in if a client is lost than if a potential client, out of the vast available number, does not actually become one. In brief, investment bankers may be at greater risk when they lose a client than they are rewarded when they secure a new one. Nevertheless, most managers of investment banking departments generally believe that a department's overall activity should be divided in spending two-thirds of its time servicing existing clients and one-third seeking new ones. This proportion, however, does not apply to every banker in every department. Rather, there are certain investment bankers who are considered to be more adept at getting new business, while others seem to be better suited to maintaining existing relationships. The split here is rather lopsided, and most agree that in any investment banking department, only approximately 10 to 15 percent of the personnel could be considered successful "new business" bankers.

In any event, there are a number of ways firms might seek to develop clients beyond their existing base. The first concept is the development of new products. Recent years have seen the development of more new products on Wall Street than ever before. New product development has been fostered in an environment consisting of many investment bankers, traders, and underwriters. Because many of the newer products are market related, they have led the firms into the creation of a capital markets concept whereby products are developed in close coordination between investment bankers, on the one hand, and trading, underwriting, and sales personnel on the other. These products could be used by both established clients and potential ones, making new products the most obvious answer to the problem of new business development in investment banking.

One of the more recent new business developments in investment banking harkens back to earlier days when firms became intimately involved with clients financially. Certain firms now have established what are called "merchant banking" operations. In its broadest sense, merchant banking involves securities firms providing upfront capital, bridge loans, or other financing packages for particular companies and then perhaps taking out those financings with the issuance of securities. The larger and better capitalized securities firms have used this technique as a way to generate new business. More importantly, this practice seems to have developed as a result of the takeovers of securities firms by corporations of substantial size. These larger parent corporate entities often already had lending facilities in house, and the combination of the two firms provided the opportunity for securities firms to develop their new business banking efforts better.

The more traditional new business development methods for investment banking operations have been rooted in creating a larger market share in a particular area of the client universe. The isolation of a particular market segment, either with regard to type of issuer, kinds of securities issued, size of company or government, competitive nature of the business, or future growth potential, is critical to directing the investment banking efforts of firms toward new areas. This approach can be used more by firms without either large resources or a substantial client base, as well as by firms seeking to penetrate further market segments in which they are already involved.

Related to this market niche idea is the concept that investment banking departments must develop their own strategic studies, specifying an organizational game plan for client development, and evaluating it on an ongoing basis. Some argue that this is an activity on which only some investment banking departments spend a lot of time. The main reason given for this is that the staffing of these departments is slim relative to the amount of work required, and senior bankers may not have opportunities to engage in this kind of activity. Most of what is accomplished in the way of developing new business game plans is done as much informally as it is formally. Yet, perhaps the most important responsibility of management in the investment banking arena today is the development of a strategic plan with achievable objectives and the monitoring of those objectives over both the short and long run. Without such a game plan, it is unlikely that an investment banking department can develop or even keep up with its competitors if those firms have developed plans and are sticking to their own directives.

BANKING AT MIDSIZE FIRMS

Certain of the largest and medium-sized firms that do not have a substantial investment banking client base present the most difficult problems to developing an investment banking capability in either corporate or public finance. Many of these firms have the infrastructure, in terms of capital and distribution capability, to support a relatively strong banking operation, but for many reasons, such a capability has never been developed. Some of these firms have attempted to create strong investment banking divisions with fanfare in a few cases, and in a quiet way in others. Such firms could, and perhaps even should, employ the strategies cited above for the larger investment banking firms, but they would have to be accomplished on a much smaller scale and should be coupled with three management strategies.

First, these firms must create a specific strategy around a market niche that they feel comfortable attempting to penetrate. Specific target clients must be isolated before embarking on a wholesale developmental investment banking effort. Second, and as in most cases in the securities industry, hiring the right people is the sine qua non of development. This is particularly important for relatively small investment banking departments, simply because so few professionals are employed. There is no other way to develop any business, especially one that is so client oriented and rests so heavily on the success of individual relationships. As a corollary to this, without hiring the right `senior banker as departmental manager, most of the department's development efforts are going to fall far short of the mark. Finally, most securities industry managers have recognized that the development of investment banking culture is critical to the success of any banking department. Such a culture is truly predicated on the people within the cultural milieu. Without a senior person at the top of the department who exemplifies the investment banking business, successful development of a department is highly unlikely, and there is also likely to be competing claims by department members for the departmental throne.

Certain regional firms and specialized securities firms or boutiques have developed the personnel, the market niche, and the clients in the investment banking field and are satisfied with their ongoing operations. As a result, they may not want to develop a larger investment banking presence. They may even fear creating monster-sized organizations over which they have no control. Management of such firms should be aware that controlled growth is always an alternative and may even be important in maintaining a market niche. This, too, requires an ongoing process of strategy development and the monitoring of objectives. Controlled growth for smaller firms might also entail working with larger firms on some financings. The success of these kinds of arrangements and the opportunities afforded to the firms involved vary from situation to situation and by no means exhaust the many other alternatives available to small, midsize, or regional securities firms for developing their investment banking departments in any way and at any rate they desire.

PREVENTING CLIENT BASE DETERIORATION

Perhaps the chief management concern facing investment banking divisions, especially those with long client lists, is the potential deterioration of their client base through efforts made by firms that are either comanagers of the account or others that are not in it. This can happen to a firm when it is either a senior manager or a comanager. When a firm is a senior manager, it can be bounced to comanagership status. As a comanager, the firm could be divested of its position and thus lose the client completely.

The deterioration of a firm's client base, however modest, may result from a number of causes. The one that concerns management the most and is perhaps the most likely cause of losing a client is the loss of senior personnel or another banker who is in charge of that particular account relationship. Very often the client and the client's personnel have come to depend so heavily on the senior banker assigned to the account that the client is willing to follow that senior banker to another securities firm. This usually occurs only in situations where the banker has been given total control over the account and the client has come to see the banker, not the firm, as its so-called comanager or senior manager. It is also likely to occur when the banker has been instrumental in bringing the client to the firm but is less likely to happen in situations where the client was already with the firm. Sufficient contact with the client by other banking personnel at the securities firm, and perhaps also by some of the firm's most senior executives and personnel from the underwriting, trading, and sales departments, can keep the loss of clients resulting from a firm's personnel defections to a minimum.

Another reason for loss by a firm of its investment banking clients or its deterioration in the underwriting rankings, especially firms that rank high in relative standings, is because firms of significant stature in corporate and public finance do not sufficiently and quickly enough develop their investment banking departments at a rate commensurate to the expansion taking place at other firms. This is perhaps the most difficult management problem in the banking area to understand and solve. There have been a number of firms that have broken into the upper echelon of corporate and municipal underwritings and have even outdistanced some industry leaders over recent years, largely as a result of an expansionist strategy, whereby the firm allocated substantial resources to its investment banking areas. For some reason, a few bulge-bracket firms have been loath to hire senior bankers from other firms with well-established records and long client lists. There may be a number of reasons for this, including the fear of hiring top people who might usurp others' positions in the department, the unwillingness of the firm's senior management to allocate resources to that department, or the fear by management that the department's culture will be upset. History shows, however, that hiring top bankers from the outside has worked, especially to the detriment of those firms that have not done so. This phenomenon is particularly interesting when considering the fact that the key ingredient to the development of client relationships and garnering new clients is, much more often than not, the individual banker. Indeed, if there is one cardinal rule to be followed in order to develop an investment banking department to the fullest extent possible, it is that the firm must hire the very best investment bankers it can. An investment banking department, moreover, is often only as good as its most senior banker or manager is, and the investment banking community bears witness to this statement.

The rankings of firms that have a proportionately large share of the underwriting business can also fall if the firms are wedded to a particular type of business in the corporate and municipal area that, for one reason or another, could have run its course. The reasons for such a development include changes in the tax laws, interest by issuers in new alternative products, and vast changes in interest rates, making products offered by firms less workable. This situation is one over which the firm may have no real control.

There are two other possible reasons for a decline in a firm's rankings, which are more the result of actions by other firms than the particular firm whose ranking is dropping. For instance, there may be mergers of securities firms that, when their underwriting activities are taken together, catapult them to the upper levels of underwriting rankings and eclipse some of the industry leaders. Similarly, certain firms that were not in the upper echelon of managers in corporate and public finance underwritings could bypass those firms that occupy higher positions as a result of a number of very large senior managed offerings that they underwrite in a year. These developments are difficult, if not impossible, for most firms to control, but they must be watched carefully nonetheless, as much from a strategy perspective as from a management standpoint, when touting the firm's underwriting rankings as an important reason for selection as a senior manager or comanager.

QUALITY PROFESSIONALS AND MANAGEMENT

In the final analysis, however, the success of an investment banking department depends on the quality of its professionals and its management. According to Samuel L. Hayes III, professor of investment banking at the Harvard Business School, "In investment banking, the most important resource is people, and it is a resource that you have to build and nurture all the time," and "managing those kind of fast track, ambitious individuals and keeping up the whole range of client contacts, is a full time job, and then some."[2]

NOTES

1. See also the annual corporate and municipal underwriting results in *Institutional Investor* magazine. For additional information, see Samuel L. Hayes III, A. Michael Spence, and David Van Praag Marks, *Competition in the Investment Banking Industry* (Cambridge, Mass.: Harvard University Press, 1983).
2. *The New York Times,* February 8, 1987.

CHAPTER 5

INSTITUTIONAL SALES: THE MANAGEMENT OF PRODUCT

Access to new issue products in the securities industry usually comes through the underwriting process, in which a group of firms as managers, with one as the lead, underwrites a new securities issue. This process thus provides the firm's sales force with these securities to sell—that is, the firms buy the securities from, say, a corporation or government, and then sell them to purchasers. If the firm is a senior manager or comanager of the securities issue, the client or issuer has decided to allow them to help structure the issue, take the greater amount of risk in selling it, and have a larger percentage of the securities to sell than other firms who are not in the management group. However, there are powerful and profitable institutional sales forces in particular product areas of some firms that are not major participants in the new issue securities business, largely because of the quality of their management.

THE NEW ISSUE BUSINESS IN PERSPECTIVE

The most difficult question facing firms that do not manage a large amount of corporate or public finance business is how to develop an institutional sales department of importance and profitability. This is not to say that a surfeit of senior-managed new issue products is all that an institutional sales force needs to be productive, service clients, and generate profits. The origination of a new issue product does not insure that it will be adequately marketed and that a sales force will penetrate all of its clients to the fullest possible extent. As a matter of fact, the concentration on new issue business by salespeople at firms that do a large percentage of their business in this manner may result in the sales force's avoidance of the secondary market and its trading opportunities in which all types of buyers may be interested. Some have argued that concentrating on new issue business may actually limit the potential relationship between the institutional client and the institutional salesperson. When the account does in fact participate in the secondary market for securities to a significant extent, and when the account believes, at the same time, that the new issue business may be available from any salesperson whose firm brings the securities to market, the relationship between the institutional salesperson and the client institution may be more apparent than real.

Every institutional sales force by its very nature, given the amount of products in the marketplace for all types of securities, such as corporates, governments, municipals, equities, mortgages, and all their derivatives, could service clients better, improve their gross production, penetrate accounts further, develop a wider client base, and, as a result, become more profitable. This will not happen by wishing it to occur; institutional salespeople sell products and help with trades on a daily basis, so that remunerative incentives alone, which are now available, will not necessarily accomplish all that could be done. To be sure, the reality of this situation is that the growth and development of an institutional sales force in many instances is as much the result of the efforts of one single individual, namely, its manager, as it is a consequence of anything else. Similarly, a sales force's success in the vast majority of cases, and especially ones without new products, is limited by the ability of the sales manager and the manager's position within the organization.

SOME MAJOR PRODUCT AREAS

Some basic products of securities firms that might be used here for analytical purposes are: equities, and municipal, corporate, and government bonds. Different firms may emphasize different products to a greater extent than others for institutional sales purposes, and this may or may not depend on the extent to which they originate securities issues of these generic products. Even within product areas of a given firm, such as municipal notes in the municipal bond department, corporate high-yield securities in the corporate bond department, or public offerings in the equity department, firms may have developed varying abilities to originate these types of new issues. In any of these cases, the firm may want to develop either its institutional sales penetration for such specific subproduct areas, the entire product area, or all major products, whether or not the firm has achieved a degree of success in originating securities issues in any, all, some, or part of these major product arenas.

Nevertheless, institutional salespeople do not necessarily have to depend on a sizable originating capability of the firm for their success. They can be successful by dealing with certain types or levels of accounts or by working more closely with their department's traders. There are other ways to develop an institutional presence in circumstances with specific constraints. For instance, some firms do not originate any significant number of new finance issues and have no real trading capability. Here, salespeople may be successful by specializing in small-size institutional accounts. Another type of firm may have only some new issue products available but have excellent traders, an established swap group, and a large inventory. This firm will cater to a different institutional salesperson who could be successful by becoming involved with institutional accounts needing to deal in the secondary market. There are small firms with some salespeople who ply their trade in a multitude of ways; but basically, these individuals have an in-depth knowledge of trading or the mathematics of some securities and have close working relationships with a small number of institutional accounts. In any event, it is worth discussing some major product areas to show what an institutional sales force faces in each and how management might be successfully developed.

Equities or Stocks

The management of the institutional equity area is complicated because so many different professionals at the firm can be closely aligned with the institutional buyer, but it affords management the opportunity to make an impact. The equity product area is split between those stocks "listed" and those traded over the counter (OTC) and considered "unlisted." There is also some cross-fertilization along client lines in the listed and OTC business. Closely allied to these areas are futures, options, and the preferred stock product department, which offer those trading, selling, and purchasing stocks myriad possibilities for sales-related activities. Each area of the equity department in most firms has position traders and sales traders. Position traders are primarily concerned with the need for order flow and the consequent commitment of capital. Very often position traders trade at a loss, although most of the time they try to at least close out flat, meaning to break even. The goal is to stimulate order flow so that institutional purchasers will buy from them and trading and sales activity will be stimulated. One of the major management dilemmas in the institutional equity area today is the potential for losses as a result of taking positions to encourage order flow from institutional purchasers. Management has been known to follow accounts closely to make certain that they are not unduly taking advantage of the firm's posture in acceding to trade with them.

Research has become critically important to the development of the institutional equity business, especially when the firm is not a major originator of new securities issues. The sales traders' relationship with the trading desk and the accounts as a go-between is pivotal in the development of a strong institutional equity business and can be helped immeasurably when the research department generates ideas that can then be used by the sales traders. For large securities firms, the research effort is seen as absolutely critical, whether the firms have substantial new issue products or not. Even some very small firms have top analysts who develop excellent ideas for the sales force.

Municipal Bonds

Municipal bonds provide a wide range of number, type, quality, and maturity options available for institutional buyers, and it is therefore an especially rich area for the development of account relationships based on acknowledged expertise in specific municipal bond areas. Management can therefore make a tremendous impact in the municipal institutional sales area by developing sales expertise slated to the type of business certain accounts do or in which some would like to have better service. Sales specialties can be developed to service institutions that deal in certain qualities of municipals, only purchase bonds in broad categories such as general obligation or revenue bonds, or buy specific types of revenue bonds or bonds and notes of a given geographic area. The complex nature of the security backing many municipal bonds also affords the institutional salespeople the opportunity to develop a business partially based on special situations or "story bonds" about which the salespersons may have developed an in-depth knowledge. In addition, the nature of municipal bonds offers opportunities for swapping them, thus providing another area of potential. Finally, because of the complexity of the municipal market, institutional salespeople and clients often work closely with the securities firm's municipal research department on issues that may raise significant questions, and the research department often provides the clients with a specialized service.

Corporate Bonds

Today's corporate bond market is roughly divided into two groups of issue types: corporate bonds issued by utilities and other corporations; and the newer high-yield bonds that have not achieved the high-quality credit standing of those issued by most corporations. In many ways, the corporate bond market is a trading game with some new issue products becoming available, most recently from issuers selling high-yield paper. This situation is in striking contrast to the one of many years ago dominated by major utilities and other companies, which frequently brought to market bond issues of substantial size.

Research has always been important in the corporate bond area, both from a credit and market standpoint. Many credits in the corporate bond area that would be considered under investment grade elsewhere are traded on an active basis, and this situation existed long before the advent of the high-yield market. Corporate bond research, therefore, is also important to the sales effort. Securities firms have long since had corporate bond analysts, some of whom specialize in the utility or telecommunications fields and others who work on the bonds issued by corporations, both industrial and nonindustrial. Recent years have seen the research activity in the high-yield area burgeon.

Government Bonds

The government bond department is unlike the former three areas because firms do have fully staffed finance departments seeking to underwrite all new issues of government securities. As a result, the institutional sales effort does not depend on product development and origination from within the firm, but it is facilitated by the involvement of the government bond department in the new issues of securities brought to market by the federal government. The institutional sales effort of a government bond department depends more on the department's trading capability, and this is only necessary to maintain an ongoing sales effort with the largest accounts in the market. Yet, even with a firm's exceptional government bond trading capability, the institutional sales effort can usually be developed much further, in much the same way as the corporate and municipal bond sales efforts. The research work done for the government bond area is largely market related because there is little need for credit research since the securities are issued by the federal government or its agencies, although the new derivative securities do need some explanation.

THE INSTITUTIONAL SALES MANAGER AS CATALYST FOR ACTION

Over the years, the role of the institutional sales manager at most firms and in many product areas has been largely an administrative one, with some minimum amount of active sales-related work. This is the result of a number of factors, but most important is the large number of administrative duties that must be done for an institutional sales force of any significant size. However, the institutional sales manager has also stayed out of the line of fire for other reasons, and perhaps has even been told to do so by the firm's senior managers. Most salespeople have developed relationships of some sort with a small number of institutional accounts. Any activity by the institutional sales manager that serves to transcend or seek involvement in these relationships has the potential to boomerang back against the manager. (This should not be so, but it often is.) Account management may, in fact, require that this be a part of the active role an institutional sales manager might and should take, but it is not necessarily more important than those discussed below. When carried to the extent suggested here, the job is not only a significant one but also a major responsibility, and it has the potential of helping generate revenues of significant size.

Major Activities

The duties and activities of the institutional sales manager described below can be done by others, and this may sometimes occur by default. In the long run, however, things do not just happen by themselves, and leaving the activities to evolve often limits their effectiveness. To be sure, the role of the institutional sales manager is somewhat different from product area to product area. For the same product areas at different firms, the institutional sales manager's role also may differ depending on the emphasis placed on the various types of securities and activities within the same product areas. What is presented below is a sort of kaleidoscopic view that brings into focus what might be considered important activities or roles that an institutional sales manager can develop to promote a sales force's success. These duties are active ones; they are not of the administrative variety nor do they involve the monitoring of accounts and account relationships, although these are important aspects of the job and are discussed later in this chapter. Among other roles, therefore, the institutional sales manager is:

1. The sales force's representative to the underwriting or syndicate area for securities allocation purposes with a view toward fulfilling institutional account requests.
2. The major allocator of securities to the institutional sales force on new issues in an effort to assure that all the accounts get the proper proportional amounts over time.
3. A point of contact for the traders by providing information about the need to position certain securities for the institutional sales force, and also an information conduit to the sales force as to why they can or cannot have securities and at what price they may be available.
4. The disseminator of information to the sales force on the available securities that the trading desk has in inventory.
5. The disseminator of information on the types of buyers as well as which buyers are in and out of the market, for what reasons, and for which kinds of securities.
6. A catalyst for action and facilitator of trades between and among salespeople, especially for those located around the country, based on trading desk products and the buying and selling needs of accounts.
7. The developer of sales strategies based on the knowledge of buyers' portfolios, their purchasing habits, and their changing requirements for securities.
8. The interface among the sales force, traders, and accounts about swap ideas and suggestions, and also a major source of information on the mathematics of these and other transactions.
9. The interface among the sales force, traders, accounts, and the research department for questions and answers as well as explanations of research material or issuers, which includes arranging meetings to solidify account relationships and present research ideas and reports.
10. The disseminator of major market-related information coming over the firm's communication systems, which includes short-term trends, significant news items, and potential effects that proposed or newly enacted legisla-

tion may have on the buying activities of accounts and on the major markets.

To be sure, these functions are absolutely critical, especially to institutional salespeople who are located out of the firm's main headquarters where the institutional sales manager is located; a few of these duties could be full-time jobs. The underlying characteristic of many of these activities is that they focus on serving the institutional client and translating this work into market-related activity. They also form the basis of managing an institutional sales operation and developing it, with or without significant new issue products originated by the firm. Sales forces do not and cannot develop totally by themselves, so it is up to the institutional sales manager to play a major role in their success.

STRUCTURAL REPORTING RELATIONSHIPS

"Form follows function," the saying goes, and nowhere in the securities industry has it become more apparent and more important than in the area of institutional sales management along product lines. Indeed, the extent to which a sales manager can successfully achieve the objectives of the job description as "catalyst for action" outlined above is also a function of the sales manager's reporting relationships within the organization and the manager's resultant job description, which most professionals expect to be operationalized on the basis of the manager's fit within the corporate body politic.

Basically, two reporting relationships are possible for the institutional sales manager in any product department at most Wall Street firms. In the first, the institutional sales manager reports completely within the confines of the product department and to its manager, so that institutional sales, trading, and underwriting is housed under one product department roof. In the other relationship, the institutional sales manager reports directly to the fixed-income sales manager for those products, the head of the equity division for stocks, or to a general institutional sales manager on a firmwide basis. This situation takes an institutional sales manager's reporting relationship outside the product departments. There are variations on these themes, with the institutional sales manager having a dual reporting relationship, reporting both within the product department and also outside it in varying degrees.

Direct Product Line and Dual Reporting

When an institutional sales manager reports within a specific product department and to the department's manager, this solidifies the manager's relationship with that department, contributing to the overall coordination of the sales operation. It subtly persuades the traders and underwriters that the configuration should foster a "one-for-all" effort. Whether or not sales revenues go into a firmwide or department pool or any other split for accounting purposes, this arrangement symbolizes a unity of effort and direction. It also provides a reasonable basis for the directed movement of securities among the underwriting, sales, and trading areas. It completes, in a way, the product management loop of a particular product area.

Most importantly, an institutional sales manager's reporting relationship within a given product area provides a rationale for the development of the sales manager's active roles as defined here and their acceptance, support, and encouragement by salespeople, traders, and syndicate professionals alike. This is the most potent and persuasive argument for an intradepartmental reporting relationship of the sales manager, or a dual one that emphasizes a close working and reporting relationship within a product department with management coordination from outside it. In other words, it makes sense from a bottom-up organizational perspective.

Additionally, when the institutional sales manager reports to the manager of the product department, the department head can more easily orchestrate the entire department's risk-taking effort. The manager can also direct the institutional sales manager's efforts toward more activity in the roles ennumerated above and do so without outside interference. Conversely, when the institutional sales manager of a given product area reports only to a superior who is on the sidelines and outside the product department and who, by virtue of distance alone, has less interest on a day-to-day basis in the product department, the institutional sales manager's efforts are usually less intense, more diffused, and more administrative in nature. Also, a direct reporting relationship of the institutional sales manager to the product department manager results in fewer competing claims by others for the sales manager's attention.

On the the other hand, when an institutional sales manager does report to a general overall sales manager located outside the product department, some significant advantages may sometimes occur. Firms are now looking to the single client who purchases different products. In these situations, a general sales manager who oversees institutional sales managers of the various product areas, some or all of which service the single client, can create a helpful arrangement. From this perspective, the firm is looking to establish a relationship with the client, and the success of this relationship is expected to be a function of the ability to service the client through a number of product areas. As a result, the client becomes the firm's focus, not each institutional salesperson who services the client in a particular product. For instance, in many cases the institutional buyer may purchase two products from the firm, such as corporate and government bonds, resulting in lines being blurred among fixed-income instruments from the client's perspective. Consequently, the relationship of the firm to the client is a result of the activity of two institutional salespeople, each covering different products. It makes sense, then, to have an individual act as an overall manager overseeing all general account relationships and to have the institutional sales managers covering the two different product areas also report, in some way, to the overall institutional sales manager. In this case, the overall manager would cover taxable fixed-income products. A dual reporting relationship of the institutional sales managers may be useful too.

It must be stressed, however, that many of the management configuration and reporting relationships of any institutional sales area are also dependent on the client. Some clients may have different professionals purchasing each product, while others may use the same professional to buy one or more securities, whether or not they are similar or related. The in-house personnel set-up used by institutional buyers for their securities purchases also varies by type of buyer and size of the institution. Consequently, no single securities firm management reporting relationship will be optimum for all buyers of every product from each department. Every firm and product department or combination of them may have to devise its own management set-up that works best for the majority of accounts it is servicing, and then handle the others on an ad hoc basis.

Nonetheless, an overall sales manager provides at least a common managerial denominator to disseminate firmwide institutional portfolio and sales strategies and to develop better compensation packages. Furthermore, the need to monitor and compare the performance of all institutional sales professionals and measure the extent to which objectives are being met might be more easily achieved if some control were vested in a single senior institutional sales manager. As a result, a dual reporting relationship, if its parameters are agreed upon by all, may be a good complement to a direct reporting one.

ACCOUNT MANAGEMENT

The assignment, monitoring, and reassignment of accounts, and the need to hire additional salespeople to develop accounts is a management problem of the first order. This goes hand in hand with the concept that the institutional account must have a continuing relationship not only with the institutional salesperson, but also with the firm, especially during times when an account is out of the market in a particular product area. Moreover, when the account is out of pocket in one product area, the client may be in the market for another product and can be serviced by a different institutional salesperson of the same firm. This further emphasizes the need for a firmwide relationship with the account, orchestrated by the institutional sales manager and developed further by an overall sales manager. Additionally, the overall institutional sales manager can speak directly to the account as a quasi-independent observer and is thus in the position to solicit information on the qualitative status of all the relationships between the account and the salespeople in all the product areas who are assigned to cover that particular institutional purchaser.

As part of the account management process, it is necessary for the institutional sales manager to assess the success of each salesperson with every account and make changes when necessary. The reassignment of accounts and the hiring of new salespeople to cover accounts are among the major responsibilities of the institutional sales manager. These functions may at times be unpleasant to perform, and therefore sales managers often shirk them. Yet, they are basic to the job, crucial to the development of any sales force, and critical to servicing clients.

CHAPTER 6

RESEARCH: MAKING AN
IMPACT

Any cursory review of the amount of research material available at a branch office of most large securities firms or at their headquarters would lead an uninitiated and independent observer to the conclusion that the firms generate perhaps more research-related matter per employee than any other type of corporation in the world. Indeed, the amount of research generated by the firm's analysts and sent throughout the securities system and even to the customers is, in most instances, tremendous. It represents a cost to the firms of millions of dollars annually, made up of remuneration for the firm's securities analysts, expenses for support staff and overhead, and many other related costs, not the least of which are printing and mailing charges.

In general, research on Wall Street involves the analysis of corporations and governments through studies of their securities as well as information on the many securities markets worldwide and the general direction of interest rates. Making sense of this voluminous information is difficult enough for many analysts, each of whom usually specializes in a particular area of research or study a select number of companies or governments. For the investor, however, both institutional and retail, keeping up with the amount of information made available even within each investor's own sphere of expertise often becomes a mind-boggling effort. Even some of the most sophisticated institutional investors throw up their hands and say, in effect, that they "can't even begin to look at all this material, let alone read it and digest it." This very statement points up perhaps the most pressing problem today facing managers of research departments in securities firms and is certainly one likely to remain important in the future.

THE RESEARCH MENU

Broadly speaking, research on Wall Street can be categorized into five major areas. Most of the research firms provide relates to information on corporations and thus will be called "corporate research." Most notably, this includes equity or stock research about listed and unlisted securities, as well as information related to the debt of companies, although this latter coverage sometimes falls within the fixed-income or bond research area. For discussion purposes here, however, corporate debt will be included in the category of general corporate research because research relating to the bond markets, as generally defined in the fixed-income milieu, is much more often market related and may best be discussed separately.

Basically then, corporate research covers two interrelated security types: equity and debt. The debt dimension includes bonds, preferred stock, debentures, and other similar types of securities, some of which do not have all the characteristics of either equity or debt but are nonetheless of a corporate nature.

The second area, namely bond market research, is one to which different firms devote varying amounts of attention. Some firms have relatively large and well-established bond market research departments. In other firms, the information related to the bond markets is provided by specialists from different departments located throughout the firm and perhaps supplemented with material from a small cadre of bond market research professionals who work either directly or tangentially with the firm's chief economist. Bond market research can run the gamut in diversity from general descriptions of the various debt markets worldwide to very sophisticated, analytical research on the bond markets and various yield relationships, both descriptive and prescriptive.

A third and somewhat related research area concentrates on portfolio research, theory, and strategy, usually of the institutional variety. Portfolio strategy has become an increasingly important research tool on Wall Street and over the years has been relied on by institutions in a greater number of ways than ever before. To some extent, portfolio strategy does in fact include corporate research coverage, both equity and debt. Very often the two can be combined, and both can be housed under one larger investment management and portfolio strategy roof within the securities firm. Some firms have a well-developed capability in this area. Sometimes the departments have a heavy emphasis on bond market research, although the extent to which it is entwined with that area depends on a particular firm's management strategy and its reporting relationships. Portfolio strategy departments related to the bond market research area, however, have become more highly developed, especially in the case of a few securities firms.

The fourth research arena, one that has developed greatly over recent years, is the municipal bond research area. In most firms, this department is located either within or closely allied to the municipal bond department. In other firms, the municipal bond research department is a part of the fixed-income research effort under which is housed bond market research, corporate bond research, and municipal bond research. Even in these situations, the municipal bond research department tends to operate in a semiautonomous manner because of the specialized nature of its activity; the research work and the information provided does not involve corporate credits and is usually only tangentially related to general bond market research. In most cases, municipal bond research focuses on the credit quality and ratings of states, local governments of general jurisdiction, and revenue authorities. In other situations, a certain proportion of the research effort is slated for tax-exempt or municipal market research.

The fifth and perhaps the most notable research area is a firm's economics department headed by the firm's chief economist, who is generally the organization's interest rate predictor and is also the firm's "window to the research world." Interest rate forecasting is surely both a science and an art. For securities firms, it has become especially significant because of the notoriety a firm can receive and the business it could obtain because of its chief economist. Over the years, it has been said that there are a few economists on Wall Street whose words can move the markets, and this may have been the case in a couple of instances. Every investor, however, whether institutional or retail, requires at least some information on where interest rates are headed in the future, both short- and long-term. To the extent that a firm's economist receives wide publicity and even is correct in predictions about interest rates, the firm would stand to profit in some form to a greater or lesser extent. It is hard for the economists of many firms to develop this kind of notoriety and capability; there are only so many people who can be quoted so much of the time. Different institutions and investors do follow certain economists, and the extent to which economists are followed may be a bellwether of the activity that their firms will receive as a result.

THE POINT OF IT ALL

The audience for the research product falls into two broad areas with segments in each area: the external and the internal audiences. The external audience segments for research include the firm's clients, both institutional and retail groups, and the press that could receive research oriented toward either the retail or institutional client base. The internal audience segments include those areas of the firm that could make use of the research. Generally speaking, these could be broken down into two broad segments: the investment banking division; and the sales, trading, and underwriting areas. With these audience segments for research kept in mind as the so called "customers" for the research product, there are three dictums that seem to be important in developing and focusing a securities firm's research effort:

1. Research cannot be all things to all people.
2. The emphasis of the research department's efforts must be placed in areas and on topics where the firm's emphasis is placed.

3. The single most important goal of research, albeit the most difficult one, is to have the greatest impact on what the firm does and how it should service its customers.

Interestingly, there are a few firms that try to have their research effort be all things to all people, not necessarily all the time and to absolutely everyone. In most cases, these firms seek the broadest possible mandate for their research departments. This is very difficult to accomplish and is often a rather costly proposition, although it is certainly a noble goal. Most firms, as well as the vast majority of other financial organizations, however, concentrate their research efforts on areas that the firm emphasizes. Surely, there is not a great number of firms whose research effort is concentrated on areas where the firm is not placing an emphasis; but there are exceptions to this rule, especially in cases where the firm wishes to develop a specific area of expertise. Nevertheless, most firms have still allocated an enormous amount of their resources toward the research. Yet, the greatest challenge and the one that is the most useful from a firm's standpoint is to allocate the research resources to achieve the greatest impact possible.

To turn the three dictums on their heads, it is perhaps best to start with the premise that research should make the greatest impact possible—that is the strategy. How this goal will be achieved should flow from that general mandate. From a management standpoint, this requires that the professionals in the research department be operating at their highest capacity, and the capacity should be judged perhaps most of all by impact. Impact must of necessity be judged by the ability of the research product to elicit responses by both the firm's external and internal audiences.

THE EXTERNAL AUDIENCE

Creating an impact through the reseach product on the firm's major external audiences, namely the retail and institutional client base, is not exactly an easy chore, given the tremendous amount of quality research presently available. To be sure, the competition is keen at the very least. It goes without saying that one of the major methods of creating an impact by any corporate business, but most especially in the research milieu, is to have the material picked up in some form by the nation's press, which includes newspapers, books, magazines, television, and radio. This is easier said than done.

Creating an impact in the firm's retail client base can be best described by the retail investor's response to the research effort, which may or may not come through to the client's account executive but is measurable by the following statements that a retail client may make or think. For instance: "The research is so clear"; "I knew just what to do when I read the report"; "It's the only report I have seen on the subject"; "This is the first report out on it"; "I never did understand that, now I do"; and retrospectively, "The analyst was right!" Although all securities firm research does not engender these kinds of responses from retail clients, such statements point up the fact that a research product has made a noticeable impact. Most important to the retail client is that the research product is understandable, clear, and even relatively brief.

For institutions, research that makes an impact must elicit comments not that different from those coming from the retail client, although the character of the research itself must be much more sophisticated given the nature of the institutional clientele. For one thing, a topic that makes an impact on institutions is harder to come by; discerning investment characteristics to look for that have previously gone unnoticed is certainly a difficult mandate to accomplish. What most institutions seem to appreciate is having a summary of the analysis in one place with a brief rationale for the investment suggestion that both encompasses and summarizes the research report and also adds an analytical dimension previously unemphasized or undiscovered. More often than not, institutions like to see some combination of credit and market analysis as they relate to a particular stock, bond, or other security. In addition, the more intriguing reports to which institutions gravitate and that interest the press are on particularly timely topics, somewhat controversial in nature. These are the research reports likely to create responses.

For the external audiences of the securities firm's research product, a few major strategic research successes that make great impact are worth more in prestige and benefits than all the other modest efforts that are made. Redundancy in research is not its most sought-after characteristic. Many institutions have long since argued that having 20 analysts on Wall Street sending them reports on the same company with only marginal differences in basic analysis and recommendations is not worth much analytically.

From a management perspective, some of the key activities deserving attention are the research department's topic selection for its reports, its work with the retail and institutional clients and those professionals who service them, and its ongoing relationship with the firm's public relations department with a view toward increasing media contact and thus achieving the greatest opportunity for impact to occur. Management needs a keen sense of the marketing aspect of the research product but also has to have a thorough understanding of the needs of its client base—its external audience—for research, and the retail and institutional segments within it. For firms with only modest resources available to fund and develop the research effort, the focus of research over time should be allocated proportionately among the various audience segments that the firm seeks to reach.

THE INTERNAL AUDIENCE

First and foremost (and surprisingly to some), the research product must appeal to its internal audience—that is, the firm's professionals, including its investment bankers, salespeople, traders, and underwriters. This need not be all at the same time and for each research report, but certainly when appropriate for each audience within the firm. If the research product will not appeal to the professionals within the firm who must use it, it is highly unlikely that it will be workable for the firm's clients; and even if it is, it certainly will not be high on the list of priorities for presentation purposes by the firm's professionals, thus limiting its ultimate utility and impact. Indeed, the response to the research product by the firm's professionals can be, and is likely to end up, more important than the response provided by any other audience group or segment. The impact of the research product on the firm's professionals might be used as a "survivability quotient" of not only the product and its use but also the research department and its staff.

For the internal audience, the research department must often make an impact through word of mouth. In the capital markets area, this involves a good working relationship between the sales, underwriting, and trading departments on the one hand and the firm's research department on the other. This is done through explanations by analysts about the firm's research to professionals who use it as well as the answering of questions asked about the research products and any one of myriad research-related items. Very often professionals within any of the groups who employ the research product connect the research analysts with their clients for similar kinds of questions that ultimately develop into discussions, sometimes covering a wide range of topics. All this activity helps professionals in the capital markets division of the firm as well as account executives in the branch system service their clients better.

Over recent years, many securities industry professionals have touted the use of the research department, its personnel, and its products as an aid to their investment banking divisions' clients as well as to the bankers themselves. More often than not, each investment banker follows or is assigned to only a certain number of clients with a given set of parameters, usually related to client type. Research personnel, for example, study situations from a much wider perspective and have at their fingertips much available data and information on a great many trends. Calling on researchers to provide this information to the bankers and to the firm's clients and prospective ones has become a useful tool for all those concerned. It not only helps the bankers develop a broader expertise in their areas of interest, but it also can be an immeasurable aid to banking clients, both corporate and government, who have a desire and a need to have someone assess them independently. The extent to which research is used in this fashion varies from firm to firm and from department to department. To be sure, this is not necessarily a new use of research personnel, but rather it is one that has burgeoned over time at most securities firms.

THE PROBLEM OF ACCESS

Probably the most significant, if not the most pressing, problem facing many research departments today is attempting to respond to the seemingly unending and unimpeded requests for information from all types of clients and professionals within the securities firm. For most analysts on Wall Street, this activity represents the ultimate juggling act of priority needs for information from all those potential recipients who believe that they have the right to know and that the responses to their requests must be immediate ones. At times this pressure cooker atmosphere, created by the onslaught of information requests, creates a tenseness within the research department. It is nice for analysts to know that what is being done within the research department is very important to others, but when a host of information requests collide at the same time, life is made more difficult for them. As a result, it is the job of the research department head and analysts to develop a back-to-back schedule that pits one information request against another and then requires analysts, the analysts' support staff, and others involved in gathering this type of information to handle the requests so that the information can be imparted on a priority basis.

There are a number of ways securities firm managers can keep the requests for research information from becoming too burdensome. From the standpoint of the investment banking areas, this boils down to what is an efficient use of the research department's time versus what could be done by the investment bankers. Also, in any large retail branch system, the potential exists for the research department to be barraged with telephone calls and requests for information and data from the account executives and their clients. Some firms allow these requests to flow directly to the analysts without any screening process, and mundane questions and information requests that could be effectively handled by others within the sales support system are funneled directly to analysts. Thus, the time the analysts spend responding to these requests is not time put to the very best use. Other firms have adopted some screening procedures for retail account executives and their clients in their quest for answers to what can be a huge number of questions. Some firms have supplemented this screening procedure with computer links to the retail branch offices, and sometimes directly to the account executives' desks, providing on-line information and answers to the more likely to be asked questions about securities and investments. For most firms, however, some kind of screening procedure becomes mandatory because of the potential, and often the actual, amount of requests for information from the sales system and its clients coming into the research department.

The screening of information requests from the trading and underwriting departments of any division is less important than it is for most of the other research department's audiences. This is so because traders and underwriters, more often than not, do their own screening. Their questions usually do require the expertise of the research analyst, because they often have sought the answers before turning to the firm's analysts. Even more important is the fact that questions and requests for information coming from these market participants are, in most instances, about their ongoing trading and underwriting activity and thus are related more to risk positions having the opportunities for profits and the potential for losses on an immediate basis. As a result, analysts are usually quite attuned to the needs of traders, underwriters, and other such professionals within the firm because of their apparent needs for high-priority information.

Somewhat related to the character of the information requests by the active market participants within the securities firm are the needs of the institutional sales staff and their clients. Although they ask all types of research questions, their needs most notably fall into two broad categories. The first consists of requests for technical information that can be about the market or specific credits and usually involve impending transactions of significant size. The second kind of request relates more broadly to conceptual or theoretical questions about the market and issuers. In both these areas, the quality of the answers provided by a firm's research department may or may not separate it from the research done by the firm's competitors. Not surprisingly, therefore, these institutional information requirements over time have received a relatively high priority in the research department's hierarchy of information requests.

ALL THINGS TO ALL PEOPLE?

Research cannot be all things to all people all the time, as noted earlier. The research department and some of its major analysts, like a top economist, are the securities firm's "windows to the world." At times, they give the firm a certain amount of credibility, and they provide all types of investors with the kinds of information that hopefully will be worthwhile, and this is the most important product of research. Nevertheless, the research departments at most firms face two significant problems: the large number of requests for information coming to them from all sources and, perhaps most important, the gyrating financial markets that provide the milieu in which the research recommendations are carried out by all those who act on them. Managementwise, one of the few important goals of a research department (and in certain instances perhaps the only goal) should be to make an impact on all segments of its audience. This is surely easier said than done, but it should certainly be the guidepost of management in allocating the firm's resources to the research area as well as within it.

PART 2

THE ADMINISTRATIVE DIMENSION: CAPITAL, ACCOUNTING, AND COMPUTERIZATION

CHAPTER 7

THE FIRMS, THEIR CAPITAL, AND RISK MANAGEMENT

THE NUMBERS GAME

Wall Street has been, is now, and always will be a numbers game. From stock prices to accounting problems, from trading positions to financing alternatives, from complex products to research alternatives, numbers are, in a phrase, the "name of the game." Management problems, their genesis, and their solutions, oddly enough, often are not. The numbers, such as profit and losses, return on equity, return on sales, and gross departmental and firm revenue are indications of progress or problems. They are a means to an analytical end, to be sure. Securities firms, however, are each individually complicated entities, and differ financially from one another, sometimes radically so, and it is worth noting how and why.

Even among themselves, securities firms, when viewed from the numbers game, are vastly different in the size and scope of their operations, as discerned by Ernest Bloch in his book, *Inside Investment Banking*. In the summary to his analysis of securities firms, Bloch reaches the following five conclusions:

1. Each investment banking firm has built a structure of particular activities for itself.
2. That structure is subject to change over time.
3. No two firms will do exactly the same things in the same proportions.
4. Although all financial statements may start from similar

reporting and analytical principles, they are not always comparable.

5. An identifiable industry does exist, and some major activities are common to all.[1]

For instance, Bloch notes how diverse the asset and liability structures are of the various firms. He suggests, by way of example, that securities firms not only use different accounting procedures, "but also that different major firms engage in vastly different proportions of the same activities," adding that "further differences in the meaning of balance sheet data may occur in spite of the availability of the AICPA's draft audit guide for broker-dealers."[2]

Interest income and expense numbers of different securities firms are also not necessarily comparable.

> Again, reporting styles vary. For some, statements may report gross interest income and expenses and may exclude income from resale agreements, client accounts, and portfolio positions. Likewise, on the expense side, statements may exclude interest costs related to repurchase agreements, commercial paper, bank loans, and other types of debt. Since activity and profit cycles may produce different levels of interest revenues and expenses, as well as significant differences in spread between income and expense, even a historically consistent treatment by each firm will generate different results in any comparison between them. Especially for some of the largest firms, interest income represents a major (if not an overwhelmingly important) source of income. . . . [For certain institutional firms] interest income represents a lower but nonetheless significant share of pre-tax income.[3]

There are no hard-and-fast rules, however. Indeed, the changing nature of the securities industry and its products also complicates the financial analysis of the firms, and various financial innovations may involve off balance sheet transactions (e.g., interest rate swaps).[4] Bloch adds that "the accounting treatment for new financial ehicles (for example, interest rate swaps) is far from uniform."[5] Also, "fitting the data for new activities to the same definitions of financial activities would require arbitrary decisions by the reporting employees attempting to squeeze new security products into the old definitions of activity."[6]

New combinations of firms resulting from the merger or takeover of securities firms by corporations that may not be involved to any great extent in securities activities has compounded the problems of broad-based comparable financial analysis. Indeed, "this further complicates attempts at comparing the remaining free-standing firms with composite firms, even using the broadest definition of the investment banking industry."[7] Finally, some firms are either partially or wholly maintained as partnerships, are employee-held, or are some combination thereof, hence not being required to make public, on a full disclosure basis, the data on all their activities.

Also, some activities that may be major revenue or expense items for some firms, such as insurance, real estate, mortgage banking, or merger and acquisition operations, may not even be done by other securities houses. Even where the activities of securities firms are identical, the differences in the extent of their engagement may be enormous. When taking into consideration how these activities are accounted for, the problem of comparability for analytical purposes grows measurably.

On the revenue side, the changing nature of both the commission structure on Wall Street and also the proportionate mix of institutional and retail investors who are in the market during any given time translates into complications in comparing the revenue base of securities firms across the board. The past seems to indicate, for instance, that stock trading is becoming more institutionalized; but with lower commissions, not many securities firms of the full-service variety receive a substantial proportion of their income from the institutional equity area.[8]

Rates of return for different securities firms covering different activities are not easily discerned because of the need to have "an unequivocal statement of the denominator of the ratio, namely the size and structure of the firm's capital."[9] This is complicated by the difficulties in comparing data derived from firms merged with financial and other corporations, and receiving such numbers from partnership firms that would form the basis for rate-of-return analysis through an assessment of the firm's capital structure.

THE ANALYTICAL PERSPECTIVE

Some research professionals on Wall Street, and undoubtedly others elsewhere, analyze data available on securities firms as the basis for stock and bond recommendations to buy, sell, or hold the securities issued by the firms themselves. Many analysts do a very good job, so there will be no attempt to duplicate that effort here. It is worthwhile, however, to discern some of the broad analytical benchmarks in the evaluation of securities firms, however uncomparable those benchmarks might be from one firm to another.

The revenue and expense sides of the ledger are the first glimpses the analyst has at the ongoing operations of the securities firm. Principal differences among securities firms often come in the form of the extent to which revenues are derived from interest income, investment banking, principal transactions, or any other wide variety of businesses such as real estate or insurance. These revenue sources will surely change in their proportionate contribution to the firm's income over a given period of years, but nevertheless, the general trend provides a good picture of what a firm's business is really all about, its diversity, and its ongoing nature. Expenses also play a big role in determining what is or is not important to the firm, although many of these costs remain of the fixed variety for any number of reasons. In most instances, employee compensation and interest expense register as the largest components of firm expenses. From these revenue and expense numbers come the income before taxes and the net income figures. All four numbers are important to the ratio analysis of the firm's financials.

Two particularly important income-related ratios are operating income as a percent of pretax income and net interest income as a percent of pretax income. Return on equity is frequently cited as a critical benchmark in the analysis of certain corporations, and this is no less true for securities firms. Return on assets is also a ratio considered to be important by many analysts. Finally, the firm's profit margin, which is measured by dividing net income by total revenues, is a ratio that is often employed as an overall performance measure.

The extent of a company's leverage is especially critical for securities firms, given the market-related nature of trading, borrowing, and managing the business. A firm's assets divided by its equity is an important measure of leverage, but one cited equally as often now is a firm's assets less its repurchase agreements divided by its equity. Total debt divided by equity is another important leverage indicator, and often separate ratios are employed using short-term debt and also intermediate and long-term debt divided by equity as analytical tools. The dividend payout ratio is also a standard measure used by securities firm analysts as well as analysts of other companies. Finally, a securities firm's internal growth rate, which is its return on equity multiplied by one minus the dividend payout [ROE(1 − dividend payout)], is another ratio worth noting. There are many other financial performance measures, but the ones discussed here are considered to be major indicators of financial performance.

THE CAPITAL CRUNCH

For many of the largest firms on Wall Street, the watchword of the industry during the 1980s has been "capital."[10] From 1982 to 1987, the aggregate capital of the industry's firms increased more than fourfold from $8 billion to $35 billion. Some of these additional funds have come from increases in retained earnings, but much of the newly found capital has come in the wake of mergers and takeovers of the securities firms themselves. There are many reasons for firms to desire more capital, and not every firm that seeks additional capital needs it for the same reasons and in the same amounts or proportions as their competitors. Taken together, the following reasons are the ones most often cited for firms requiring additional capital:

1. To facilitate order flow.
2. To execute institutions' buy and sell orders.
3. To aid in firmwide trading.
4. To maintain positions in securities worldwide.

5. To act as an originator of new issue business.
6. To provide for major cost outlays, such as those incurred to upgrade computer and information systems.
7. To provide funds for certain merchant banking activities requiring the securities firm to inject capital into deals for bridge loans, etc., and for other financings, such as leveraged buy outs, and venture capital transactions.
8. For regulatory purposes.

In 1975, the Securities Exchange Commission (SEC) adopted a uniform net capital rule, established minimum net capital requirements as well as debt/equity guidelines, and set criteria for debt subordination agreements and requirements relating to consolidation of subsidiaries.[11]

To be sure, not every firm could use additional capital for any or all of these reasons. Only a handful of firms have sought the huge amounts of capital needed for them to be, at times, many things to many clients, and perhaps all at once. Without these seemingly gargantuan needs in some situations, the vast majority of securities firms have become content to develop their capital base in a slower and much more modest fashion. A few are satisfied to be so-called "niche" players, developing specialized skills or catering to certain clients, which does not require vast capital resources.

Access to huge amounts of capital, however, is no guarantee of success at any of the activities requiring it, and the misuse of large amounts of capital can result in huge losses for the firm making mistakes in employing this "two-edged sword" resource. Capital, for instance, is only one of the ingredients of a solid institutional business. A survey assessing the institutional activity of securities firms employed six evaluative measures showing that capital, in and of itself, was not enough to build powerful institutional presence, although it certainly helped. The study's measurements included:

1. Willingness to commit capital.
2. Research.

3. Ability to handle block positions.
4. Order execution.
5. Accessibility of buy personnel.
6. Best overall service.[12]

RISK MANAGEMENT: PROBLEMS
OF EMPLOYING THE FIRM'S CAPITAL

The term "risk management" sounds like a classic committee function when, if done properly, everyone applauds the successful operation. It fits anything but that description. The management of risk is perhaps one of the most technical and challenging tasks facing securities firms today: no one cheers when it works, and heads roll when it does not.

In its most basic form, risk management seeks to limit the downside risk or potential losses accruing to a securities firm from engaging in certain activities with its capital or taking specific trading positions. The tool has grown in importance over recent years as a result of the demands for greater trading, buying, and selling activities placed on securities firms by institutions that came during a time of wildly volatile securities markets, thus compounding the difficulty of firms in meeting service requests. The complicated nature of the process also arises from a number of inherent structural elements of the securities markets themselves, how the activities are handled within the firms, and who handles them.

Risk management begins with the need of a particular area of a securities firm, such as stocks, government bonds, or corporate bonds, to reduce its potential loss on a transaction. Conceptually speaking, then, it is a specialized activity that requires a total understanding of a given security and its marketplace. In some instances, the activities that mitigate the risk of a transaction in one security involve a countervailing activity in the same security. In other cases, limiting risk in one security can be accomplished through a transaction in a different security. This produces an "intersector" risk management tool, requiring not only the expertise of specialists in the other security but also the cooperation and support of another department in the securities firm. Finally, when the risk of a transaction or series of transactions becomes enormous, the attention and support, in capital and human terms, must be provided by the firm's senior executives. This raises problems of capital allocation priorities predicated on a relatively certain range of capital requirements needed in the immediately forseeable future. It also involves understanding the relative risks of all the transactions when taken together if they occur during a limited time frame and within the near future.

The Hedging Process

One of the most important risk management tools employed over recent years is the technique of "hedging," which is similar to the familiar concept of "hedging one's bet." The need to hedge a firm's position in a particular security could arise from a number of circumstances, most notably the following:

1. The firm's unsold bonds or older inventories are affected because interest rates are rising and the price of the securities is consequently dropping.
2. The carrying costs of the firm's securities inventory is increasing as a result of interest rate increases.
3. In the underwriting of a new securities issue, the price the firm paid for the securities drops, as a result of deteriorating market conditions, and falls below the cushion provided by the risk component of the gross underwriting spread or discount.
4. In the underwriting of a new securities issue, the senior underwriters have to purchase unsold portions of the new issue or may acquire a larger portion of the issue than originally anticipated.

Hedging, used to accommodate these and other situations, usually involves the use of options or futures as a price-balancing tool for a transaction that is slated to occur at the same time, at a later date, or even before the hedge is in place. An interest rate hedge might offset or balance out changes in a transaction's profit or loss position (resultant assets or liabilities) with a profit or loss from a futures or options transaction. To eliminate the effect of interest rate fluctuations on a transaction, the assets or liabilities must be matched by all the appropriate characteristics of the hedged security; they must correlate as closely as possible to the interest rate changes and resultant price changes. In the case of number 1 above, for example, the firm could sell treasury bond futures of, or on, the firm's unsold inventory. To counter the problems of excess inventory exemplified in number 4, the excess inventory can also be hedged with treasury bond futures.

Managing Risk

There are certain concepts relating to risk management at the securities firm that should be highlighted before delving into the problems associated with this activity. First of all, at the present time different firms have developed widely varying capabilities in the risk management field. They range from those firms that have been doing it on a sporadic basis to those with good-sized staffs involved in the activity as well as sophisticated techniques to limit risk. Even within certain firms, there exists widely varying expertise in risk management, and demarcations of expertise run along departmental lines. For instance, at a single firm, the stock trading area may be heavily immersed in the development and implementation of risk management strategies; but in the corporate or government bond areas, risk management practices may be largely absent for any number of reasons.

Also, at firms with large retail branch office systems, risk management may be somewhat more complicated than at securities houses that are heavily, if not entirely, institutionally oriented. In retail systems, there are complexities in charting the status of the firm's inventory because many sales tickets of the firm's securities transactions are sometimes put through the system beginning at the branch level. It is easier to get a handle on the firm's inventory at institutional firms because of the relatively centralized nature of their operations, even though most of these firms have a few branch offices. It is also usually more critical to firms emphasizing their institutional business to have a relatively sophisticated inventory-tracking capability and risk managment system. The same is true for securities firms with large retail systems that also have highly developed institutional capabilities.

A few other development strictures of the risk management field are important to note. Equities usually have their own system of risk management, their own hedging techniques, and their own management structure to support the operation. Risk management for fixed-income securities (corporates, governments, and municipals) can be handled either within the same management structure or by separate structures for each. This is the case largely because hedging in one area is often done to offset risk in another, although municipal bonds present some challenging risk management tasks. Most risk management professionals also agree that it is difficult to hedge fully and successfully all the firm's securities at once on a firmwide basis. Someday this may be possible, but at the moment, it is a somewhat elusive objective.

There are also some specific management problems, both conceptual and practical, relating to risk management, which are important to consider when embarking on a major risk management operation. These include:

1. Expecting too much from the risk management technique or the hedge.
2. Doing too much hedging too quickly.
3. Engaging in intersector hedging without adequate and agreed upon goals, objectives, and position and hedging limits.
4. Operationalizing risk management techniques without generally agreed upon time frames or limits of activity, such as when to take a loss and the limits of a loss, and when to and when not to purchase and sell the underlying securities.

MANAGEMENT CONCERNS
IN RISK MANAGEMENT

Management concerns in the development of the firm's risk management operation have as much to do with personnel as they do with strategies and their coordination. Among the major management concerns noted below are a number of potentially interrelated staffing considerations.

1. Critical to the establishment of an ongoing and effective risk management capability is selecting or hiring specialists who have proven track records in the management of risk for specific securities. A broader firmwide capability requires additional professionals who have a wider range of knowledge and experience with a number of securities.

2. There should be a risk management chief because most firms find themselves in the position of attempting to develop strategies for different areas of the firm, and therefore overall coordination is essential, especially in situations where different product areas have progressed to varying levels of success in the risk management business. The risk management chiefs should also have an in-depth knowledge of each security under their jurisdiction to adequately supervise intersector hedging operations and to oversee the development of new and sophisticated risk management products. This latter job often requires a conceptual understanding of specialized techniques only found in individuals who have been exposed to, and have experience with, the cross-fertilization and development of risk management ideas that cut across product lines.

3. Through these professionals and with the advice and consent of the various heads of the product departments as well as the firm's most senior management, in-house risk management strategies must be developed and agreed on for each product area and also on a collective basis.

4. Following this, each product area's personnel must be made comfortable with the particular overall strategy adopted as a precursor to those to be operationalized. This is especially important in the case of intersector hedging, where it is possible that a product area could lose money as a result of a hedge accomplished to limit the downside risk of another product area's transaction. Conversely, if in a similar situation, the product area doing the hedge registers a profit, there should be some compensatory arrangement agreed upon in advance, as there would be in a loss situation. Some sharing of profits and losses as a result of any risk management techniques is an important consideration.

5. The risk management staff, both within and outside the product departments, must be available on a "first alert" basis to deal successfully with the often unpredictable and episodic requirements for the management of risk.

6. Periodic evaluation and review measures must be undertaken by each department engaging in risk management activities and by the risk managers themselves, including all those involved, whether they do it as members of a particular product department or whether they are outside the product areas. The melding of goals and objectives must be charted and evaluated, and resultant changes in the activity should be made if necessary. This kind of ongoing analysis and review is critical because of the amounts of capital usually employed in operationalizing these techniques.

RISK MANAGEMENT AT A MINIMUM

Many firms are interested more in minimizing risk than in managing it, although each effort has elements of the other within it. The minimization of risk at the departmental level, however, emphasizes a number of operating modes unlike those of firms or departments that assume a moderate risk posture based on their capital position and the degree to which they opt to put their capital at risk. Firms seeking to limit risk emphasize:

1. The securities trading function as an adjunct and facilitator for the firm's distribution system.
2. The role of the trader as one who does not engage in transactions as a market anticipator.
3. The limitation of losses as a primary goal with the elimination of loss as a key goal.
4. The development of strategies to reduce the need for risk management of any sort.

There is nothing wrong with a minimum risk posture, but it is critical to understand that it demands as much coordinative effort, and sometimes more, than the work involved in full-scale risk management.

NOTES

1. Ernest Bloch, *Inside Investment Banking* (Homewood, Ill.: Dow Jones-Irwin, 1986), p. 40.
2. Bloch, p. 28.
3. Ibid., p. 33.
4. Ibid., p. 27.
5. Ibid., p. 32.
6. Ibid., p. 27.
7. Ibid., p. 27.
8. Ibid., p. 32. See also "Where Will Wall Street's Commission War Lead?", *Institutional Investor*, February 1985, p. 51.
9. Bloch, p. 27.
10. See also "How Much Capital Is Enough?", *Institutional Investor*, November 1986; and "Wall Street Is Solid—But Very Nervous," *Business Week*, January 12, 1987.
11. Bloch, p. 27.
12. "Seats of Power," *Financial World*, January 20, 1987.

For additional information on risk management, see Nancy Rothstein and James Little, eds, *The Handbook of Financial Futures: A Guide for Investors and Professional Financial Managers* (New York: McGraw-Hill, 1984).

CHAPTER 8

CONCEPTUAL PROBLEMS IN SECURITIES FIRM ACCOUNTING

FROM A PROFIT CENTER TO FIRMWIDE ACCOUNTING MENTALITY

One of the key problems facing securities firms in their ongoing evolution is the movement from a profit center accounting and compensation mentality to a broader firmwide one. This has by no means been a smooth process in any firm, and not all firms are at the same stage in this general trend. As a broad conceptual framework representative of most firms within the securities industry, the apparent movement by management to place greater emphasis on firmwide income results and to distribute expense items on a more precise accounting basis among the various departments are among management's most important jobs today, and they are not easy ones. They affect the motivation of securities firm employees, their compensation structure, the understanding and implementation of firmwide and departmental goals and objectives, and also the development of managers and other professionals within the firm. This is certainly where what some might consider to be relatively simple accounting concepts have had great impact on securities firms and their personnel.

Historically, the profit center mentality of securities firms has been rooted in the individualized and entrepreneurial nature of the activities in which most professionals and managers engaged, resulting in a quantitatively measurable compensation structure. From a bottom-up standpoint, securities firms have been, and are now, composed of individuals who in effect ply a certain trade providing financial advice and products to customers from a sales standpoint and also from a trading, underwriting, and investment banking perspective. Each professional or group of them, particularly in the sales and trading areas, is capable of generating profits for a net revenue stream to their own small business units and ultimately to the firm. As a result, the profit center mentality, based on individual productivity, has been the bedrock of the firm's net revenue stream.

Most professionals in the firm have been compensated on a quantitative basis as to how much revenue they ultimately generated. This can be seen in the commission remuneration structure for sales professionals who are by far the largest percentage of revenue-generating professionals in the securities firms. This concept has also spilled over to the investment banking and capital markets areas, and management has been able to isolate individuals who are considered to be revenue generators and has compensated them on that basis. Thus, while this type of compensation system has been rooted in individual productivity, especially at the branch office level, it has carried over and become an entrenched part of the way management has viewed the success of other small business units or departments within the firm and also the method by which professionals in these areas have been compensated.

This perspective of departmental and individual success has collided, over recent years, with the problem of market volatility, which has affected individual and department production levels, and also with the need of firms to account for revenue and expense items better because the interdependence of many small business units and departments has become a larger part of the overall workings of the securities firm. To be sure, the movement from a profit center to a broader firmwide revenue stream for compensation purposes and for the evaluation of small business units has hit particularly hard in a number of areas within the firm because managers and professionals alike have had to restructure their approach to, and the view of, their own activities vis-à-vis the needs and objectives of the firm.

This metamorphosis in the attitudes toward, and perspectives of, individual and departmental achievement has greatly impacted the capital market areas of most firms, where compensation for professionals was usually a set salary and a quantitative- and qualitative-based bonus depending on the net revenue of the small business unit or department and a professional's contribution to it. In these situations, net revenue really mattered, and in most cases, it could be attributed to an individual or a group of professionals. Regardless of how other departments within the capital markets area fared on a net revenue basis and certainly without much regard to other departments and divisions within the firm, this semiscientific method of allocating compensation and also measuring overall success was also based on the net revenue of the small business unit or the department.

In the investment banking areas, it was relatively easy to attribute revenue generation from particular clients to the bankers or the groups who were responsible for it within the investment banking department. In some ways, this has given way to a departmentwide revenue effort. Firms interested in developing an investment banking department often view that department, for a certain period of time, as a loss leader, similar to the perspective applied to newly hired professionals who are only expected to cover themselves on a financial basis some years in the future and not immediately. Likewise, remuneration in the institutional sales area of most firms has been traditionally based on a commission compensation structure like that of the branch office account executive system. At many firms today, the institutional sales commission system has been changed to a salary and bonus plan that emphasizes the salesperson's overall relationship with the account and the progress made toward goals and objectives established by the sales manager and the department head. Implicit in this arrangement for individual compensation as well as the resultant effect that the set-up has had for management's view of the institutional sales net revenue stream is a broadening of the profit center orientation of that department to more of a divisionwide or firmwide approach.

Even the individualized entrepreneurial nature of the branch system has been somewhat muted. Once solely an individualized net revenue generation effort by the account executives themselves through specific securities transactions, the branch office system and each branch office are beginning to develop a closer relationship with the firm, certainly in accounting, whereby individual production and the resultant revenue stream are also a product of fee-based services developed by the firm such as financial planning and packaged products like mutual funds and unit trusts. Interestingly, many departments that were previously cost centers of the firm, in the sense that they only provided support activities and were thus registered in the expense component of the firm's income statement, have shown that they too can generate revenues by documenting their successful efforts to save the firm money and also by marketing some of their services to other firms and companies for a fee.

These developments, many of which are at different stages in their own evolution, have markedly changed the way individual professionals at the securities firms and managers of the firm's departments and branches view their own efforts to bring net revenues to the bottom line, vis-à-vis the firm's expenses and costs incurred for support. What has evolved is a much broader concept, both in how revenues are accounted for and in the extent to which they are attributed to departmentwide and firmwide efforts.

This evolution has been reinforced by the cyclical nature of the revenue stream of many important departments at the securities firm, as a result of volatile financial markets, clients who are in and out of the market at different periods of time for their own reasons, and the need of the firm to maintain relationships with those clients and develop others, while compensating all of the firm's professionals at a justifiable level. Indeed, many firms have recognized the need to maintain client relationships in times of volatile financial markets and when clients are out of the market, as well as the necessity to keep the departments and business units that service such clients intact during these times if the firm is to proceed successfully along its broader corporate mission. In situations like these, when individual production may not be high and a department's net revenue stream may not come in at the numbers expected (which may be a result of situations beyond the control of the professionals in that department), the firm has had to compensate individuals in ways that do not penalize them, thus paying less attention to the net revenue stream of their departments. Here, the compensation and departmental planning process is based more on a perception of what was accomplished within the given set of market and other parameters than what was actually so on a more quantitative measure of relative success. This perspective is a much broader one because it entails a view of a department's success and that of its professionals that is more of a firmwide contributory nature than a specific bottom-line profitability standard. This has aided in moving the mind-set of the securities firm management away from the previously more prevalent profit center mode.

This discussion does not necessarily mean that all firms have found it problematic to adjust to this new mind-set or that all firms have had to go through this evolutionary process. Certainly, many firms have not had difficulties in doing so, others have not had to, and much of the success or difficulty is largely the result of an individual department's or a firm's view of this matter and thus is not necessarily applicable across the board for all the departments within any firm. In firms that highly compensate professionals, these problems have not been that pronounced; in such cases, the firm's organizational ethos has resulted in muting the effect of potential difficulties because of its "all for one" concept by which the professionals work. In other cases, regardless of how highly paid professionals at a particular securities firm have been, analysts have attributed tremendous problems to the interdepartmental rivalry for firm resources and remuneration that has occurred when professionals claim responsibility for parts of the firm's net revenue stream. This has resulted in departments being pitted against one another in claims for better compensation as a result of relatively greater success. Fortunately, in most cases and for most firms, this has not occurred.

ILLUSORY REVENUES AND EXPENSES

The move to a broader firmwide mind set of revenue generation and resultant individual compensation has been coupled with a desire by management at securities firms to account more precisely for departmental revenues and expenses. This includes the allocation of corporatewide functions as expense items, such as administration and research, on more of a firmwide basis. In a broad sense, it also includes a better accounting for costs related to transactions occurring both in the branches and at the home office and for expenses incurred to support those transactions that are in place all the time. This is a classic accounting problem. From a pragmatic viewpoint, it generates basic conceptual problems in attempting to assess the relative productivity of departments, small business units, and individuals. Also, if not handled and explained correctly, these accounting difficulties could result in problems in motivating, keeping, and hiring personnel as well as in making accurate assessments of the relative productivity of departments.

Laying claim to revenue has been a major preoccupation of departments within securities firms. This has been especially so for interdependent departments, such as those that, during the course of a securities transaction, become involved in the sales, trading, or underwriting of the security and thus can have a claim to the resultant revenue less the commission paid. In some cases, when every department in a securities firm claimed the revenue to which it thought it was entitled, the securities firm would net something like three times more revenue on a firmwide basis than it would with an accurate accounting system in place.

A single example might suffice. One of the most critical management problems affecting some bond departments in the capital markets area of a securities firm that trades, underwrites, and sells certain products, is the accounting system employed by which the monies available on a net revenue basis for profits to the firm or to the department are distributed after the sales force is paid. In the case of a bond department, after the sales commissions have been paid to the sales force, there is a certain percentage left over for the bond department and the firm, usually hovering somewhere between 60 percent of the gross sales commission when 40 percent was paid to the retail sales force, or approximately 80 percent of the commission when 20 percent was paid to the institutional sales force. Traditionally, the remaining amount was split between the bond depart-

complicated new financial products. Every firm has had a brush with these problems at one time or another, and some organizations have had greater difficulties than others. The first is the need to update the firm's entire accounting system and integrate it with the operations department so that the firm can immediately locate any major faux pas in either the accounting for revenues or in the processing of securities transactions. This is especially important in the government securities area where enormous amounts of funds are traded by most firms every day and where the complex new products seem to have financial tentacles stretching throughout the firm's operations and securities processing departments. In these instances, funds are traded in such huge amounts that there are numerous opportunities to lose large amounts of money either through mistakes being made because of the complexity of the instrument or in the cost-of-carry of the securities. Management must, in a sense, wed the accounting and operations departments into a well-oiled machine by making sure that they work closely with one another through all phases of the securities transactions process. Thus the "revenues will conquer all" mode has given way to one that seeks increased revenues but also decreased expenses through the minimization of mistakes.

Another seemingly more mundane accounting problem that has arisen at most firms over recent years is the need of every department to keep expense accounts as up to date on a consistent basis as possible. In accounting lingo, the goal is to have "no prior year adjustments in the current year," which means that there must be an effort to avoid the possibility that a department, and thus the firm, would be hit with an unanticipated charge after the end of a fiscal year that throws off the bottom line to a noticeable degree. To some, this problem may seem like an unimportant one, but in a securities firm, prior year adjustments can sometimes be of such a large size that they decrease a department's profits in a way that is not only upsetting to managers and professionals alike but that also significantly impacts their own remuneration.

CHAPTER 9

COMPUTERIZING WALL STREET: WHITHER THE INFORMATION FLOATS!

Computerization and its derivative technological advancements have so quickly swept onto the Wall Street scene that it is a dizzying task for most managers to keep current with the advanced applications of information processing, let alone totally understand, apply, implement, control, and plan for these cascading changes in corporate communications and information dissemination. If one thing is certain, however, it is that in a post-1980s world of computerization, the lives of account executives, traders, investment bankers, and managers industrywide and their clients will hardly be the same.

Wall Street has become so jargonized with computer lingo that some suggest it has turned many managers off rather than on. To carry the jargon one step further, the micros must be user friendly because the workers may be computer illiterate and not understand how to use global data-based networks and real-time workstations. As a result of these and other testaments, some department managers fear an invasion of the technocrats. To be fair, however, people naturally fear what they do not understand. If management does not fully comprehend the processes of and the development in communications and information processing in the securities industry, it can hardly be expected to be able to grapple with its most pressing short- and long-term problem—the management of information systems. Indeed, this is likely to make or break many securities firms as time marches on.

The limitations of time and space do not allow a lengthy

sojourn into all the complexities of computerization from a technological standpoint. Such a discourse would be voluminous, and like the development of computers themselves, could be outdated once on the market. Instead, it is simply worth discussing the evolving world of Wall Street's computerized activities and the management and organizational problems relating to these technological developments.

LIFE ON THE MAINFRAME: IT BEGAN WITH OPERATIONS

Computerization on Wall Street began with the mainframe computer, a so-called first generation type, employed principally for trades processing. Still, problems came fast and furious. During the late 1960s when the then record volume began taking its toll, Wall Street managers, argues Carrington, "were not, as a rule, much interested in the functions of the 'back office,' where the business was processed, nor were they disposed to invest in the computers, management and planning efforts needed to ensure a smooth handling of the paperwork."[1] Indeed, it was not long ago that operations difficulties resulting from trades processing threatened the stability of certain firms. The root cause was inadequate computers for rudimentary processing functions done on a large scale. Not only were the computers overloaded, but also humans were involved in coding and recoding trades resulting in geometrically increasing costly mistakes. Many operations were still completed by hand in the face of greatly increasing volume.

Later, computerized operations developed wider usage, from trades and order processing to securities clearing to cash management to the cashiering function and then to the stock loan and margin areas of the firms. This was not an ordinary growth development. It did, however, represent the use of the firm's main computer for support functions absolutely vital to the day-to-day activities of the firm—the "life blood" of the system. For the purposes of conceptualization, these functions may be termed "after-the-fact computerized transaction processing systems." We need not go further here; there are a couple of works that discuss in detail the nature and breadth of these functions for a host of securities. The major computerized operations of a securities firm, from mainframe, to mini-, to microwork, are housed in the following departments: orders, purchase and sales, cashiering, margins, stock record, dividend, proxy, stock record, and new accounts.[2]

Certain firms have recently developed sophisticated services as outgrowths of their own in-house capabilities that are being made available to other companies on a fee basis. The development of securities clearing procedures for new products such as mutual funds is one such example. For a long time, some securities firms relied on others for their clearing operations, while other firms did their clearing in house. With the vast proliferation of securities firm products over recent years, many firms could not keep pace with workable clearing methods for trades. The problem was compounded by the complicated nature of the products, many of which were derivatives of securitized or collateralized debt obligations, loans, and the like. For those firms that were either inventive or simply determined enough to allocate the time, money, and personnel to the clearing cause, some now have a new product to sell—one that is not securities related. This has resulted in some firms having an operations department that technically generates some revenues. (The analysis by a firm of the profit-making potential of this effort to allocate a part of its operations staff and computer hardware and software to the development of a system for sale outside is a management issue. It demands an assessment of the effort's potential and the ability of the department to succeed as well as allocation procedures and commitments for staff and other resources. It demands, too, the establishment of goals and objectives, and it requires feedback by monitoring the entire process.)

Concurrent with computerization of trades processing and clearing was the wholesale use, or perhaps better yet, underuse, of the firm's mainframe computer for large-scale accounting and data-processing purposes, including departmental "actual versus budgeted" (AVB) monthly revenues and expenses, other multitudinous procedures, and customer and bank services. Computerization today, however, has far surpassed what many believe to be these rudimentary functions. The ability of a firm to centralize these tasks for all departments, thus reducing the firm's overall operations costs and paperwork, improving communications, and storing information to be later disseminated firmwide, shows the need for managerial control, and most importantly, for reducing the firm's "information float."

WHERE DID THEY GO FROM HERE?

Some $1.4 billion is projected to be spent by securities firms in 1990 on computers and communication and information processing systems, which is a threefold increase since 1984. During the early 1980s, most of the capital outlays for systems were made by only very few firms, almost all of which had developed large-scale plans for integrated systems to be placed on-line over the following three to five years. Computerization on Wall Street at that time reduced itself neatly to the "will haves" and the "will have nots."

Monies spent up to the mid-1980s went to pay for new management information systems, more highly developed data-processing tools, state-of-the-art computer software (which like the computers themselves, remained state-of-the-art for only short time spans), and most importantly, integrated systems. The objective of these historic expenditures was to make virtually every usable amount of information immediately available to everyone who needed it. From the CEO to the account executive, from the branch manager to the securities trader, from the audit and control department to the product development area, and from the traders in London to those in New York and elsewhere around the globe, those who needed information and those who had to communicate with others, both in and outside the firm, would be able to do so in an on-line time frame.

On-line Trading and Beyond

As a natural outgrowth of computer use for trades processing and the monitoring of trading inventories, "on-line" trading capability was management born and bred. It was designed to quench the thirst of traders, institutional salespeople, and account executives to have at their fingertips an accurate, up-dated trading inventory of any security. Functionally, in an on-line system, trades are recorded immediately right through to order processing, and the inventory is updated right away. In some on-line trading systems, securities firm branches are capa-ble of accessing the trading inventory. Many systems also have on-line posttrade telecommunications channels in an effort to achieve accurate input information and feedback for corrective purposes. Clearing operations for trades have also been injected with a dose of high-tech computerization. Security transactions have been integrated with the Depository Trust Company (DTC) for clearing efficiency. The National Association of Securities Dealers Automated Quotations (NASDAQ) systems and some other entities have also developed highly sophisticated small-order execution systems (SOES).

These developments may seem less than volcanic to those who are somewhat unfamiliar with the ways of life in the securi-ties business before large-scale computerization, but developing and implementing these on-line systems is no easy feat, and they do serve important purposes for management. Although on-line trading systems are management tools to increase trad-ing and sales productivity, they also are foundations for the management of risk, the monitoring of product sales, and the tracking of revenue, all of which will be discussed later in this chapter.

Enter the Computer Generation

To this point, computerization probably still sounds dull. Cer-tainly most of us do not feel content only when every little microchip is in working order and when we are generating reports only for the firm's managerial accountants. That was not the idea of these systems, but it may have been perceived as such. Computerization, however, has led to one development now in the process of changing the nature of the financial ser-vices and securities industry. This will be done through the development of a firm's nationwide integrated communications networks and so-called broker or intelligent workstations.

Account executives, as discussed earlier, usually have anywhere from 50 to 150 financial products to sell their clients. Within these generic product types are different stocks, corporate or municipal bonds, and the like, bringing the total into the thousands. Additionally, there is market information that must be understood and digested, not only relating to such daily concerns as interest rate directions, but also to stock and bond price directions and volume. On top of this information heap is perched the firm's research recommendations, which include market predictions, securities buy, sell, or hold suggestions and credit evaluations, and economic and interest rate predictions. This information can be reflected against available data from the securities rating agencies and other information services. Add to this information glut the firm's suggestions about the viability of different products for certain client types based on their willingness to take risk or on their relative financial status. The account executive is thus in the throes of a veritable information hurricane. Is all this information digestable, understandable, and then usable by and for a single individual? Possibly it is, but only in selected circumstances where account executives have focused their efforts on particular products and specific types of clients. First, however, where is all this information? It is everywhere—in financial manuals, in the newspapers, on the quotron, on firm communications' wires, and in hard-copy research.

FROM MAINFRAMES TO MICROS: ON-LINE INFORMATION FOR ACCOUNT EXECUTIVES

The personal computer is the securities industry's answer to the delivery of on-line information in one single place to the account executive located anywhere around the globe. It is perhaps the most significant communications and information dissemination development that is likely to hit an industry in so short a span of years. Microcomputers, linked to branch or minicomputers and integrated to the firm's mainframe computer system located at headquarters, form the basic hardware that most firms view as the key to their information system in the future. Certain firms expect to integrate this system with satellite communications for global sending and receiving capabilities to relieve what is expected to become congested terrestrial communications lines.

Aptly dubbed the "intelligent workstation," the micro or personal computer (p.c.) would come equipped with a host of software packages and appropriate applications allowing the system to perform a vast array of functions and provide a flood of on-line information. Three activity areas would be impacted by this type of integrated branch communications and information network, tied to the firm's worldwide system.

First, office-related work could be accomplished by this set-up. Such mundane functions as word processing and filing could become an important part of this operation, releasing support staff as well as account executives to perform more leveraged duties. Branch back office functions might be more efficiently handled by computers. Also, electronic mail systems could be developed linking all account executive workstations together and tying them to headquarters.

Second, access to all or part of the firm's data base could be made available to the account executives via this integrated system. Important available information might include a client's buying predispositions, historical purchasing patterns, client financial profiles, and an evaluation of a client's transactions based on a host of criteria, from type of product to size of purchase to the timing of the transaction, and so forth. This arrangement would provide the account executive with client-related information from which a better match between products and clients could be made. Such information could be used in conjunction with the firm's product information services and marketing advice. Workstations could also provide customers on-line information about their own account.

Third and most important, the workstation would be the vehicle to provide account executives with on-line securities-related information both from within the firm and from outside sources, and this could be relayed to clients. Market data could be made available globally, including on-line securities prices and global market information. Firm research of all types would be easily accessible, as would on-line data about the firm's products. This information could be integrated with that available from other financial and economic services. The computers' graphics and report-writing capabilities would provide account executives and their clients with useful tools for evaluating their entire investment picture or particular strategies on a comparative basis.

THE NEXT WAVE: INVESTMENT ANALYSIS

The onslaught of available information is thus making quasi-analysts out of account executives and their clients in ways that go far beyond their information courier and information recipient roles of yesteryear. This is being accomplished by the personal computer and could be made available to both account executives and their clients through sophisticated software programs providing stock screening techniques, on-line information services, trading techniques, and portfolio management services for both account executives and their clients. Much of this is also useful to the institutional investor.

Stock Screening

Stock screening packages offer analysts, account executives, and investors the opportunity to select and compare stocks across myriad characteristics and variables from data supplied by any number of services. Prior to the mechanism of stock screening, data on stocks were only available on a mainframe computer, and users had difficulty in accessing and employing the data because the software programs were less than user friendly. Today, advances in both hardware and software technology have conquered most of the earlier problems.

The stock screening industry is essentially divided into two groups of service providers: those firms that collect raw data, and those that distribute data with "value-added" analyses. The systems themselves may be categorized as either "open" or "closed." Open systems allow the users to input their own data and make use of information provided by their firms, among other sources; closed systems do not offer these possibilities.

Users essentially call up from the system stocks of their

choosing, but most access is through company or stock characteristics that yield a cross-section of stocks for perusal and analysis. Variables may include stock prices, earnings forecasts, operating ratios, return on assets, return on equity, return on sales, and so on. Smaller systems have a limited number of stocks and associated variables; larger systems have much better screening capabilities, including much greater stock universes from which to choose, larger varieties of data and research sources, and better evaluative capabilities. Analytical tools for larger systems run the gamut from mechanical reporting techniques, including computer graphics, flexible printing methods, and various ranking and sorting capabilities, to software-based analytical processes such as the statistical techniques used for comparing stocks and prognosticative measures for predicting stock performance. Information systems, in short, have brought users the opportunity to better their own analyses.

On-line Investment Management

The personal computer, together with information tie-ins for data available from inside and outside the firm, left only one more place where this entire system could be useful, that is, the home. With many households purchasing personal computers, securities firms began efforts to isolate customers who would be interested in having at their disposal the same kind of information that was being made available to their account executives. The vehicle would tie the home computer to the firm's information system. Some firms also endeavored to develop on-line trading capabilities for their customers through the use of their "home workstations," and other firms selected a middle-of-the-road approach, whereby trades could only be made after the client spoke to the account executive. Yet, trial and error, as it often does, reduced some of these plans to corporate reject status. A few firms, in the course of attempts to develop "home workstation" pilot programs, abandoned their efforts because of technological problems and the inability to make the program work from a long-term bottom-line standpoint.

In any event, as originally conceived, home workstations are a customer convenience. The market niche was those investors who liked to do some of their own analytical work or who, because of demanding jobs or unusual workloads, could not make easy contact with their account executives. Home workstations also afforded clients, just as it provided their account executives, the opportunity to access the firm's research and information about their own account on an on-line basis. As firms could monitor a customer's access to the firm's data, account executives could use the information to determine the client's interest in various investment information and vehicles, and also analyze, for whatever reason, the times that the client used the system. Some firms expected that workstations could also be used to confirm orders and to send and receive electronic mail—both similar to the capabilities of the account executive's workstation.

It is worth noting that some firms viewed the ultimate use of this system as a way for clients to bypass account executives. Many firms, however, believe that there are ways to prevent that possibility, and many clients view this system as an adjunct or supplement to the financial service of the account executive and not a means to supplant it. Whatever the case, the financial services industry of tomorrow will probably make some use of the home financial workstations being developed today.

TECHNOLOGY-INSPIRED MANAGEMENT CONCERNS

The development, implementation, and application of information and communications systems, especially those of a large scale, cannot be made serviceable in a managerial vacuum. The systems just described and their ultimate capabilities may sound larger than life but are at the least worthwhile. Unfortunately, management problems could occur during implementation simply because of that one organizational dilemma—namely, that somewhere along the line, humans must become involved in the process.

Indeed, management concerns in the information dissemination arena may be divided into a number of categories. Not all these groupings are totally unlike difficulties encountered by other corporate organizations wrestling with the complexities of information and communications life in a "post-p.c." world. What should become strikingly clear, however, is that the nature of the securities firm and its corporate structure exacerbates the information dissemination problem, making management crucial to the successful implementation of any system. The end users total thousands of professionals, and the amount of information that must be disseminated on an on-line basis is enormous. For the securities firms, these problems are less technology inspired than they are derivatives of organizational structure and user needs. Some of these potential management concerns are discussed below.

Planning for Computerization

As trite as it may sound for those familiar with the basic principles of corporate management, planning emerges as the number one prerequisite for developing an integrated computer system for the securities firm, given the total amount of data to be dispersed, the number of systems on-line, and the average daily volume of information that must be disseminated. Flexibility of the system should be a paramount concern of management together with maintaining the system's capability to on-load new and useful applications.

Computer systems planning should involve three management overseeing functions: assessment, integration, and monitoring. Every securities firm, no matter what business it specializes in and regardless of how large or small it may be, is at a different stage in the development of its computer system. Making matters more complex for managers is the fact that, more often than not, different departments and divisions within the firm are also at different stages of systems development and computer use. As a result, questions should be asked about the general level of the firm's computerization. Is the firm principally using data-processing technology, or is there a need for computerized on-line trading? Does the firm require high-volume trades-processing technology, or is the firm barely past the order-matching stage? These questions, and others like them applied to divisions and departments, may sound simple enough, but answering them in detail for any securities firm or business unit is a task of enormous proportions.

Building a computer infrastructure requires that management oversee the design and creation of an integrated computer hierarchy. For the securities firm, this generally involves three levels of computers stretching from headquarters to the account executive's desk—mainframe to minicomputer to microcomputer. (In today's world, the capabilities of each level of computerization are advancing so rapidly that it is often hard to tell the difference between a mini and a micro and so forth, if size were not a factor, and soon it probably will not be.) Basically, management must supervise a network of dissemination levels, all integrated, flexible, and compatible.

Misuse Through Decentralization

The extremely specialized nature of functions in the securities firm and the myriad ways end users ultimately make use of the firm's information systems present unusual problems for management in resource allocation, coordination, and control of the entire operation. The principal problem is the system's likely movement to a truly decentralized computer operation. Decentralization of computer use, applications, and service is certainly important; after all, the users are deeply decentralized in securities firms. Too much decentralization, however, could result in disaster.

Senior management must control automation in the securities firm. Management must be involved in staffing the information and communications team at the upper levels, buying new major equipment at every organization level, and approving the development of important applications. Headquarters should not surrender control to end users for budgeting and the development and use of corporate data bases. In a few words, management must control the automation process.

The problems associated with a decentralized computer operation or one that gives end users an oversupply of independent authority fall into three categories. First, when account executives or other end users employ their own hardware and software, problems of system and support services compatibility crop up immediately. Second, over time, the independence of end users results in the production of computer applications similar to those readily available through the firm. This is costly and time consuming for everyone involved. Third, a deeply de-centralized computer system often results in a loss of total control through bureaucratic inertia. Large-scale computerization, especially in a securities firm, has a way of centrifugally pulling the computer system into its own orbit far away from centralized managerial control. Many users of very different hardware, soft-ware, and applications systems results in users arguing for even more and different systems, which must be grafted onto those in operation. This has the potential to develop into a costly opera-tion and result in a state of confusion and loss of managerial control, especially when users become wedded to their own sys-tems. Once user independence starts in a specialized organiza-tion like a securities firm, it can become virtually unchecked and uncheckable.

Computer Illiteracy

The phrase "computer illiteracy" is very familiar, and unless management takes a hands-on approach to solving this problem, nothing short of job loss will rectify it. This is particularly important for the securities industry, because the future suc-cessful delivery of financial services will be largely, if not whol-ly, dependent on a knowledge of the computer for gathering information, analyzing data, and processing securities transac-tions. Securities firm personnel must become computer literate, and they can be; unfortunately, many are technology shy. This has resulted in computers being used for the most mundane functions, far below their capabilities. Many mainframe com-puters in the industry are used largely for transactions process-ing, and most microcomputers are employed for the simplest functions, such as quote retrieval and word processing. For those securities firms making good use of their computer capabilities, management must move the organization from being computer productive to being user productive. Conversely, industry per-sonnel, particularly account executives, must also guard against becoming too computer dependent. When the system stops functioning, will the professional also?

Applications upon Applications

Professionals at securities firms have the need and the ability to make use of hundreds, if not thousands, of applications of computer software in their daily businesses. This comes as a result of the tremendous number of financial products in the capital markets and the need to assess the appropriateness of each investment in the context of market activity and investor need. System users in these organizations could dream up literally an endless number of applications for computer use. Management's job is to monitor and control the computer applications process to help insure that applications will focus on the proper area, and make certain that management will have a say in the applications approval process. To be sure, users, computer and information systems staff, and management should all be involved in monitoring the development of computer applications in the securities firm. Applications should be created by computer personnel with the help of users and should be subject to oversight by management. This system seeks to limit duplications of applications, helps make certain that applications are modified when possible and not recreated, and aids in preventing the development of applications that seem far-fetched, difficult to implement, and unnecessary, all of which could drain the resources of professionals attempting to develop them.

Computer applications had their genesis in the operations area of securities firms, and many application opportunities still exist there. Most firms have eliminated much human work in the trades processing areas; computers can now talk to computers throughout transactions processing. Problems do arise, however, in processing transactions of the many new derivative products which are being manufactured by securities firms on a seemingly daily basis. Processing transactions of these products is often so complicated that it requires a concerted effort of management of the product areas, senior sales staff, information and operations personnel, and the users or those who will sell this merchandise. Critical to this effort is close communication and control between the operations personnel and the product development group. Generally, computer technology use will be more efficient for firms with smaller, simpler, or standard product lines, but it will be indispensable for firms with complex products. Another key applications use of the computer, and one becoming standard at securities firms, is for the departments' monthly "actual versus budget" statistics. Although it seems like a natural outgrowth of computer use, receiving accurate numbers from the systems at securities firms is not as easy as it may sound.

THE COMPUTER MANAGEMENT STRUCTURE

Computer-driven Reporting Relationships

A key management problem facing firms developing information and communications systems is structuring the overseeing department and its allied areas into the firm's organizational hierarchy. In most firms, the data processing chief reports to a financial executive, as do the firm's chief information and communications officer. Sometimes these departments have a single manager but usually they do not, and "turf" problems may arise. Some firms have these departments together with the firm's accounting, auditing, and legal staff, report to an administrative chief of the entire services group. However, any structural reporting relationship will necessarily depend on the development of the firm and its computer systems. For those firms planning or in the midst of large-scale development, it makes some sense to have the designated head of the information services department—the chief information officer—whose area might include data processing, telecommunications, and information systems, report directly to one of the firm's top three executives, or even directly to the CEO, depending on the CEO's expertise in the area of computer systems development. For large-scale programs, however, the computer system's chief should report directly to the top of the firm. Too much is at stake in the system's arena bearing heavily on a securities firm's future for it to be otherwise.

The Information and Communications Department

The management structure within this department is critical to its success. The area is usually best divided into five separate units: hardware and software acquisitions; installation and testing; servicing with or without in-house technicians; departmental and individual applications; and education. The important dimension here is that departments or business units firmwide be assigned, to the best extent possible, the same individuals on an ongoing basis to provide advanced education and applications service. Departments and individual users become accustomed to working with the same computer specialists, which leads to more interaction and greater consequent use and production on the part of the end user. Also, the computer applications specialist becomes thoroughly conversant with the particular needs of a given department and the subtleties of the computer applications that must be employed. Thus, better service is likely as the result. At some point in the development of a computer system, firm management together with the computer systems development chief will have to decide whether to (and if so, how to) stock hardware and software and hire full-time servicing technicians. The pros and cons of each decision for management should become clearer when a cost-benefit analysis is completed.

Macromanagement Concerns

The point of these newly developed computerized data-processing technologies and information and communications systems is to provide the best and most up-to-date information to all parties to the transaction, from the firm to the client. These systems should then release professionals at the securities firm from performing many unnecessary tasks, thus allowing them more time to act as better informed financial professionals and to develop client relationships.

Beyond computer systems development, management faces three major concerns that can only be addressed through an ongoing process of review and evaluation. The first question is whether the computer systems can be cost effective. The second is whether the firm has the best system for it. The third is whether the system is meeting its objectives. These are major issues that management must grapple with as it seeks to keep pace with technology and employ it as a means to achieving better service and greater productivity.

THE INTERNATIONALIZATION OF THE SECURITIES MARKETS

The internationalization of the securities markets via computerization has given rise to "globalism" as Wall Street's watchword. Trite though the term global may be, the concept is quickly becoming a reality, carrying with it far-reaching impacts on the world financial markets and the securities firms themselves. Largely an outgrowth of computerization and satellite communications systems, the integration of different financial markets around the world comes as a result of this technology creating a 24-hour securities trading day. Financial data and pricing information are updated and disseminated on an on-line or real-time basis, and securities firms transmit their trading inventory books electronically from one market and one exchange to another as each closes and the other opens. Firm trading positions are also updated from a global standpoint as a tool for risk management.

As one might imagine, fully operationalized internationally linked securities markets and firms do not come about without technological and management problems. Macromanagement concerns include language differences, currency exchange problems, and time zone variances, all of which are problems endemic to international financial markets. International exchanges must establish linkages among one another as well as regularized operations and order-processing procedures, including 24-hour clearing and settling rules. Complicating matters further is the need for regulatory rules accepted by all worldwide markets, exchanges, participants, securities firms, and clients alike. On a larger and more sweeping scale, corporate reporting rules should be standardized because the regulatory reporting requirements in the United States appear, in some cases, to be stricter than those of other countries and regulatory bodies.

NOTES

1. Tim Carrington, *The Year They Sold Wall Street* (Boston: Houghton Mifflin, 1985), p. 47.
2. For a detailed discussion of the securities transactions, see David M. Weiss, *After the Trade Is Made: Processing Securities Transactions* (New York: New York Institute of Finance, 1986).

For some discussions on computers and information systems of securities firms, see the *Wall Street Computer Review,* especially the following articles:
"How Automation Is Fueling Intercontinental Trading: The Sun Never Sets on the Financial Empire," October 1986.
"Information Technology Yields New Clout for DP Professionals," February 1987.
"Wall Street's Computer Spending Plans," August 1985.
"Wall Street's Electronic Future," October 1985.

PART 3

BEYOND CAPITAL, COMMITMENT, AND CAPABILITY

CHAPTER 10

MOTIVATING THE HIGHLY MOTIVATED

In addressing a meeting of some senior managers of a securities firm, a member of the firm's executive committee told them that he believed some professionals within the organization were not highly motivated enough. He said, "Let me tell you how I think people should be motivated. If you have ten guys trying to pull a cannon up a hill, and they are having problems, and it does not look as if they're going to do the job, the only way to motivate them is to shoot one of the guys. Then you will see how fast the other nine pull that cannon right up the hill." At another meeting at a different firm, one top-level manager suggested that she believed there was only one single way to motivate securities industry professionals. She said, "Those who want to be with us and produce will be paid and paid very well. It's the only way I know how to motivate people." Within these two anecdotes are the basic ways most believe professionals on Wall Street are motivated—namely, by fear and greed. The examples wed the concepts of both motivation and compensation. They are really two separate ideas, however, and should be dealt with in different terms, although they do have related aspects to them.

Motivation, to be sure, is certainly more than what can be stimulated through increased compensation or even fear, and on Wall Street, motivation runs far beyond the Pavlovian response created by a potential reward. Indeed, motivating people who are usually first-rate professionals, are already fairly well motivated, and are also sometimes very well paid is a complex task. Many industry professionals have also achieved a relatively high degree of success and thus have developed a significant amount of self-esteem. Most of these individuals perform at a high level of their own capacity, and a good percentage of them may actually be overachievers. Motivation itself is often difficult to understand, hard to operationalize, and of especially enormous importance if successfully achieved on a large scale within any organization; but it is complex to activate in organizations like securities firms.

The general literature on motivation, both for individuals and groups, is vast and has been one area in the study of management and organizational behavior that has developed to a fairly sophisticated degree. The comprehensive nature of the field owes its growth, in large part, to the fact that it does span so many different academic disciplines and is sometimes an interdisciplinary type of study. Motivation theory and practice occupy important parts of the literature on psychology, management, sociology, and even in philosophy. Without rehashing the voluminous material published on the subject to date, it is worth noting that motivation studies have also spanned the gamut of those dealing with single individuals performing tasks unilaterally to the hows and whys of motivating small groups of professionals within an organization and even entire organizations themselves. Substantial work has been done by Maslow, Herzberg, Skinner, McClelland, Vroom, and McGregor, among others. Analysts and managers alike owe a tremendous debt to these individuals as well as many other distinguished academics who have studied and written about the subject, and also to those managers and professionals within organizations who have taken a keen interest in this field and have launched programs aimed at developing employee motivation.

To even argue that, all things considered, the more highly motivated a company's professionals are, the better the company will do based on almost any measure compared to other similar entities may be generally considered true. In its application to professionals within a securities firm, the concept of motivation thus assumes enormous importance. This is the result of several reasons: the entrepreneurial nature of the business; the fact that revenue generation can often be pinned to the performance of individuals and those who work closely with each other in small business units and interrelated ones; the competitive nature of the business itself; the fact that it is so people oriented; the idea that its bedrock of organizational life is the relationship between the securities firm professional and the client; and the simple fact that the securities industry seems to attract and seek highly motivated individuals.

THE GATEKEEPERS AND MOTIVATION

"You've got to be a little different to want to be in this business, stay in it, and be successful in it," said one securities firm recruiter to an incoming class of investment bankers. This theme has been echoed time and again by the securities industry's gatekeepers, from those interviewing newly minted M.B.A.s, to those looking for lateral entrants with sales-related experience for employment as account executives, to those selecting computer whizzes for a firm's operations or information processing area or even for the capital markets division. Just because the gatekeepers think that these applicants should be different (and once they are employed the applicants think they *are* different) does not necessarily make them so. Surely many collective groups of professionals such as astronomers, computer salespeople, accountants, trial attorneys, marketing executives, and industrial engineers think that they too have different makeups, and maybe they do. Yet, what the gatekeepers in the securities industry are saying is that the kind of individual who the industry attracts and ultimately hires is different from the average working person in some very important ways, and this indeed may actually be so.

Securities industry professionals are usually considered to be relatively intense and highly motivated individuals who move at a much faster pace than most other people, have well above average intelligence, and are, in fact, interested in remuneration. They do not necessarily expect themselves to move up the corporate hierarchical ladder largely because of the individualistic and entrepreneurial nature of their jobs, which allows them to develop clients and earn progressively greater compensation whether or not they are promoted up into the higher levels of the firm's management structure. Thus, what a securities industry manager is confronted with is a group of individuals who may or may not respond to traditional motivational techniques. The problem then becomes one of keeping the individual's motivation at a high level, developing the motivation of others when it is not at what managers perceive to be their capacity, and also motivating highly motivated professionals so that they can continue to produce at a high and perhaps overachieving level.

An in-depth analysis of the motivational characteristics of securities industry professionals in different departments and divisions and for different jobs, while interesting and informative, is certainly beyond the scope of this volume. Perhaps it is sufficient to say it is generally agreed that within a representative sample of securities industry professionals, both managers and employees, would be found a highly motivated group of individuals, who enjoy the fiercely competitive environment in which they work. In a sense, this milieu feeds their high level of motivation.

THE "WE'RE GOING TO WIN" PHILOSOPHY

Securities industry professionals, regardless of how well they are paid, are among the few workers in the United States who, no matter how you describe it, must have an almost insatiable inner drive that motivates them and an undying determination to win. This is a function of the fact that on the average, securities industry professionals are either their own revenue generators or major contributors to a small group of individuals who generate revenues in their small business unit, usually with some help from others in similar organizational units located throughout the firm.

Much of the literature on management and motivation has confined the incredible motivating drives of certain corporate professionals to those with so-called "type A" personalities or who occupy the upper strata of management within corporations. Securities industry professionals up and down the corporate hierarchy, most especially those who have on-line revenue-generating jobs or are considered to be moderate to big producers, seem to have a built-in behavioral mechanism that virtually insures a high level of motivation beyond the capability of many corporate professionals, and in some ways, is not understandable to most working people. There have been many anecdotes and discussions of this type of individual, who seems to pervade Wall Street securities firms, in the press, in the national magazines, and in a number of books about the industry. Interestingly, this is not a recent phenomenon and was noted in books written over a hundred years ago. James McCabe, in his book *Light and Shadows of New York Life* written in 1872, stated, "It has been remarked that men who do business in Wall Street have a prematurely old look, and that they die at a comparatively early age."[1] McCabe suggested further that

> This is not strange. They live too fast, their bodies and brains are taxed too severely to last long. They pass their days in a state of great excitement. Every little fluctuation of the market elates or depresses them to an extent greater than they think. At night they are either planning the next day's campaign, or are hard at work at the hotels. On Sundays their minds are still on their business, and some are laboring in their offices, screened from public observation. Body and mind are worked too hard, and are given no rest.[2]

Some things never change.

If this type of individual has been in the securities industry for so long a period of time, perhaps even since the industry's inception, it bears some significant thought and study about why this is so, what is motivating these individuals, and what will continue to do so. Obviously, these professionals are competing with others for all types of securities industry business. Professionals at other corporations, however, also compete with other professionals and companies who sell like products or market similar services, and some of this competition may be as fierce as the level at which securities industry professionals compete. Yet professionals at securities firms must be competing with more than just professionals at other firms to sustain these high levels of motivation and resultant production. For instance, they may be competing with themselves to provide better service and to generate more revenues for the firm, which is ultimately translated into higher compensation. It takes a certain kind of person to continue producing in such a highly pitched way for so long, perhaps for a lifetime, even when most outside observers and even the professionals themselves believe that their basic financial needs are already met.

As a result of these general prescriptions, three questions present themselves. The first is: How do the firms isolate these individuals to become employees if it is taken as a given that they are among the large group of individuals who apply for employment? The second question might be: How are they motivated once employed, especially those professionals whose motivation and consequent production is lagging for some reason? The third question is related to the second: How are these professionals kept motivated to produce at a level so as to exceed production of most other professionals with whom they compete in the securities industry?

All these questions are ones with which personnel directors of securities firms and managers wrestle on a daily basis, and they are not easy ones to answer. Indeed, most professionals in the securities industry would probably agree that the questions, at this point in time, really have no definitive answers. There have been few studies of them in controlled circumstances, and few individuals have ventured into writing anything that truly conceptualizes what might be the answers to some of these issues. As a result, all that can be provided here is a series of answers in the form of descriptions based on what is believed to be some important aspects of motivating securities industry professionals. Answering these questions is so difficult because there are too many variables to control, and there are probably not enough acknowledged motivational benchmarks in the securities industry for use as analytical tools. For those individuals and analysts who believe they have a generalized view of the answers to these questions, they might say this situation is like the statement, "I can't describe greatness, but I know it when I see it." With that in mind, it is probably best to proceed to a conceptual discussion of these issues, if only to develop a framework for other analytical studies of much larger dimensions on this topic.

SOME ANSWERS TO MOTIVATION ISSUES

Selecting the kind of individual with the traits that will ultimately lead to success in the securities industry is particularly hard because it is difficult to define those traits. To some extent, the hiring process is a self-selecting one, whereby certain types of individuals solicit interviews with securities firms based on what they perceive the securities firm to be, what its managers are looking for in potential employees, what they know of actual employees, how they believe their makeup would fit within a securities firm, and what they like to do. However, if the process of self-selection was all there was, then almost every individual in the securities industry interviewing pool would be successful at a securities firm if and when hired. Nothing could be further from the truth; simply isolating those candidates within the applicant universe who seem to be highly motivated or possess some other personality trait or specific skill is not all there is to the hiring process, even though this is an important part of it.

As a consequence of these conceptual guidelines, the responsibility for the rest of the entire hiring process remains with those who do the interviewing. This is particularly significant because it is at this level that the ultimate selection as to who will or will not be a securities firm employee is resolved. There is perhaps no more aphoristic comment about this activity than simply to say "it takes one to know one." This implies that the very best professionals in each securities firm department should be involved in the interview process. These individuals may have a sixth sense about who has the requisite motivation to be molded and appropriately directed so as to achieve success within the industry.

Many agree that only the most highly motivated professionals can truly understand and intuitively feel the degree of an interviewee's motivation, which seems to be necessary for success in many competitive fields, especially those within the securities industry, whether it is expressed in determination, overt aggressiveness, a subtle continuing determination, or an overpowering desire. It is this intuitive selection process and one-on-one relationship between the interviewer and the prospective employee that elicits information leading a sophisticated and highly motivated interviewer to isolate a candidate as one who could potentially be a big producer. The development of this entire concept is summarized by Morse and Lorsch when they state that

> Even with our limited knowledge, however, there are indications that people will gradually gravitate into organizations that fit their own particular personalities. Managers can help this process by becoming more aware of what psychological needs seem to best fit the tasks available and the organizational setting, and by trying to shape personnel selection criteria to take account of these needs.[3]

How can individuals be motivated when they are already highly motivated? How to motivate individuals is a classic management question, but how to motivate those who are already highly motivated, especially during periods when their motivation, and thus their production level, is not as high as it would ordinarily be, is a difficult question to answer, but it is a particularly important one to discuss and analyze for managers in the securities industry. The firms select individuals with relatively high levels of motivation, those professionals who want to be the best, set constantly higher standards, goals, and objectives for themselves, and those who simply just want to win.

Dealing with motivational problems of professionals within the securities industry who seem to have "topped out" is a speculative type of exercise. There has not been much work done in this general area, but

> research conducted by management scholars at M.I.T., Columbia University, and elsewhere strongly suggests that workers at all levels who continually face new jobs will be more vital, more productive, and more satisfied with their work than those who stay in one job, even though the changes in the job do not include a promotion but are entirely lateral.[4]

It is hard to envision applying this concept on a broad scale to securities industry professionals, especially those who have developed expertise in specific areas or who already have a list of clients they must continue to service and need to develop others. It is also difficult because so many of the tasks within the securities firm are of such a specialized nature that cross-training is virtually undoable.

What does become clear, however, is that motivation, or the lack of it, is very important in situations where individuals perceive, or in fact are, doing a repetitive type of function. Even with highly motivated specialists within the securities firm whose jobs are subject to the vagaries of market conditions and the unquantifiable and unpredictable aspects of client behavior, highly motivated individuals may still subconsciously or even consciously perceive that their job is a repetitive task. The situations may result in a sort of high-level boredom that dampens what would normally be the high motivation level of the professionals, thus reducing their production. This would seem to account for motivation being depressed in such professionals even when compensation is high or relatively so; take away increasing interest in their jobs, and their motivation drops off, sometimes precipitously so.

While wholesale cross-training of securities industry professionals is probably not feasible, managers should isolate those individuals whose performance and production levels are below par because of a seeming lack of motivation and should adjust their job functions slightly to develop their interests in what might be considered new opportunities. In the investment banking area, for instance, this might be done through assigning bankers different targets to solicit for new business purposes or even having them work with different bankers whose expertise and abilities are not the type with which the banker has been used to dealing. Branch managers may suggest that account executives develop their knowledge of new product areas and apply it to a totally different type of client. Traders in any capital markets area may develop an interest in investment vehicles tangentially related to those they are actively trading, and new responsibilities and assignments may be made. A similar concept could be applied to the product service areas when professionals grow tired of marketing the same products.

This idea is also applicable to other areas within the securities firm, but these examples should suffice. Yet, this has only been done on a sporadic basis in the firms, largely because most managers have believed, and perhaps rightly so, that the more expert professionals are in a given specialized area, the better they will be able to perform. The process of job enrichment, however, flies in the face of this concept and is an activity likely to obviate some of the motivational problems now surfacing in some well paid, exceedingly intelligent, and once highly motivated and productive securities firm professionals.

Beyond the problematic situations where highly motivated individuals have not been operating up to their capacities, the securities firm as an organization must provide for the ongoing motivational needs of its professionals to maintain their already generally high levels of motivation and achievement. Put differently, it is not only professionals whose motivation has been depressed who should be of concern to management, but also all professionals should receive at least some type of reinforcement so that their motivational needs are satisfied and their production does not perceptibly drop as a result of something the organization is not doing. This is not to say that over time a professional will or should not exhibit less motivation than at others; keeping individuals operating at high levels of peak performance over long periods may either be an unrealistic goal for management or may give rise to other problems as a result. Also, aside from the professional whose motivation drops to a noticeable degree, there are probably many others within an organization, especially one whose employees are generally highly motivated, who operate at a lower motivational level. This may not necessarily be noticeable to management. If such is the case for a large number of employees, management may believe that their lower level of production is the norm rather than the exception. Thus, the organization must grapple with the problems of sustaining a higher level of motivation in all of its professionals to prevent this kind of situation.

Some believe that there is an atmosphere that could be created within a department or a small business unit of a securities firm that would result in fostering a high level of motivation within the firm's employees. Many securities industry managers argue that the firm must structure a quality working lifestyle for its highly motivated professionals, one that promotes achievement by treating the individual in a relatively hands-off way, but provides positive reinforcement over and above the usual compensatory kind. This might include the bestowing of special ranks and creating the feeling that the individual is part of an ongoing team effort or, in the words of Sherwin, giving individuals a sense of "the attraction and excitement of pursuing a shared mission."[5]

Securities industry professionals seem to view their goals as more immediate than do professionals in other corporations who think of their career objectives in terms of a longer perspective—namely, that there is a goal or a rank or a series of benefits they will receive much later on in their careers if they continue to achieve at a respectable level. Most corporations are also much more hierarchical in nature than securities firms. In many companies, individuals develop at a slower and more predetermined pace with a view towards movement up in a management hierarchy. For highly motivated individuals, especially those in the securities industry, where professionals usually do not view their careers as a series of pyramidal steps running up the organization, the tools for positive reinforcement of their motivational systems are very important. Thus, highly motivated individuals need additional reinforcement of self-worth and the feeling that they are pursuing a more important goal than just their own increased productivity.

MOTIVATION AND COMPENSATION

Although compensation will be treated in the next chapter of this text, it must be differentiated as a motivating factor and an important one in the industry. In most cases, increased compensation provides an incentive for an individual to perform at a higher level, although the extent to which it permanently alters an individual's motivation remains an open question. In situations where compensation is relatively high and also is not a significant contributor to increased productivity, compensation is only part of the process in developing incentives for employee performance. This is not to say that at extremely high levels of compensation individuals do not desire to be paid more; there are enough indications in the real world to show us that even at excessively high compensation levels, the drive for greater remuneration often feeds on itself. In those situations, however, it takes on much different dimensions because, although the precise amount of compensation may not be that important, the relative amount may be and the organization still needs to continually reinforce patterns of behavior to keep motivation at an optimum level and thus sustain a high level of productivity.

Indeed, many individuals in the securities industry who are earning a relatively good income encounter periods where their motivation is low or relatively so, as noted earlier. Others simply reach a lethargic state, even though they are producing revenues for the firm and are earning a substantial amount. At a low level of compensation, most individuals are normally under stress so that remuneration in those circumstances is extremely important and is likely to produce higher levels of motivation and greater production. At high compensation levels, it has been found that increases in remuneration can only sometimes motivate professionals to higher levels of production. The point is that securities firm managers have been presented with situations, sometimes in large numbers, where the professionals who earn a decent income, and some who earn a relatively good-sized one, have not been particularly motivated. This represents one of the more intransigent motivation problems within securities firms.

Also, two other important principles run counter to the proposition that compensation is the sine qua non of motivation in the industry. The first is that, in many cases, the greatest unhappiness and the real power politicking causing the greatest clashes and conflict may occur within the firm among professionals who are the highest paid. Second, most professionals believe that if one is doing well at a particular securities firm and has the support of management, it would take a large increase in remuneration from another firm to lure them away from their present employer. Most individuals are not willing to prove themselves again at another firm over the long period of time required to earn the respect and appreciation not immediately accorded. These ideas support the concept that motivation also comes from within an individual, especially when it is at a high level and the individual is already well paid.

MOTIVATING THE MOTIVATED

The study of motivation in the literature on organizational behavior, psychology, social psychology, and general management has had a long history. There have been some landmark works in this field, which has spanned many years and, perhaps in nonwritten form, runs back to the beginning of time. In situations such as those presented by securities firms, where there are highly motivated professionals who are working in incredibly competitive environments, who are already well compensated, and who perform some very specialized tasks often with and for their own clients, the "how to's" of motivating employees assume some very complex dimensions. These are not easy to discern, let alone treat adequately or even fulfill successfully within the confines of securities firms. In the future, there may be much more work done in the area of motivation analysis that will study complicated milieus such as securities firms. More than anything else, however, managers in securities firms must be particularly aware of some of the concepts involved in motivating their already highly motivated employees in their fiercely competitive environment. Motivation on Wall Street certainly runs far beyond the results of fear and greed, however humorously attributed to the high levels of productivity and underlying motivation of the firms' professionals.

NOTES

1. James D. McCabe, Jr., *Light and Shadows of New York Life* (New York, 1872; fac. ed., 1970), p. 280; quoted in Robert Sobel, *Inside Wall Street* (New York: W. W. Norton, 1982), pp. 38–39.
2. McCabe, p. 280.
3. John J. Morse and Jay A. Lorsch, "Beyond Theory," in *Harvard Business Review on Management, Vol. 1, Classic Advice on Aspects of Organizational Life* (New York: Harper & Row, 1985), p. 139.

4. William G. Ouchi, *Theory Z: How American Business Can Meet the Japanese Challenge* (New York: Avon Books, 1981).

5. Douglas S. Sherwin, "Strategy for Winning Employee Commitment," in *Harvard Business Review on Management, Vol. 1, Classic Advice on Aspects of Organizational Life* (New York: Harper & Row, 1985), p. 289.

CHAPTER 11

MANAGEMENT BY COMPENSATION

If you turned to this chapter first because you think it is going to tell you how much more you should be paid or will provide a listing of comparative salary ranges of Wall Street professionals, you are in the wrong place. Some of these questions, however, are important to understand because many believe that compensation is the glue that binds a securities firm together. As a result, the issues involved in compensation on Wall Street—namely, how much an individual is worth and why, as related to others within the firm and professionals at other firms who do the same job—are the raison d'etre of many professionals and managers. This has made compensation the most talked about topic on Wall Street, and it has been for years. It is mulled over by professionals during, before, and after work; it is a potential conflict generator as well as an incentive for production; and it has also been a major reason why professionals leave their firms for others. Yet, compared to its critical importance within the industry and the attention paid to it on an informal basis, management and most professionals at securities firms spend a comparatively small amount of time actually dealing with it, both from a macroorganizational standpoint and within small business units.

A PANORAMIC VIEW OF WALL STREET COMPENSATION

On Wall Street, compensation often assumes important symbolic dimensions. "The money is a point system," suggests a Wall

Street professional. "Ego counts more. Arguments here always revolved around what the other guy got, not what you needed to live on."[1] Implicit in these statements is a type of relative theory of compensation in which, regardless of the amount an individual is earning, compensation is seen as a signal of status and of worth as perceived by that individual and when compared to fellow employees and professionals at other securities firms.

Indeed, compensation stories abound on Wall Street, and like the fish that got away, the compensation packages get bigger as the rumors circulate further. Invidious comparisons are made by many and have been known to cause serious management problems. Compensation problems can rock a department to its foundations with discontent and perhaps result in the eventual departure of a large number of the department's very best people with no formal or informal notice given to management. In situations such as these, the replacement costs for equally good individuals, if they can be replaced, could be enormous. When big producers who are respectfully looked on by others at the firm leave, it is often very upsetting to the organization and is a signal to others that this firm may not be a good place to work.

One of the more dramatic changes that has occurred on Wall Street affecting the compensation of professionals has been the general dissolution of the partnership form of major securities firm enterprise. Securities firm partnerships afforded those professionals, who were fortunate enough to gain access to that upper level of firm management, the opportunity to accrue substantial wealth. Yet, the partnership form has fallen by the wayside today, as virtually all major securities firms have gone public, been partially or totally bought out, or merged with other entities. While every conceivable reason has been given for why partnerships are no longer as viable on Wall Street as they once were—from the need of the firms to secure larger capital bases to the desire of the firms' management to use the resources of larger institutions that want to or have developed ownership interests in it—some individuals believe that there are many reasons that partnerships have been sold.

Indeed, one reason sometimes cited by many is that members who were partners had a desire to get their capital out of the firm so that their funds would not be subject to use as part of the firm's capital base for trading purposes and be subject to potential losses. In the volatile financial markets of recent years, which have a bevy of complicated securities vehicles, this reason is a particularly important one. While there is potential for large investment gains, the possibility of enormous losses looms large. Also, some industry observers suggest that another reason was the premium over book value that was paid for the ownership shares of the firm, although many people would certainly disagree with these hypotheses. In short, some analysts argue that there were many reasons that the partnership form of securities organizations are fading on Wall Street. Most would agree, however, that in the final analysis, this changing situation is a result of a convergence of forces.

The selling of these partnerships has also worked to the compensatory disadvantage of soon-to-be-made partners, who would have wanted to sell had they made partners, but are now faced without the opportunity of earning multiples of their money through a partnership sellout. In short, this single evolutionary process has made compensation even more important because most professionals are now denied the opportunity of securing wealth through securities firm partnerships.

There are basically two types of compensation packages on Wall Street—the commission structure set-up and the salary plus bonus plan. Remuneration by a commission set-up is one based on a percentage of each transaction's profit, and most securities salespeople are usually paid in this fashion. The salary plus bonus plan is the compensation structure applied to most other professionals, and the specific bonus arrangement can range in amounts anywhere from a small percentage of a professional's base salary to multiples of it. Thus, the commission pay structure is a more quantitative way of compensating employees, while the salary plus bonus plan is more qualitative, although it does have some quantitative aspects to it, and the extent to which it is more quantitative than qualitative depends on the firm, the department, and the manager. In addition, there are all kinds of other compensation arrangements for professional employees on Wall Street, but they are all variations on these two themes, depending on the production of professionals, their level in the firm's hierarchy, or any contractual arrangements they may have with the firm. There are also other

ways to provide employees with additional compensation monies, and some of these are related to plans allowing an individual
to defer compensation or purchase an interest or share in their
company.

RETAIL COMMISSION COMPENSATION

Traditionally, securities salespeople on Wall Street, particularly
account executives, have been compensated through a commission-based pay structure that is quantitative in nature. Most
securities firms have set retail account executives' commission
payouts at approximately 40 percent of the gross commission
(sales) credit. If the production of account executives is lower
than a particular level set at most firms, then the commission
rate is usually lower than 40 percent; and if production is higher, then account executives receive an increase in payout on a
graduated basis above the 40 percent level, all calculated with
downside and upside limits. These figures are the general
parameters of commission-based pay for account executives; but
as noted in one study, "comparisons among the firms are difficult, . . . not only does the payout vary with a broker's gross
production level, but it also depends on the nature of the product
sold, and it may be calculated on a monthly or yearly basis."[2]
Over recent years, firms have been continuously revamping
their commission pay set-ups to achieve better incentives for
higher production and to reflect more accurately the effort, abilities, and input of account executives as well as firmwide goals.
In particular, some securities firms have changed in part from
commission-based pay structures, which are transaction
oriented, to ones that are fee based, are more related to garnering "assets under management," or aimed at keeping client
relationships over longer periods of time. These have been ways
not only to develop relationships with clients that go beyond the
single transaction but also to provide the firm and even the
account executive with income that is less cyclical than that
usually related to transactions partly dependent on market conditions. In addition, many firms have either cut commission
payouts for small transactions or developed in-house sales
groups to handle transactions under a certain size.

There are a number of key problems that have arisen as a result of this commission-based pay structure for retail account executives. Primarily, it is difficult to arrange a compensation program that provides incentive for higher production. Usually this is accomplished by increasingly graduating the payout as production is increased. At the upper levels of pay, however, some additional motivating factor must be provided. Furthermore, firms have had to wrestle with the problem of developing a compensation structure adequate enough to lure top account executives into the firm, while not being disruptive to the account executives presently at the firm, especially those in the branch office that would provide a future home for the new employees. Another difficulty is designing an additional part of the compensation plan that helps to effectively retain the new employees. Overshadowing all these issues is the illusive one alluded to earlier—structuring a pay plan for account executives that is workable, on a relative basis, for all the different kinds of products that the firm is offering. This would take into account the difficulty in selling them and the desire of the firm's management to modify its pay structure to compensate better for the cyclical nature of the securities business.

INSTITUTIONAL COMPENSATION IN FLUX

Institutional sales personnel usually have been compensated on a basis similar to that of retail account executives—one that is commission oriented, although the payout percentage has hovered between about 10 to 20 percent of the gross commission credit because of the larger sales that the institutional salespeople usually transact. Over recent years, however, there has been a movement to compensate institutional sales personnel on a salary plus bonus basis. This system provides a base salary and a bonus, based on the quantitative amount of production achieved and also on a qualitative basis, which takes into account whether or not accounts were in the market during the year, whether the account packages were rearranged with easier or more difficult accounts to cover, or any number of other similar possibilities. This arrangement was designed to control particular aspects of the institutional sales business, compared to those of the retail sales process, where an institutional salesperson may adequately cover only approximately 15 to 30 accounts and has a total account base of only about 30 to 50 accounts. An individual retail account executive sometimes has hundreds of accounts; some have perhaps a few thousand, although clearly not all of these are active at any given time. Retail account executives thus move from one account to another over very short periods of time, while institutional sales personnel must concentrate on establishing and continuing relationships with those accounts assigned to them whether or not the accounts are in the market. Some argue that in doing this institutional sales personnel are establishing a relationship both on their own behalf and also on behalf of their firm. This is not to say that clients of retail clients do not have a relationship to both the account executive and the firm. It is important to note, however, that an institutional salesperson cannot take a big institutional account, such as a bank or insurance company, totally away from the firm if the salesperson leaves. As a result, there are good arguments to be made for compensating institutional sales personnel on a salary plus bonus basis. Some individuals believe this leads to a politicized environment, is probably only best for mediocre salespeople, and does not hold as many opportunities for the very top people. These criticisms, however, are not necessarily valid.

Institutional sales compensation plans present a number of problems for management. The first and perhaps one of the most prevalent ones is in firms that do not senior manage or comanage a substantial amount of new issue products. The problem surfaces in cases where amount of product or the payout percentage is not large enough to keep the very best salespeople at the firm or to entice other salespeople from other firms. In situations like these, management should seek to arrange the level of commission payout to result in enough remuneration to retain salespeople or bring others into the firm, even if the firm does not have access to large amounts of new issue products.

Some firms are in a transition stage as they move from a commission-based institutional sales compensation system to a salary plus bonus remunerative system. In these instances, it is usually the biggest producers who become concerned about the future level of their compensation, often believing that the salary plus bonus plan will not result in the compensation levels to which they have become accustomed. In the transition stage, which usually begins around the end of the year when the compensation system is about to be changed, the largest producers often seek employment at firms that have retained a commission-based pay structure. It is at this point that management should become involved in a communications process with the entire sales staff, but especially with the departments' biggest producers, in an effort to retain these professionals. Sometimes the movement to a salary plus bonus plan for institutional sales personnel is attractive as seen from the standpoint of salespeople at other firms, so that firms in a transition stage can often use this as a "carrot and stick" to lure others into the firm. Professionals who have not covered the accounts they would have liked or are covering ones they believe will not be as productive in forthcoming years tend to feel more comfortable with the new system.

A firm whose institutional sales force is paid on a salary plus bonus plan and has been for some time has one additional burden to carry from a management standpoint. To retain its sales force, particularly the very best people, the firm must regulate the salary plus bonus system so that it results in compensation competitive with the better plans, some of which may be commission based. The goal here may be to have the biggest producers in a firm with a salary plus bonus plan receive remuneration closely equivalent to the largest producers at competing firms whose compensation system is commission based.

RETAIL-INSTITUTIONAL COMMISSION COMPENSATION

Some firms have a group of account executives who handle large-size retail accounts and small to midsize institutions. The firms usually provide these account executives with a designation such as "retail-institutional" account executives or another similar name. These account executives are usually paid through a commission-based pay system and have a payout roughly equivalent to that of the firm's retail account executives. Management is usually presented with the same types of compensation problems for these account executives as it is with regular account executives; but, in some ways, this situation places these account executives, as well as managers who oversee them, in a sort of compensation bind. One important difficulty is the possibility that retail-institutional account executives can alienate the institutional sales force and its managers by virtue of the fact that they are actually servicing institutional accounts but are doing so with a much higher payout, even though the small to midsize institutional clients require a greater amount of labor-intensive servicing than is required for the larger institutional clients. In addition, regular retail account executives can also become somewhat disenchanted because they realize that these retail-institutional account executives are permitted to service institutional accounts but receive the higher retail payout. These are all-important compensation considerations for management.

Such situations have led to some alternative arrangements. Some firms have suggested that account executives who handle largely small and midsize institutions should be transferred to the institutional sales force and have their payout adjusted accordingly. At other firms, account executives who are in the retail-institutional category have been asked by management to drop their small to midsize institutional clients and concentrate solely on retail ones. There have also been cases where institutional salespeople have wanted to service small to midsize institutional accounts that were being handled by the retail-institutional personnel. These issues go far beyond the questions related to compensation but have part of their genesis in the compensation arrangements and are therefore worth mentioning here.

THE SALARY PLUS BONUS COMPENSATION SYSTEM

The salary plus bonus system is widely used in the securities industry, particularly in the capital markets and investment banking areas. Although it might be a good system because it provides incentives to professionals in their quest for higher year-end bonuses, it is also laden with a number of complications that have led to significant management problems at some securities firms. Many argue that the bonus system can become rather political, and that some individuals who receive higher bonuses than others are more politically adept at successfully claiming credit for revenues generated and convincing others, principally management, that they have caused this revenue inflow. To be sure, this system does have a politicizing nature, but most industry professionals contend that this is a fact of organizational life. Others suggest that the political posturing and other types of behavior designed to alter the conception of who is and who is not the department's major producers has already been discounted in the manager's view of the department and its inner workings.

A positive aspect of a salary plus bonus plan stems from the fact that many of the revenue-generating jobs under these types of remunerative systems result in group tasks that make it difficult to pinpoint the individual who has been key in creating the revenue stream. More often than not, revenues have been generated as a result of a team effort. Consequently, a salary plus bonus plan appears to be the kind of compensation program that best fits in these situations because it is both quantitative and qualitative. It also provides managers the opportunity to subtly and privately give hints to select individuals that they are not performing up to management's expectations and reward others who are top producers.

One of the key problems in the salary plus bonus plan is getting professionals to understand that their bonus is tied largely to their own production but also to that of the individuals with whom they work and to the results of their division and the firm. The effort here, on the one hand, is to insure that the professionals feel comfortable that their input is recognized and that their compensation could not necessarily be impacted greatly on the negative side because of chance or because others within their department or division have not produced according to expectations. On the other hand, the concept also stresses that the professional is indeed part of a small business unit, department, and firm and that collective efforts also have to be taken into account. Thus, there are three broad parameters that securities firms professionals suggest will indicate how well paid they will be under such a plan. They are: the extent to which the professionals contribute to the revenue generation; the extent to which their department is successful; and the extent to which the firm is profitable.

The key to the success of this compensation arrangement is an ongoing communications effort between the individual professional and the manager. This is rarely ever taken to heart by managers and employees alike to an extent that will alleviate the anxiety involved in getting a bonus, help a professional's development, and ultimately prevent the degeneration of this process into a political one. Consistent feedback between the manager and the professional over time results in a common understanding of goals that are set and the professional's successes or lack of them. Yet, for the most part, securities industry professionals are given annual reviews by their managers that last an hour at most, with a minimum amount of give and take, and that conclude with the bestowing of an already decided on bonus amount. It is unrealistic to expect that in this short timespan and in such an anxious and often tense meeting about an individual's livelihood that true constructive criticism can be dispensed by the manager and digested successfully by the employee in order to upgrade the individual's capabilities. Professional development is not a once a year cause. Because success in the securities industry is so dependent on communication, motivation, and individual development, it should come as no surprise that an ongoing dialogue, both formal and informal, with professionals under a manager's jurisdiction, is critical.

It is also important that these discussions be done with a manager who is in a position to make decisions about a professional's bonus. Too often this process takes place between a professional and a manager who cannot really make those decisions and can only make recommendations. Even if a more senior manager makes the final determination about an individual's bonus based on the recommendations of a lower level manager, the senior manager is often unaware of the relative production levels of individuals under the lower level manager's supervision and is thus in a position to have much of the comparative analysis obscured by the immediate supervisor. This situation is yet another unusual one in the securities industry and is also endemic to companies with a number of specialized small business units where many compensation recommendations are left to managers, but the ultimate decision is made higher up in the management hierarchy. In any event, for many securities industry managers and professionals, the salary plus bonus plan is likely to remain a fact of life for years to come; alternative systems either have not been devised or could be much worse.

REGIONAL PAY DIFFERENTIALS

Few securities industry managers calculate precisely the cost of living differences in different areas across the United States when arranging compensation packages. This is particularly important in developing compensation plans for professionals in the capital markets and investment banking divisions because, in most of these instances, the salary plus bonus plans usually only attempt to take into account revenues generated but do not factor in cost-of-living differences. As a result, there may be investment bankers living in New York and other cities who are earning the same amount in compensation; but because it is far more expensive to live in New York, there may be inherent inequities in remuneration. There are no professionals more sensitive to it than those who believe that they have been shortchanged because their cost-of-living has not been taken into account in their department's compensation arrangements. This could lead to an environment replete with claims and counterclaims for revenues generated by professionals and small business units in a department that has offices located in different cities. In actuality, these business units are supposed to be working together but, in fact, they begin to work at cross purposes with one another because of the perceived inequities of compensation when year-end bonus calculations are made.

SUPPORT STAFF COMPENSATION

Absolutely critical to a well-oiled securities machine is a quality support staff, and many believe that most profitable securities firms on Wall Street have the very best support personnel. Having quality support staff is important because they often have as much, and sometimes more, contact with clients than do the professional staff members who are either tied to their telephones or are even traveling on the road for a large percentage of their working time. Support staff in the industry is therefore critical to its ongoing operations and success, and it should come as no surprise that a major production incentive for support staff is a well-paying compensation plan. If a comparative informal analysis is any indication, those firms that are the most successful pay their support personnel better than many other firms.

The relative profitability of public securities firms, and in many cases, the specific bottom-line net income at year end, is usually available and published in newspaper accounts nationwide. With this has been published the relative percentages of salaries firms have provided their support staff for year-end bonuses. The provision of bonuses for support staff is by no means a hard and fast rule on Wall Street, but it has developed into common practice over recent years. It is therefore in the interest of Wall Street managers to provide bonus packages for support staff that in some way reflect the general profitability of their firms in relation to that of others. Many managers believe that the cost of additional bonuses or somewhat larger ones for support staff is well worth the expense.

MANAGEMENT REMUNERATION

Perhaps the most delicate compensation arrangement that can be devised in a securities firm and one that deserves special attention is the pay provided for management. This is usually done through a salary plus bonus plan and therefore has quantitative and qualitative aspects to it. It is important to understand conceptually because it affects how lower and midlevel managers relate to senior managers and also how managers compensate all employees who report to them. Yet, the complexity of management compensation in securities firms is compounded by classically unusual situations that are by-products of the firms' organizational structure.

The first is the possibility and indeed likelihood, that any given manager, especially one at the mid- to upper levels, supervises on-line big producers who generate large amounts of revenue and often earn more than the manager. When managers in any organization are paid less than, at the same level as, or close to the level of professionals under their supervision, the situation has a potential, in a worst-case scenario, to breed difficulties. For instance, some managers may tend to minimize the accomplishments of their biggest producers or take credit for them. Others may attempt to get hooked into the revenue-generating activities of their big producers in an effort to be associated with them. There are many other potential problems that could arise from such situations, and one need only use some imagination to conjure up some of them. Nevertheless, the situation is a delicate one, and unless handled correctly, can spell trouble for the manager, the department, and even the firm.

One of the key ways to circumvent these difficulties and one not generally used to the fullest extent possible is ongoing discussions between a manager and the manager's superior about specific short- and long-range goals. To be sure, most managers work on a collegial basis and develop relationships that are more informal than formal. Although the formality is apparent in conversation and perhaps in the year-end review process, the setting of goals and objectives for a manager and the manager's department within the confines of this relationship is often pushed aside as something too rudimentary to spend time on. Yet, this single process, which also ultimately translates into an ability to compensate managers more accurately, is one critical means of developing a goal orientation in a department and from the top of a securities firm to its lower levels. It is this interplay, exchange, and communication among managers running from one level of a firm to another that keeps the whole operation in check and as close to its strategic critical path as possible, while the organization remains composed of specialized and relatively autonomous, although somewhat interdependent, business units that usually have their own revenue-generating capability. It is this interstitial tissue of organizational life within the securities firm that very often makes or breaks its long-range success—and it is compensation-related.

COMPENSATION VARIATIONS ON A THEME

In the wake of the seeming demise of the partnership form of organization as a major organizational structure for Wall Street securities firms, many firms have attempted to design compensation programs that incorporate the wealth-building potential inherent in the traditional partnership arrangements. Most firms trying to structure new compensation plans and graft them onto their existing programs have had some notable difficulties in making them work. A major problem, which is more of a mind-set one, is that many of the firms' professionals believed that the arrangements supplanted the existing compensation plans rather than supplemented them. This is so because many of these new plans had a forced deferral of compensation as part of the package, whereby a certain percentage of an individual's compensation, usually considered to be part of the bonus plan, was held by the firm for five years or more, and it was only at that time that the professional could take out funds. This was done every year, while the individual's money earned the same rate of return or interest that the firm did or some similar arrangement.

From the firm's standpoint, this was an especially good system because it provided what might be called the partnership "golden handcuffs" for professionals; they could not take their funds out of the firm if they left. The difficulty with this system was that it was usually not enough of a deterrent to prevent professionals from moving to other firms. In many cases, very little money was left within the firm if a professional quit, and in other cases, the resources of the firm hiring away the professional were usually of such size that the firm could easily cover the amount of money one left on the table.

Nevertheless, there is no magical formula for successful

compensation arrangements to supplement or supplant those already in place. Sooner or later, firms will devise some that are truly successful in keeping top producers as close to home as could reasonably be expected. Ultimately, a professional's rationale for remaining with a firm will have as much to do with the firm as it does with anything else, even compensation plans.

EQUITY THEORY AND COMPENSATION

One of the major themes about compensation on Wall Street, as noted earlier, is that it is a way of keeping score or a point system, and as such, it has an already built-in theory of relativity. Many securities industry professionals are content with their own level of compensation until they hear that others within their department, or holding similar jobs at competing firms, earn substantially more. At that time, satisfaction goes out the window as harmful comparisons are made. This may sound simple and obvious, but it is central to equity theory in the literature on compensation. To be sure, the problem is a classic one, but it is particularly important to understand in designing all types of securities firm remuneration programs and plans.

Why employees are satisfied or dissatisfied with their compensation is often a result of perception. According to Edward Lawler's argument, as restated by Wallace and Fay, "the immediate cause of satisfaction or dissatisfaction with pay is the distinction between the amount employees think they should receive and the amount they think they are actually receiving relative to others."[3] They argue that "the amount of pay an individual judges that he should be paid depends upon the amount of input he sees himself contributing as compared to the input of another."[4] Indeed,

> the perceived amount of received pay is a relative amount, based on a comparison of the perceived pay of referent others to the actual pay one receives ... If an individual is consistently denied pay satisfaction, dissatisfaction will result, and it will be increasingly difficult for the organization to attract and retain valued employees.[5]

This is a typical pay dissatisfaction model that can be applied to problems in compensation, especially within the securities industry when comparisons are made.

An individual's perception of equity in compensation may also drastically affect decisions about work. Indeed, Wallace and Fay state that

> the relative way in which management treats an employee's compensation is at least as important as the absolute level of pay. Perceptions of equity, then, influence the decisions people make about organizations: to accept or reject a job offer, to stay with or leave an organization, and to expend more or less effort on the job.[6]

This is particularly applicable to the securities industry because of the scoreboard compensation mentality, compounded by the largess of certain firms in doling out additional remunerative rewards as a way of luring professionals away from competing firms. Compensation arrangements should be equitable, but should also be perceived as such.

NOTES

1. Ken Auletta, *Greed and Glory on Wall Street: The Fall of the House of Lehman* (New York: Random House, 1986), p. 135.
2. "New Ways to Pay Brokers," *Institutional Investor,* May 1986.
3. Marc Wallace, Jr., and Charles H. Fay, *Compensation Theory and Practice* (Mass.: Kent Publishing Company, 1983), p. 84; see also Edward E. Lawler III, *Pay and Organizational Development* (Boston: Addison-Wesley, 1981).
4. Wallace and Fay, p. 84.
5. Ibid., pp. 84 and 86.
6. Ibid., p. 19.

CHAPTER 12

A FIRM'S ORGANIZATIONAL ETHOS

Shortly after I started working on Wall Street, I asked a close friend of mine, who was also a new recruit, what it was like to work in a corporate finance department of an investment banking firm. I wanted to know the feeling of the firm, its culture and way of life, and what was expected of employees from professional and social standpoints. My friend quickly retorted, "That's easy. You want to know what it's like? Well, I'll tell you. To really fit in, you come to work with brightly colored suspenders, walk around smoking one of those expensive cigars, and have a fully packed suitcase next to your desk. Sometime in the late morning, right after you get a telephone call, you pick up the suitcase and run out of your office, past the elevator, while bellowing to your secretary, 'I'm late and the elevator's too slow!' Then you push open the emergency staircase door, and run down some stairs, finding your way in time out of the building."

This was a first-impression view of a firm's corporate culture as experienced by a newly minted business school graduate and corporate finance neophyte. Yet, many people outside the securities industry still have this myopic perspective of what a securities firm's ethos is all about. Cigars and suspenders may be part of it, if only a symbolic part. An organization's ethos is much more than these kind of seemingly required accoutrements, and it means much more, especially on Wall Street.

IN DEFINITIONAL TERMS

Webster's Dictionary defines ethos as "the distinguishing character, sentiment, moral nature, or guiding beliefs of a person, group, or institution." Some management experts have generally defined organizational ethos in a more restrictive way as "corporate culture," and others have developed articles and books based on various aspects of these terms. Quite obviously, for every manager and scholar there is a somewhat different definition of culture, beliefs, or what is called here organizational ethos. Subtle shadings of meanings of these words are noteworthy but do not change the general character of Webster's definition. Yet, what the literature has shown managers and management analysts is how important organizational ethos is to the ongoing success of the modern corporation.

In many instances, industry observers as well as management scholars have attributed the unabashed success of companies, both small and large, to the highly developed nature of the company's organizational ethos or culture. However defined, what is critically important to understand is that an organization's ethos is becoming more accepted as a significantly important, if not major, foundation through which to propel a corporation to financial achievement. Perhaps nowhere is this more apparent than in the securities firms on Wall Street.

All firms on Wall Street, to a greater or lesser degree, exhibit an organizational ethos in a variety of forms, however difficult to describe, pinpoint as to origin, explain as to composition, or even define specifically. Many of the firms' professionals wear their organization's ethos on their sleeve as a imprimatur or showpiece for professional colleagues and clients alike; it is certainly something everyone reacts to, for better or for worse. To be sure, each firm's ethos may be characterized differently, having its genesis in many different roots, such as the firm's skilled intellectual financial advice, its big market trades through the use of huge amounts of capital, the strength of its worldwide distribution system, the so-called "way the firm does business," who the firm's clients are, how selective it is in hiring, or its economist's ability to predict interest rates. Indeed, there is hardly a securities industry professional who does not acknowledge the ethos of a number of firms as seen and exhibited by its employees. In some cases, even among industry colleagues, professionals of other firms are held in awe because they are members of a particular firm whose ethos is recognized throughout the industry. It goes without saying that sometimes ethos leads to arrogance; this is not a usual result, but it may happen.

Generally speaking, and though there are no quantitative ways to prove this, there appear to be three ways a firm's strong organizational ethos helps: it attracts the best people; it helps secure the best clients; and it improves company spirit. For the securities industry, put simply, it works. Thus, three significant questions flow from these attributes, which are also an important part to understanding securities firms:

1. What is an organizational ethos in the securities industry?
2. How is it developed?
3. How is it maintained?

WHAT IS IT?

Beyond most definitions and without being trite, it may be argued that organizational ethos, as applied to the securities industry and certainly from what most professionals have observed, is a certain pride, exuded with fearless confidence and indeed some pleasure, about what the organization has done in the past, what it represents, and of what presumably the professional is now an example. A securities firm's organizational ethos is presented in an effort to inspire clients and professionals within the firm, and perhaps even to impress other colleagues at competing organizations. Although truly difficult to describe, the fact that it works says something about what it is. This is not to say that everybody at every firm wears their organization's ethos on their sleeve; some make a habit of not doing this in an effort to be as inconspicuous as possible. Ironically, the ethos may become even more conspicuous by its absence, when taking into account what most people perceive the securities firm to represent. In some firms, the ethos permeates the entire organization up to the chair of the board in somewhat varying degrees.

Finally, an organization's ethos is not always entirely of the firm's own making. Books about Wall Street and its firms and stories about deals, sales, and trading results on the news and in the tabloids promote and tout it but most of all publicize it, perhaps making it larger than life for the media's readers and viewers. The organizational ethos of many securities firms that emanates from its wood-paneled corridors and boardrooms, is something of which popular novels are made. The simple fact is that Wall Street allows it to flourish and perhaps promotes it, enjoys it, and even requires it. Oddly enough, professionals at firms that do not have a highly developed organizational ethos talk about it more than those at firms that do. In a way, the ethos of many Wall Street firms has a tendency to get bigger by the day. Those professionals who do not have it want it, and others who are not involved with it are interested in reading about it. In a few words, it is also the aura of the firm projected to the outside world and, in many ways, it is maintained by the media, as will be discussed.

HOW IS IT DEVELOPED?

Surely a securities firm's organizational ethos, or the culture of any corporation, is not created in a vacuum. The firms had to do something to acquire their character, organizationally speaking, but not every employee helped in the process. Yet, most securities firms have a characteristic tone, and if you ask those who visit different firms from financiers to clients to interviewees, they will tell you that the tone of some of these firms is markedly different from others, which presumes that an ethos actually exists. What the observer does encounter is that the firm's ethos is, more often than not, a result of results, not surprisingly. It is also a function of the firm's size, its abilities, and its accomplishments, all of which foster a perception of the firm inside and outside.

Most people believe that the ethos, described here as a tone, is developed or set by the firm's senior managers; but an organizational ethos for a firm of thousands cannot truly be set by a few people. Indeed, it has to be established by the firm's managers throughout the organization, and this is at once reflected by what others within it perceive the tone of the firm to be, and what those outside it believe it should be. In this way, it is sort of an ongoing process of mirror-created images, established largely by what the firm has accomplished, acted on by the firm's managers up and down the firm's hierarchy, and reflected on the firm's personnel to such an extent that very often it is even carried through to the professionals' body language. Finally, it even becomes apparent within the media and at times is an important part of the firm's advertising. The phenomenon of organizational ethos within a securities firm feeds on itself and tracing its development becomes a sort of "chicken-and-egg" situation.

HOW IS IT MAINTAINED?

An organizational ethos is maintained in three principal ways. First of all, it is maintained in the same way it was developed, reflecting from management to personnel to the outside world and back to the firm. It is maintained then with momentum that often does not come crashing to a denouement but rather is more representative of a steady stream of reinforcement by the firm's senior managers, its personnel, through the firm's activities, and the media, when appropriate.

Second, a securities firm's organizational ethos is maintained through a sort of implicit system of nondenial. In this way, by not denying the organization's ethos projected to the outside world, the firm perpetuates its existence, and in a sense, even promotes it. Nondenial, in any event, is an important way to perpetuate what might be denied.

The third way an organizational ethos is perpetuated, and one especially important in the securities industry, is the aura created by the media surrounding a firm's activities and the lucid descriptions of what the firm's organizational ethos actually is. Professionals within the securities industry, as well as industry observers, for some reason seem to enjoy reading about the securities industry and its firms. The media feeds that appetite, as stories abound of the inner workings and machinations of Wall Street's securities firms, all replete with detailed descriptions of the cultures of the firms, their styles, and their most notable professionals. This process, perhaps more than anything else, helps maintain an organization's ethos. In many ways, it may even make the professionals within a securities firm try to live up to what has been created by the media, and therefore what they believe others would like to see.

The maintenance of an organization's ethos is easier said than done, however. Over the years, the ethos or culture of firms within the securities industry has both faded and grown as much, if not more so, than those of other corporations. This is important because securities firms have been noted for their in-house cultures since their inceptions. One of the major reasons that the ethos of some firms has faded measurably is that many partnerships no longer exist as such. Partnerships on Wall Street implied a clubhouse atmosphere with an "all for one, and one for all" culture. For most firms, the days are gone when taking trading risks meant actually risking one's personal wealth, which was tied up as part of the firm's capital. Gone also are the times when most major firms were of such small size that, while the partners were surely not blood relations, in many instances they acted as such—with all the familial problems usually associated with that type of in loco parentis organizational umbrella.

As an offshoot of this situation was the tremendous increase in the number of employees of most of these many securities firms over the last five to ten years or so. Although some firms have indeed remained relatively small, other securities houses that previously numbered 1500 to 2500 in total employees have grown in size to 4000 to 7000 in number. Consequently, it is often extremely difficult to maintain the kind of ethos that previously characterized a much smaller firm. This is especially so because the vast proportion of the influx of new employees has come within a relatively short period of time.

When a securities firm has merged with another securities firm or when it has been taken over by a larger institution, its ability to maintain its organizational ethos remains an open question; in most cases, it is not easy for the firm to retain its culture. In instances where securities firms have merged with each other, the firm with the least strongest ethos stands the greatest chance of having it evaporate in a relatively short period of time, or at least be modified as the intermingling of employees occurs and professionals leave to join other organizations. Where a securities firm was bought by a larger and different type of entity, it was more easily able to retain its corporate culture, if any. It is possible, however, that the securities firm's ethos would be modified, but this would occur over a much longer time period.

The point here is that an organization's ethos, particularly those of firms in the securities industry, is both an organizational feeling and imprimatur—developed by its managers, worn by its professionals, and shown to the world with some dignity. Most important, however, is that it can change or die; but it can be maintained, and for securities firms, perhaps it should be.

CHAPTER 13

POWER POLITICS CAN BE PROFITABLE

SOME BASIC CONCEPTS

To most observers of the Wall Street scene and to readers of contemporary books and periodicals about it, the words power, politics, and Wall Street appear to be synergetic. Indeed, these three concepts come center stage when talking about securities firms; but in some very important ways, the management activities that flow from politics and power have some useful and important by-products, especially when employed in the context of the organizational structure of securities firms. To most individuals, the words "power politics" inevitably conjure up the image of corporate internecine warfare replete with cloak-and-dagger routines, thus isolating the seamy side of organizational life. This unsystemized and impressionistic view emphasizes the negative aspects of power politics and thus, in large part, may be an unrealistic view of the process.

Some would argue that the nature of the securities firm gives rise to a working life of potential conflict in competitive situations that provides a foundation for the kinds of concerns implicit in power politics. The firm's characteristics might include the profit center mentality of many business units and their managers as well as the seemingly contradictory aspects of it that lie in the fact that many of these departments, particularly those in the capital markets and investment banking areas, are interdependent. Claims often arise as to who or which area was most responsible for the generation of a particular revenue stream. Also, there is an autonomous and entrepreneurial nature to departments and many professionals reinforced by the decentralized nature of most business units within the firm and by the fact that very often the biggest producers in the firm do not occupy the mid- and upper levels of management.

As a result, many management experts and industry analysts believe that these securities firm characteristics provide a fertile field for the development of organizational politics of the power variety to thrive virtually unchecked until they develop an ongoing life of their own. This may or may not be the case, and whether or not this scenario is ultimately actualized certainly varies from firm to firm and from department to department. Yet, the potential problems of conflict, competition, and control of departments within investment banking firms is, in fact, noted by Ernest Bloch. He argues, for instance, that

> within an investment banking firm, strong institutional sales and trading departments and equally strong managements of customer assets compete with each other for scarce resources within the firm, namely, capital in human and financial form. It is unlikely that one department of any investment banking firm will assist another to its own detriment either in performance or in the earnings that may be claimed by the partner (or vice president) in charge.[1]

However, even if the nature of securities firms does provide a foundation for the development of power politics to a greater extent than the milieu of most corporations, the use of power politics within the firm can also be turned into a profitable way to manage conflict and compromise in the kinds of situations that are relatively decentralized and allow individuals a great degree of autonomy. Indeed, here power politics can mold departmental policy, can aid immeasurably in developing a more cohesive working relationship among professionals within a small business unit and also among larger departments and even divisions, and can also provide an informal influential force in directing the activities of professionals or redirecting them in accordance with the goals and objectives created by department managers and the firm's top management team. Within an organization whose component parts are rather autonomous, specialized small business units and departments, such as those characterized by securities firms, the use of power politics by managers may be one of the most important means by which the managers can successfully control and develop the business units under their supervision.

To be sure, the acquisition of power and the use of it is certainly not all bad (as noted in editorial introductions to the following articles). In an article, McClelland and Burnham generally suggest: "Good managers are not motivated by a need for personal aggrandizement, or by a need to get along with subordinates, but rather by a need to influence others' behavior for the good of the whole organization. In other words, good managers want power."[2] Power may be a necessary condition for managerial control within the types of organizations prevalent today. John P. Kotter maintains generally that "as organizations have grown more complex, it has become difficult, if not impossible, for managers to achieve their ends either independently or through persuasion and formal authority alone. They increasingly need power to influence other people on whom they are dependent." Furthermore, "effective managers tend to be very successful at developing power which they use along with persuasion to influence others," and they do so "with maturity, great skill, and a sensitivity to the obligations and risks involved."[3]

DEFINITIONALLY SPEAKING

The literature on organizational behavior and development is especially rich in its discussion of the concepts of both power and politics in organizations and their use by employees and managers alike. Even more significant is the fact that in most organizations, managers and employees spend significant amounts of time discussing these ideas as they are applied in daily situations by colleagues. In typical business settings, however, these concepts are very rarely, if ever, defined conceptually, and they are usually lumped together to form the phrase "power politics," even in light of the fact that the classical definitions in the literature usually separate them and define each in different terms. For discussion purposes, therefore, it is probably best to review each concept's definition through the literature on organizational behavior and define both as a basis for applied study.

The concept of power as defined by Salancik and Pfeffer is "the ability of those who possess power to bring about the outcomes they desire."[4] Pfeffer goes on to suggest in another publication that "most definitions of power include an element indicating that power is the capability of one social actor to overcome resistance in achieving a desired objective or result."[5] Most important is that some analysts conceive of both power and politics as concepts that are not unidimensional. They argue that there are two sides to power and politics. McClelland has suggested that there are in fact "two faces of power." In paraphrasing McClelland's ideas, French et al. suggest that

> The negative face of power is characterized by a primitive, unsocialized need to have dominance over submissive others. The positive face of power is characterized by a socialized form of leading and initiating that helps others reach their goals as well as helps the person exercising power to reach his or her goals.[6]

This twofold conception suggests to analysts that power is not really an either/or situation, but rather a relative one.

Many years ago, Harold Lasswell defined politics as the study or the analysis of who gets what, when, and how.[7] Pfeffer, in a later discussion, suggests that "organizational politics involves those activities taken within organizations to acquire, develop, and use power and other resources to obtain one's preferred outcomes in a situation in which there is uncertainty or dissensus about choices."[8] And like power, many analysts believe that politics also has two faces, both a negative and a positive one. French et al. suggest that the negative face of politics "is characterized by extreme pursuit of self-interest; . . . and predominant use of the tactics of fighting such as secrecy, surprise, holding hidden agendas, withholding information, deceiving." They suggest further that "the positive face of politics is characterized by a balanced pursuit of self-interest; . . . engaging in open problem solving and goal clarification and then moving to action and then influencing; a relative absence of the tactics of fighting; and a socialized need to lead, initiate, and influence others." They also argue that "organizations can be arrayed along a continuum of how political they are and whether the organizational politics show a positive or negative face."[9]

There is much speculation in the literature on organizational behavior about the extent to which organizational politics can provide a motivating force for the firm, its departments, and its professionals. The question is: Is the absence of organizational politics best for any given business unit or corporation, with the knowledge that a total absence of organizational politics is so pure a corporate concept that it is probably an unrealistic goal in a practical situation? A more important issue is the extent to which organizational politics can be a positive force within any organization. French et al. say that "in extremely political organizations so much time, effort, and energy go into internecine warfare that the organization does not get its job done well; . . . and it loses many of its best people either through purges or self-initiated flight." They state further that "in extremely apolitical organizations little productive or innovative work gets done; complacency is widespread, tough decisions do not get made, and the organization loses ground to its external competitors." Thus, the conclusion they reach is that "a modest amount of organizational politics is necessary to produce optimal individual and organizational performance."[10]

When coupled with the concept of power, organizational politics becomes a particularly potent force in influencing and controlling professionals in any organization. Some consider politics to be the operational concept behind those two terms taken together, and this might be so. The use of power, which implicitly includes a concept of strength and an ability to get something done above and beyond the use of individuals as simple communicative mediums or as building blocks to accomplish a goal, becomes an organizational force driving the actions of personnel. Thus, in a few words, power politics is an effective way to peddle influence.

A SECURITIES FIRM POWER MATRIX

Power within a securities firm, as in most other organizations, can be used or unused, and it can be provided by those with either legitimate or formal authority or those with implied or informal authority. Formal leaders are those who have legitimized power such as managers of departments. Professionals who are informal leaders and have implied power are individuals such as big producers. Professionals with legitimate or formal power can exercise it through directives; professionals with implied or informal power can use informal communications channels such as the corporate grapevine or cliques of cohorts to solidify and activate their power. Holders of legitimate power exercise it in a variety of ways such as through the doling out or withholding of remunerative rewards or through the crediting of revenue generation. Informal leaders can also exercise power in a number of ways; big producers, with or without their associated colleagues who believe in "their cause," can exercise influence within an organization either by explicit suggestions to management or by a general overall political power game plan.

In the literature on organizational behavior and development, there are many examples of the kinds of situations that seem to promote or cause organizational politics to develop at a faster pace and in a greater degree than what might normally be the case. To be sure, one of the related studies on the topic is by Culbert and McDonough. They suggest that there are six principal reasons or situations that promote organizational politics. These include: competition at the top; the erratic boss; too much hierarchy; insufficient respect for the individual; too much job security; and fixation with the bottom line.[11] To be sure, not all these situations will ultimately cause the disastrous results from organizational politics of the negative variety. Surely, not all of them exist at once for every department or every firm that has a high degree of organizational politics. What these situations do from a conceptual standpoint, however, is to provide at least an understanding of the kinds of conditions in any organization that might prove to be a fertile field for the development of divisive organizational politics. They lay the groundwork for an understanding of power politics within the securities firm.

POWER POLITICS AT
THE INTRADEPARTMENTAL LEVEL

Power politics in securities firms within departments may have a number of causes. Among them are the following situations that underscore the specialized nature of the firm's activities and the individualized orientation of revenue production of the firm's top professionals.

1. The managers are unfamiliar with the area they supervise.
2. Management tolerates and pays well the nonproducers.
3. Certain professionals are not sure of their own status within the organization or believe that they are under attack by peers or their managers.
4. Departmental decision making is actually incorrect or the perception by departmental members is that it is incorrect.
5. The departmental manager is too autocratic, thus stifling dissent and developing phony loyalties in certain professionals.
6. Professionals who are not that competent are often promoted or given more responsibility by managers.
7. Senior managers within the firm are too easily or not easily enough accessed by lower level staff members.

Power politics can result from all of the above in a securities firm, although it is not limited to these situations. Very often, however, situations like these result in the development of a clique syndrome within the department with the informal leader who, in many cases, is the biggest producer within the group or with another individual who is accorded the role of the informal leader for any number of reasons.

Because the root causes of power politics within a securities firm are really the result of people problems, solving a political difficulty with power implications should focus on the individuals involved and employ the manager as the professional who would interface with all in that situation. Communication is the absolute key to resolving these difficulties, and the manager should immediately have a number of meetings for the department or small business unit, separate meetings for senior people within the department, and meetings with the lower and midlevel professionals. This helps to develop a team atmosphere at each working level within the department, and the group meetings can provide the forum to break down any barriers among the department's different levels of professionals. This should be standard procedure, but the competitive and high-powered nature of the securities industry usually provides little time for these activities, especially if they are considered unnecessary or unneeded. However, when problems of power politics develop within a department, these group sessions are especially important in countering the potentially devastating political environment that could impact the department's production level and its personnel.

POWER POLITICS AT
THE INTERDEPARTMENTAL LEVEL

Conflict between or among departments that gives rise to power politics within the securities firm is often the result of the bureaucratic nature of its corporate form of organization. In the securities firm, conflict usually arises over the desire of department managers to take additional responsibilities and departments under their jurisdiction or extend their authority to matters, issues, and clients presently beyond their control. For instance, power politics could result from the desire of departmental managers to receive as much credit as possible for revenue generation, even when departments and small business units are interdependent. In the capital markets area, for example, there are sometimes conflicts between the trading and underwriting small business units in a department that handles securities of a single type. Similarly, there are often some problems within capital markets departments between the trading desk and the institutional sales area over the stocking of securities to be made available for institutional sales purposes or the extent to which a trading desk should limit that activity in favor of trading its own positions or providing a secondary market primarily for the retail sales effort. Furthermore, when a new hybrid product has been developed, there has been some conflict over which department should handle the underwriting, trading, and sales of it.

From an accounting standpoint, interdepartmental conflicts that result in power politics can have their root causes in the allocation of expenses and the crediting of particular departments for the generation of revenue. There are numerous examples that may be presented showing how conflict is caused by these management decisions, all subject to the competitive processes of organizational compromise, and interdepartmental conflict can result from a number of problems beyond those mentioned here. The point, however, is that they are not only endemic to the securities firm but also are the result of life in human-made organizations and are simply likely to remain so.

Solving interdepartmental conflicts that result in power politics can be somewhat more difficult than working with similar situations within a single department. This is so because problems at the interdepartmental level inevitably involve the manager of each department and, more often than not, require a third party to intervene. The third party, who is often a senior level executive at the firm and usually the one to whom both managers report, is responsible for either reaching a compromise for acceptance by the two managers or making a decision in favor of one of them. When the problem is a result of the need to divide responsibility for new projects or functions between the two managers more effectively, the third party is often in a pivotal position to make the decision because it is probably one that has not been a factor before in the relationship between the two departments. The decision becomes much more difficult and the situation much more contentious when the departments have been vying for control of a function for some time, especially when the result of the decision is likely to affect the future revenue stream of either department. This is when the role of the third party becomes more critical and also much more difficult. Here, the intervening authority assumes the function of revenue allocator, as when two managers are in conflict over which of their departments should be credited for the generation of a particular revenue stream.

Another problem in the solving of interdepartmental conflict that has bred power politics in the securities firm is the fact that there are two managers usually involved having their own constituencies, namely the professionals in their departments. As a result, the managers would like to show their departments that they have actually come out the victor and not lose credibility or the respect of professionals within their departments. It is important, therefore, that whatever decision is reached that the manager of each department as well as the third party senior manager who may be involved as a referee either meet with the professionals in both departments or couch the decision in memo or verbal form, so as to retain the respectability of both managers and the reasonableness of each department's position in the particular situation. Furthermore, it is especially important to limit the amount of political fallout from such a situation, because it is likely that two departments will be involved with each other in other activities if they were involved earlier. The managers must minimize any potential long-term destructive effect on the relationship between the professionals within each department who often have rather strong opinions as to what the causes of the conflict were and what would be the appropriate decision to resolve the situation.

POWER POLITICS IN RETROSPECT

Power politics in any organization, corporate or otherwise, is a difficult thing for most people to handle; few individuals seek out involvement in these types of situations, although many may have input into the conflict, knowingly or unknowingly. Some believe that the nature of securities firms provides a fertile field for the development of power politics, but this question is likely to remain an open one. However, the use of power politics is not always bad, and many top analysts and management experts believe that it is perhaps the only way managers can exert influence within the complex organizations in which they work. Many also believe that a moderate amount of power politics can be a motivating force for the organization. This is especially so for securities firms because of the nature of that corporate form of organization.

It is crucial to understand, however, the causes of conflict in a securities firm, both within departments and between departments, that can give rise to power politics and may not have important positive results. It is equally as important to recognize that the success in solving conflicts, and thus the minimization of power politics to an acceptable level, can be particularly useful in providing the informal influence on individuals necessary to carry out corporatewide and departmentwide goals and objectives. In a securities firm, power politics can be as destructive as it can be helpful and creative. It may turn departments or small business units into armed camps, or it may be the single most important way a manager can develop a cohesive team effort. Power politics can be disastrous or profitable. Whatever the case, it is ultimately up to the management.

NOTES

1. Ernest Bloch, *Inside Investment Banking* (Homewood, Ill.: Dow Jones-Irwin, 1986), p. 272.

2. David C. McClelland and David H. Burnham, "Power Is the Great Motivator," *Harvard Business Review on Human Relations, Vol. 4, Classic Advice on Leadership,* p. 103, comments about the article; see also the entire article in the *Harvard Business Review* (March–April 1976), pp. 100–110.

3. John P. Kotter, "Power, Dependence, and Effective Management," in *Harvard Business Review on Human Relations, Vol. 4, Classic Advice on Leadership,* p. 121, comments about the article; see also the entire article in the *Harvard Business Review* (July–August 1977), pp. 125–136.

4. Gerald R. Salancik and Jeffrey Pfeffer, "Who Gets Power—and How They Hold on to It: A Strategic-Contingency Model of Power," *Organizational Dynamics,* 5 (1977), p. 3.

5. Jeffrey Pfeffer, *Power in Organizations* (Marshfield, Mass.: Pitman Publishing, 1981), p. 2.

6. Wendell L. French, Cecil H. Bell, Jr., and Robert A. Zawacki, *Organization Development: Theory, Practice, and Research* (Texas: Business Publications, Inc., 1983), p. 372; see also David C. McClelland, "The Two Faces of Power," *Journal of International Affairs,* 24, no. 1 (1970), pp. 29–47.

7. Harold Lasswell, *Politics: Who Gets What, When, How* (New York: McGraw Hill, 1936).

8. Pfeffer, p. 7.

9. French et al., p. 373.

10. Ibid., p. 374.

11. Samuel A. Culbert and John J. McDonough, *Radical Management: Power Politics and the Pursuit of Trust* (New York: The Free Press, 1985), pp. 54–69.

CHAPTER 14

THE "BIG PRODUCER": WHO'S REALLY THE BOSS?

THE BIG PRODUCER IN NAME ONLY

A treatise on the securities industry would not be complete without a section on the so-called "big producers" of the securities firms. These professionals, who generate revenues of sometimes awesome dimensions, are at once heralded by management for their contributions to their firm's bottom line and also feared by superiors and others for the potential clout they wield in the firm. They are the professionals who often keep departments and branch offices afloat during bad times as well as being the largest revenue producers in their respective business units most of the time. The nature of the securities industry and the firms themselves provide the big producer with a intangible cloak of political armor within the firm that, at any given time, may be used with all the potential possibilities that it could normally entail.

The term "big producer" assumes different dimensions from firm to firm, from department to department, from branch office to branch office, or from departmental unit to departmental unit. The big producer normally generates a large amount of revenues, usually far exceeding those produced by other professionals who hold similar jobs or responsibilities within any business unit. A big producer who is part of a revenue-producing team is generally considered to be responsible for the largest percentage of the revenues generated or the professional without whose help most of the revenues would not be generated. The big producer then, can be a "big fish in a little pond" or a "big fish in a big pond" and can exist almost anywhere at any firm. A big producer can be an account executive in a branch office, a trader on a municipal bond trading desk, a government bond salesperson in a government bond department, the manager of an over-the-counter stock area, a head of a public power group in a public finance department, a head of a utility section in a corporate finance department, or an equity trader on the firm's main stock trading desk. The big producer can be at a large wire house, a midsize investment banking firm, a small regional firm or a large one, a large full-service firm, a very small financial advisory firm, or a small retail or institutional securities house. A big producer can be at any of these institutions or can be in virtually any department in a securities firm. Thus, the concept of a big producer, and the application of it to any securities firm, is first and last a relative one.

The securities firm's biggest producers are the industry's most sought after employees and the ones securities firms, not surprisingly, can least afford to lose. Their loss does not reflect well on management in many instances, and in others, big producers often have the capability of taking other employees to their new place of employment. The potential ability of big producers to pick up and leave their firm for any number of reasons does not have to be explicitly stated by them during periods of problems or conflict; it is implied and is always there as an informal but formidable threat that can be operationalized quickly in the securities industry. This is a significant basis of informal power that the big producer wields within securities firms. Some big producers do, in fact, have the formal management authority to go with this implied or informal clout; but that does not necessarily have to be the case, and in most instances, it is not. This is so because big producers are usually in on-line revenue-generating positions and are allocated only a moderate degree of overall managerial authority and responsibility, lest too much of their time be spent on management duties and not enough on the generation of revenues for the firm.

Big producers are recognizable in the securities firm, largely because word of mouth spreads the tales of who is and is not in that category. More than most other securities firm professionals, big producers usually have a paved road of access to many other professionals in the firm whether they are peers or subordinates, direct superiors of the big producer's immediate manager, or others of management rank often right up to the firm's number one executive. Nobody at a securities firm would like to incur the wrath of big producers, especially the big producers' immediate bosses, and nobody at a firm would like to be the professionals whom the big producers point their fingers at as the reason for their discontent with or departure from the firm. Similarly, managers and others in and around big producers want to encourage them in their efforts, support them in any way possible, and provide them with the motivating forces necessary to keep them operating at a high level of productivity. Thus, the access of big producers to other professionals in the firm, especially those in the top of the management hierarchy, is not only an open one but also is welcome and often with a degree of enthusiasm, which puts the big producers' immediate superiors in somewhat awkward, if not defensive, positions.

Although difficult to quantify, most securities firm managers agree that if there are rules to be bent or changed or if there are new rules to be made to accommodate a professional's particular situation, they are usually bent, changed, or made for the big producer more than any professional at the firm. It is a rationalized management approach to what some consider to be a complex business, and often it just leads to better production for the big producer and the small business unit. The point here, however, is that for every organizational unit in virtually every firm, there is usually a professional who can be singled out as its biggest producer. Most senior managers in relative proximity to this individual know who the firm's big producers are, and if not, the big producers can make themselves known to the managers without much difficulty.

THE VULNERABILITY OF MANAGEMENT

The Account Executive as the Big Producer

When most securities industry analysts and observers think of a big producer, a firm's high-level producing account executives in the retail branch system usually come to mind. In some firms, they are designated as on the president's or chair's council, which represents a group of top-producing account executives in the firm based on some quantitative measure of performance over the previous year or so. Big producers may also include many other account executives in different branches located throughout a firm's retail branch system, who are not necessarily within the firm's designated uppermost rank of highest producing account executives. While the biggest producers in the firm's retail system often have access to the CEO and others in the firm's top management group, most other big producers in the branch system are relatively well known to the branch management executives, especially the regional managers and the managers in the upper levels of the national branch system. If they are not immediately known, an on-line account executive information system can make knowledge of their status immediately possible.

One of the more interesting traits of some branch office managers is their ability to harbor a feeling of vulnerability within the firm's organizational structure and at the same time to appear to have a position of unusual formal authority within the firm's management structure. The feeling of vulnerability can come through their perception of relative worth, as viewed from the perspective of senior management, when compared to that of big producers in their branch office. The managers' apparent stronghold of supervision and responsibility comes through their formal authority as heads of the branch offices in which the big producers may work. Nonetheless, the important aspect of this analysis is the feeling of vulnerability on the part of branch managers inherent in their status as a result of the strength, within the organizational structure, of their largest producers, whether formal or informal, or whether explicit or implied.

As noted earlier, big producers in a firm's branch system are accorded such respect and status that they very often have a direct line to the president and chair of the firm as well as to other managers of significant stature within the organization. As supervising managers, the branch managers thus, in general, often feel ill at ease when placed in that situation, and in many cases, are loath to do anything to irritate the big producers in their branches. Indeed, branch managers are often at a loss to do anything that would result in their authority being challenged or directives being circumvented by big producers under their supervision as a result of access to higher levels of authority within the firm or even by the pressure that can be exerted on the branch managers by a big producer in a simple informal conversation. All this is the result of the unique characteristics of securities firms in which account executives have or appear to have their own franchise as independent operators of their own businesses.

The Big Producer in Capital Markets and Investment Banking

The concepts involved in managing professionals who are big producers in the capital markets area are not unlike those in the retail branch system; but very often a big producer's success is a result of a team effort here, and in most instances, there is no direct quantitative remuneration structure with which to reward big producers. For instance, as head of a trading area, a big producer might not only successfully trade a position but also could be acknowledged as a big producer because of the success of all the traders under the producer's supervision. In a corporate or public finance department, a big producer may be the key individual in bringing in a client or maintaining that relationship, yet more often than not, there are a number of investment bankers involved in the process, and it is unlikely that the big producer could generate the same amount of revenue without the help of others. Also, in this investment banking new business effort, it is usually the case that the bankers use information from the trading area or traders and underwriters themselves in presentations or even use their successes as examples to potential clients of the kind of system the investment banker's firm brings to the party.

   Although this team effort makes difficult the quantification of the extent to which a big producer in the capital markets and investment banking areas is actually successful, it does help the big producer develop an informal power base with peers and subordinates that could ultimately be even more effective in making their manager feel vulnerable than if the big producer was a single salesperson, such as in the retail or institutional sales areas. In instances such as these, and when direct access to others higher up in the firm's management hierarchy is sought by the big producers and their associates, this group effort can sometimes be very effective.

The other problem facing managers supervising big producers in the capital markets and investment banking areas is the vulnerability they feel as big producers get better, and the managers must rightly tout the accomplishments and the successes of those particular individuals. Thus, professionals who manage big producers in these areas (as well as perhaps other areas throughout the firm) often wonder if their managers will ask them, "Well, if this producer is so good, knows so much, has all these great ideas, and even has good management qualities, what do we need you for?"

The feeling that managers have in these situations is not unique to the securities industry and surely has its place in most organizations. In securities firms, however, where big producers are bringing in a large amount of revenues, and the managers are relegated to professional managerial roles, the managers, whether realistically or not, tend to feel vulnerable with big producers under their supervision. The extent to which any manager is uncomfortable in these situations depends on the psychological and emotional makeup of each. Some managers feel more vulnerable than others, and most feel more vulnerable than is necessary, although there are probably some who feel less vulnerable than they should.

CIRCUMVENTING THE CORPORATE HIERARCHY

Although one of the key securities firm organizational problems results from the big producers' apparent access to upper management, this can at times have positive aspects. Access to upper management by any employee can be a useful and productive tool for the employee and management alike. Carried to extremes and in contentious situations, however, it can lead to organizational chaos.

In most other types of corporations, top individuals in departments do not have the kind of easy access to upper management that seems to be prevalent in securities firms. Most other corporate managers are simply not that responsive to it, and there is more of an ingrained management hierarchy than seems to have developed in securities firms. There are probably other corporations in specific industries that do allow professionals, who are seen as very important to the company, access to senior managers on an informal basis that circumvents their immediate superiors. In most companies, however, hierarchical relationships seem to be more strictly observed than they are in the securities industry, and perhaps for good reason on both sides of the aisle; but it does create some interesting situations at times for the inner workings of securities firms. Nevertheless, the potential of access to senior management by big producers establishes a mind set in the way of life in securities firms and thus guides the behavior of the big producers' immediate superiors. This situation is not likely to change drastically because of the nature of the firms. As a result, the answer to this problem becomes more one rooted in organizational development as a behavior modification tool for personnel rather than some managerial dictums of "what to do."

Minimizing Problems in the Branches

First and foremost, the big producers in branch offices must have strong loyalties to branch managers, and the branch managers must have helped develop this and instilled it in the office's account executives. In addition, branch office managers must have the support and confidence of their regional managers and others in the upper management orbit as seen through memos and actions taken on behalf of them at the securities firm. Without these types of strong signals to branch managers and their big producers and without the managers and big producers in the branches operating as teams with total confidence in each other, the possibility for difficulties from a management standpoint remains an open one. In cases where big producers who are retail account executives are having difficulties with professionals in the capital markets area of a firm, it is best that the branch manager and the manager of that particular capital markets department remain in close contact with each other and begin ironing out the misunderstanding at that management level rather than starting the process at some other level that could result in circumventing other managers.

Minimizing Problems in Capital Markets and Investment Banking

One key to developing top-producing professionals in the capital markets areas who must work with others in interdependent business units is to create a mind set that does not view individuals as their own profit centers. Also important is a prohibition, however loose, against allowing professionals to go above their immediate superiors until they have worked with them on the difficulty at hand. These concepts may seem simple enough, but they are rarely ever enunciated as management dictums in a capital markets or investment banking area; rather they are implied, and that alone is often not sufficient to do an effective job of melding a group of professionals together, some of whom are markedly bigger producers than others. Without these management edicts, the potential for tremendous problems arising in departments is a real one. While they seem easily isolated and relatively simply solved, what usually occurs is that these difficulties simmer in one form or another. Management's concern should be to make sure the flame on the stove is so very low that the simmering is either not apparent or inconsequential. The ideas behind this thesis are that these entrepreneurial difficulties do exist, and management's job is to minimize them, thus limiting their impact on the ongoing operations of any area within a securities firm.

THE BIG PRODUCER AND THE FIRM

The securities industry will always have big producers as will most other corporations. Presumably, the more big producers a securities firm has, the better off it is. Yet, managers should not live in fear of what top people might or could do. This is indeed one of the intransigent difficulties facing management in the securities industry today, whether or not some realize it or it is verbalized in industry management circles. Most analysts agree that it is simply a fact of life, and that it does have the potential of upsetting departments and divisions within the firms. Nevertheless, by management emphasizing that no professional at the firm is bigger than the firm itself or even its managers, much will have been done to maintain the positive attributes of organizational life that make it an optimum situation for the firm's big producers to achieve to the greatest extent that they can.

CHAPTER 15

HIRING THE RIGHT PEOPLE

In the narrowest sense, there is only one mistake a securities firm or its managers can make and that is to hire the wrong people. Almost everything that occurs in the securities firm, whether positive or negative, whether wildly profitable or financially disastrous, is usually the result of on-line decisions made by its professionals, especially when all securities market-related factors are controlled. To be sure, no organization, public or private, can be helped by hiring the wrong people. Let there be no mistake, however, more than any other industry in the world, hiring the wrong professionals in the securities industry cannot only be problematic, it can also be catastrophic, both in the immediacy of results and in long-term divisive effects on the organization. To some extent, this dictum may sound trite, but firms on Wall Street have not been immune to hiring the wrong professionals regardless of how profitable the securities firms have been.

Hiring the wrong professionals results in the making of incorrect decisions that, when compared to other industries, can have a greater and more immediate impact, especially in situations like securities trading or investment banking. It can also cause the misuse of personnel resulting in lost opportunities and client alienation, largely a result of the fact that most mid- to high-level professionals within the firms are virtually autonomous actors within the corporate body politic. In some other industries, most professionals who are limited in the autonomy with which they can make decisions and also the kinds of activities in which they are involved usually do not have the potential of immediately causing disruption. Hiring the wrong people in most companies can result in losses from unnecessary fixed costs such as salaries and fringe benefits as well as secretarial help, office space, health benefits, and to some extent, lost opportunities, money, time, and clients. A wrong decision can be made, but it is usually one that is overseen by other individuals and may not necessarily have the kind of immediate or long-term potential for disruption or financial disaster as do the bulk of the decisions often made unilaterally by professionals in securities firms on a daily basis.

INCREMENTAL MIS-DECISION MAKING

From a purely definitional standpoint, incremental mis-decision making is the result of decisions or directions from a manager or other professional staff member that when carried out result in a series of actions each consecutively falling wide of the desired outcome. These can be costly, especially in a securities firm, and can result in the poor use of the firm's resources, its capital, and its personnel. Not every decision made by those who have been successful in a particular securities firm area will be the right one, but they usually will result in the minimum of incremental mis-decision making. The effort here is to keep their particular decisions as close to the correct one as possible so that, over the long haul, there are a minimum of decisions that result in costs to the firm in one form or another. If this discussion were placed in graphic form, a professional's decisions, as signified by dots on the graph, would be made so that they would fall as close to the critical path of the manager's goals as designated by a straight line on that graph. The closer the dots fall to that line, the fewer problems in decision making are likely to occur.

There are a number of notable situations in the securities firm that could result in incremental mis-decision making of a most costly sort. Incremental mis-decision making can be particularly so in areas such as investment banking. Here it could assume rather problematic dimensions. For instance, a senior investment banker could decide to pursue a particular client or issuer who, it is expected, will issue securities in significant size. The banker then spends substantial time during the year pursuing this business and employing the department's and the firm's resources. As time goes on, a number of other professionals become part of the banking team seeking this business, almost on a full-time basis. Later, the computer support area becomes involved in the effort, and the new products unit devotes substantial time in creating financial vehicles for use by the potential client. During this phase, the firm's top management gets involved, making the appropriate appearances and assuring that the firm's resources are allocated to this important project when there are questions about other competing priorities.

Throughout this entire process, each additional decision results in another one being made to further the effort, and over time, tremendous departmental and firm resources are siphoned out to support the project. In the final analysis, however, it is found that the financing was originally not feasible or another investment banking firm is selected or the project is scaled down to a small proportion of its originally intended size.

Later, at an investment banking department meeting, it is discovered that the top bankers in the department could have detected that the financing was unlikely to be accomplished for any of the reasons cited. Thus, the entire process could have been avoided if the senior banker who initially became involved was knowledgeable about new business efforts and the particulars of this financing. Each successive decision made to back the project further was an incrementally wrong one, costing the department and the firm enormously in any number of ways. The hypothetical new business effort described here is exemplary of incremental mis-decision making of the most fundamental sort.

Another example might be when a senior professional in a public finance department requests a competitive underwriter to buy a particular issue at a level that may incur a loss because the manager believes that buying the issue would be helpful in the department's efforts to secure negotiated public finance business from that issuer. The underwriter then purchases the issue and does in fact incur a loss, but the public finance investment banker is later unable to secure negotiated business from the issuer for any number of reasons, all of which could have been taken care of before the underwriter purchased the competitive issue.

Another possibility is when the head of an area in a corporate finance department tells staff members to suggest a particular financing mechanism to a corporate client because the client has probably not heard of it and is likely to be receptive to this idea. After the corporate finance staff develops a proposal and presents the concept to the senior executives of the corporation, it is found that the real decision maker for selection of the underwriters has already heard of the financing technique and does not think it is appropriate for the company's financial situation.

Yet another problematic situation is where an institutional sales manager suggests a particular strategy as a method to develop accounts where there was presently no real relationship. After much time and effort is expended on developing the concept, the idea does not work because the sales manager did not realize the firm does not have the type of product appropriate for this strategy or the kinds of institutions as clients who would like that particular type of product. Incremental misdecision making is certainly not restricted to the management levels. Very often, the autonomy granted to many professionals in a securities firm results in their making incremental misdecisions that are not likely to happen at most other corporations to the extent to which they do in securities firms. Trading losses are a major example.

MANAGEMENT DECISION-MAKING PROBLEMS

From a management standpoint, a number of other problems can immediately occur at securities firms if managers are not sufficiently knowledgeable about specific areas under their jurisdiction. These situations are, by their nature, a result of hiring the wrong professional for a particular management job, but they are also more conceptual than the types of problems occurring on a daily basis. That is not to say they are ultimately less costly or less problematic; rather they can be equally so, and perhaps even more disastrous from an organizational standpoint. Nonetheless, they are very important, and it is critical that they be understood as such.

Senior managers who are not knowledgeable about areas under their supervision might develop a hands-off policy towards the business units. In such situations, managers of the small business units, all under the senior manager's jurisdiction, assume a larger management role and more autonomy in their own activities. The manager thus winds up as more of a departmental caretaker than a manager or leader. In most cases, strategy is difficult to develop for the department, and as a result, the department usually ends up marking time. As a corollary to this situation, the locus of decision making moves much lower in the management hierarchy. There develops more of a profit center orientation for the small business units and, to some extent, of individuals within those business units who see their own goals as more important than those of the department, division, or even firm. In these instances, it is difficult for managers to "wrap their arms" around the department and imbue it with a broader organizational directive, because many question the manager's authority, ability, and knowledge to do so. Moreover, this type of situation basically stymies motivation and limits enthusiasm and support for the "all for one" team concept.

Most important is that managers who are not viewed by their subordinates and others as generally knowledgeable will have extreme difficulty in hiring the very best professionals to work for the firm in their departments. This represents, perhaps, the major impediment a firm must face in developing a first-rate department of any type. In the securities firm, the potential employee views the manager as the key to the department's success, in terms of developing strategy, attracting other top professionals to the firm, and garnering the attention, approval, and resources provided by top management. If potential employees believe that the department head is not an expert, then they are likely to feel that upper management will also view the manager similarly, will not have an interest in the department's development, and thus upper management will not allocate firm resources to the area, whether in capital, human, or remunerative form.

This is not only important in the competitive product development areas, such as corporate and public finance, but is also critical in the branch office system. Account executives seeking employment at other firms look to the firm's capital, its products, and its personnel for support and stability. More than that, they look to the branch manager for whom they will be working as the kind of individual who is knowledgeable enough to understand the intricacies of the business and thus support them to the best extent possible; who is able to hire other top account executives so that clients and potential ones within the general geographic domain of the branch will see the branch and its professionals in the best possible light; who will be fair to them; and who will represent their interest in the most professional way to senior management, both in the region and at headquarters.

In short, if a firm has hired the wrong professionals as managers, those who are not experts in their fields, and who are not recognized as such, it is an indication to a potential employee that senior management may not care about that particular department or area within the firm. Needless to say, under these conditions, disruption and upheaval are likely to loom large.

HIRE ONLY THE BEST FOR THE JOB

From a management standpoint, perhaps the most important thing a securities firm can do is hire the best people at any level of the securities firm hierarchy. Hiring the wrong ones obviously results in problems for corporations of all types; but for securities firms, the impact can be immediate and far-reaching because these individuals usually have the authority, either explicitly or implicitly, to make decisions that could result in tremendous losses or costs to the firm. Making decisions over a certain period of time, each of which is somewhat incrementally wrong when compared against the correct one from an organizational standpoint, can lead to confusion, annoyance, lost opportunities, the inability to keep good people or hire others, and perhaps most importantly, the promotion of professionals who are themselves not competent. Circumventing these problems is especially important in companies such as securities firms, where client contact and cooperative efforts are the keys to the successful implementation of business plans, the servicing of clients, and the garnering of new customers.

CHAPTER 16

SELECTING SECURITIES FIRM MANAGERS

Everybody in every kind of business has the desire to, or should want to, select the very best managers up and down the corporate hierarchy. Firms want to isolate those individuals who are the most knowledgeable, have the widest experience, have the best track records, and whose personal goals and objectives fit those of the corporation. Yet, choosing managers who will ultimately be successful is a task that is much easier said than done and is one of the biggest dilemmas facing top management in securities firms, but it is rarely recognized as such a major problem. To be sure, there are two widely divergent schools of thought about how to select securities firm managers, both of which are the result of the specialized nature of the business and the individual entrepreneurial environment the securities firm fosters.

Basically, the first school of thought argues that only those professionals who have been exceedingly successful at a particular job are the ones who can best manage those who do it. The second philosophy suggests that the autonomous nature of many departments and the individualized aspect of the professional's activities should make securities firm management, on a large scale, one of the hands-off or laissez faire variety. Consequently, those who are best adept at managing small to midsized business units in a securities firm do not necessarily have to be those professionals who have been exceptionally capable as individual producers but rather may be those who are professional managers and whose job would therefore involve more general overseeing and less on-line responsibility.

SHOULD THOSE WHO HAVE DONE IT ALSO MANAGE IT?

There are many vociferous proponents of the argument that only those who have been especially successful at a particular job can effectively manage an operation of that type. The argument is particularly applicable to management jobs in the securities industry, because most of the tasks are specialized in nature and require the manager to understand thoroughly both the job and a professional's developmental process so as to be effectively capable of not only guiding that individual but also of managing a group of individuals whose jobs are slated to achieve a de-partmentwide or corporatewide mission. This line of reasoning is particularly potent when applied to management jobs that are located at the small business unit or departmental level of secur-ities firms. Managers of such areas include those who handle public and corporate finance departments, any specific trading, underwriting, or sales department, and even the firm's branch-es. The argument may also be applicable to managers who supervise product departments such as those originating, de-veloping, and marketing the firm's products. Furthermore, many of the support areas of a securities firm require such an in-depth technical knowledge of defined tasks that some believe they would be difficult to manage by those relatively unfamiliar with the jobs to be carried out.

A few examples should suffice. For instance, key to the development of an investment banking area, either corporate or public finance, is the creation of a strategic program for the department's personnel and its potential target clients. This may sound simple, but it is one of the most difficult tasks facing investment bankers today, particularly a banking department's manager. It requires the manager to understand totally the investment banking environment and the myriad ways to get clients successfully through the securities firm's door. All of this is based on thorough understanding of and long experience in developing accounts in the investment banking field and formulating and working on strategic departmental plans, which, of necessity, require adjustments over time based on market conditions and the relative success in achieving the plan's goals. The job of the manager of an investment banking department is clearly not one for a novice or one who is relatively unfamiliar with the field.

Branch management is also more of an art than it is a science, and it is naive to think that a group of branch office account executives will go along developing accounts and increasing the branch's market share to the greatest extent possible without adequate management by a professional who has had significant experience in the field. There are innumerable administrative and compliance difficulties that may crop up, as well as problems with client relationships in which the branch manager may have to become involved, most of which are extremely delicate in nature. In a macrosense and for the development of the branch as a whole, it is the branch manager who is responsible and is the professional to whom others look for the branch's orderly development and profitability. Branch management is a 24-hour job, and the manager must sometimes be all things to all people, from psychologist to investment advisor to administrative expert to lightning rod for the hiring of other account executives. Ultimately, one argument goes, the branch is only as good as the branch manager, and the only branch manager who can be exceptional is one who has a thorough understanding and knowledge of the job.

Managing a securities trading department obviously also requires great expertise. Indeed, one cannot successfully be a head trader without an acknowledged ability to do so; but there are a great many ways responsibility is allocated in different trading areas at many securities firms. The head trader can be an on-line professional who not only trades a position but also supervises an entire desk. The head trader can also be one whose role is simply supervisory in nature and who coordinates the risk position for the home office desk as well as for those traders who trade the same securities at the firm's offices around the country. Another situation might be where the head trader has on-line responsibility but reports to a manager who may get intimately involved with trading decisions, on the one hand, or may assume the role of a hands-off supervisor, on the other. There can be other numerous permutations of the degree to which the managers can allocate the responsibilities for risk within their department. Somewhere along the line, so one argument runs, a manager who is in close contact with the trading effort or a head trader with on-line risk responsibility must be an acknowledged expert in that area or the securities firm is leaving itself open to potential financial vulnerability. There may be other examples too numerous to detail here that support the statement that only those professionals who are experts in particular areas can and should be permitted to manage them. These illustrative examples should suffice, however.

SHOULD MANAGERS ONLY ADMINISTRATE?

The second school of thought on selection of securities firm managers argues that those professionals in a position of responsibility at a securities firm do not necessarily have to be experts in the area they supervise. This argument also suggests that the firm's biggest producers may not possess the necessary managerial skills to assume positions of supervisory responsibility in the organization, and it may not necessarily be in the best interests of a securities firm to have those individuals do so. The securities firm may even function best with managers who have a hands-off philosophy and allow the firm's specialists and entrepreneurs to develop their businesses with a minimum of interference and with great autonomy so that they can fully actualize their optimum potential success. Seen from this perspective, management is clearly an adjunct to those professionals who actually bring hard dollars down to the bottom line; management's major role is to be supportive, helpful, and involved when important decisions are made, during conflict and crisis, and when and if called on. Under this scenario, management is also expected to set goals and objectives for the firm's professionals, its departments, and divisions but is not supposed to ride herd on the professionals who are mandated to carry out the mission.

Moreover, this school of thought suggests that management in and of itself is a professional occupation, and development is best accomplished by having managers rotate from one related area of the firm to another in order to gain both experience in the management of a securities organization as well as knowledge about the various areas within the firm. The development of managers is more a process than it is based on an individual's expertise and knowledge of any given number of specialized functions or services the firm provides. Management then, as seen by this second school of thought, is separate and distinct from the ability of an individual or group to generate revenue, and it is best suited to those who are professionals at it and are schooled as such.

Underlying these ideas is the concept, ironically, that most functions within a securities firm are of such a specialized nature that they can, and indeed should, be accomplished by those individuals who are on-line, with a minimum or just a moderate amount of guidance from the firm's managerial staff. For instance, the heads of the corporate and public finance departments should only be involved in the broadest strategic decisions, and the managers of the units within these investment banking areas should actually be the professionals who have hands-on responsibility for the development of their groups organized around specific industries or companies, types of governments, or kinds of financings. Put differently, the locus of decision making should be adjusted to a lower level and be given to professionals who are involved in the day-to-day operations of client and personnel development and relations. Similarly, on the branch level, minimum interference by the branch manager is perceived to be best for creating an atmosphere that results in the individual development and creativity needed by the kind of professionals who ultimately become successful as account executives. Likewise, this line of reasoning suggests that traders and underwriters who are involved in moment-to-moment market-making decisions should have the autonomy and responsibility for their decisions; any major interference by managers who are once removed from the pulse of the market could have problematic consequences not only on the moral level but also on the bottom line. The list of examples supporting this school of thought could go on, but it is probably not necessary, for argument's sake, to describe any more here.

AN ANALYTICAL FRAMEWORK
FOR MANAGEMENT EXPERTISE

What must be developed is an analytical framework that shows the expertise needed by securities managers in the areas they supervise to direct, control, assess, and develop the departments and their personnel adequately. This should not be taken as a dogmatic dictum of precisely which managers should have a certain degree of expertise under their belts. Strict observance of those rules would be foolhardy, especially given the fluidity of job descriptions at the management levels in securities firms as well as the seemingly endless combinations of shared responsibilities that could work well in a number of situations but not necessarily in all of the firm's specialized departments. Nevertheless, setting forth a broad framework is useful because it focuses the managerial mind on the particular jobs within the firm that demand an inordinately specialized capability.

At the divisional or group head level of a securities firm, it is not necessary, and indeed may not be possible, for senior managers to have an in-depth knowledge of all the areas they supervise. Most managers at this level have risen in the securities firms ranks because of an expertise in a particular specialized area such as government or corporate bond trading and sales, and as they progressed, they assumed other departments under their jurisdiction about which they may have had a limited knowledge but which seemed organizationally appropriate to be placed under their supervision. In some of these cases, managers at lower levels may have had sufficient expertise to handle their own departments with only a moderate amount of supervision. Over time, however, division or group heads may develop sufficient understanding of all the areas they supervise, while lower level managers whom they oversee and who have on-line responsibility have the additional capability and expertise that is required.

Managers at the department level, however, must be experts at what they do and what they supervise. As defined here, these departments include such areas as municipals, governments, corporates, stocks, corporate finance, public finance, and equity research. Even at the departmental subset or small business unit level, which in some firms are departments in and of themselves, managers must have developed an acknowledged expertise in those areas. Such small business units may include municipal trading, government institutional sales, mergers and acquisitions, over-the-counter stock sales, or the branch offices, and all such similar level managerships throughout the firm. Still, many firms have not developed analytical frameworks for their major operating divisions and departments.

In the final analysis, the best securities firm managers are those who have been experts at what they supervise and have a hands-on approach to the areas under their supervision, provided that they are not located so high up in the management hierarchy at the firm to make that expertise difficult to develop in a short period of time.

CHAPTER 17

THE HOWS AND WHYS OF DISMISSAL: A CONCEPTUAL VIEW

Terminating someone's employment is perhaps the second most difficult thing to do. The first, for most people, may be getting dismissed themselves. While people really do not need any lessons in how to get dismissed successfully or how to dismiss someone creatively, the concepts involved and the issues raised concerning what should and should not be done from a management standpoint in these situations, and why and how it should be accomplished, are critically important to corporate life and are especially so in the securities industry. Having established the critical need for individual competence at all professional levels in securities firms—in on-line positions, in staff jobs, and in managment posts—it follows that the converse, namely the unimportance of individuals who are not competent, who should not be in particular jobs, and who must not be, results in the unequivocal statement that appropriate managerial action must be taken. Yet, it does not always happen like that.

People who are occupying a position at a firm and who should not be cost the firm money. From the standpoint of fixed costs, the employees receive salaries and perhaps bonuses, health benefits, secretarial help, office space, and supplies and equipment. They also cost the firm in important other ways. They occupy a space that others might otherwise more effectively use, take up the time of other employees, use resources of the firm, often become problematically involved with clients, and cost the firm lost opportunities. In a securities organization, as noted earlier, hiring the wrong professionals leads to incremental mis-decisions that can present major difficulties and revenue losses in a very short period of time. Miscalculated trading decisions, the indelicate handling of institutional and retail customers, and the misallocation of resources for developing corporate and public finance clients are among the many problems created by individuals who should not be in the positions they hold. It is therefore incumbent on managers to evaluate these situations and arrive at conclusions about their personnel, and if necessary, to act expeditiously, especially in securities firms, because losses incurred in trading securities and problems in client relations can be costly, occur very quickly, and be difficult to rectify.

Perhaps even more importantly, having professionals making mistakes on an ongoing basis is counterproductive to the kind of enthusiasm and momentum that must be generated within each department or business unit for it to reach its goals and even surpass them. For other personnel who must work with these individuals, it is a demoralizing experience, and in the atmosphere of a securities firm, it is noticeable and spreads quickly. Thus, the role of management assumes new significance, and managers who do not act quickly when all the appropriate results are in are hurting the department and firm on a daily basis, perhaps far more in a week or a month, when measured quantitatively, than the cost to the firm of the manager's entire total compensation package for the year.

WHY IT IS HARD TO DO

Despite the immediacy of problematic personnel situations, managers in the securities firms, like those of most other corporations, have nonetheless not always acted quickly once all available data are in. This, once again, is a result of the somewhat peculiar circumstances in which securities firm managers find themselves. Some attribute this situation to the fact that of the securities firm senior managers who can almost unilaterally make those decisions, many are not on-line producers on a full-time basis or have developed an expertise in all the areas they supervise. This is certainly not true in situations where the managers have been chosen because they are acknowledged experts in particular areas, such as those who become branch managers as a result of their meteoric rise as account executives or those who become heads of taxable fixed-income divisions because they have been especially successful in the trading of government and corporate bonds.

There are, however, three general reasons that may lie behind the fact that, in some situations, management has prolonged action on dismissing the individuals who, over relatively long periods, have either not produced up to expectations or have caused problems that, though not necessarily disastrous, are sufficient enough to impede organizational progress. Stated briefly, the reasons may be: (1) a manager's fear of retaliation by others who are exogenous to the problem situation; (2) a manager's fear of losing departmental personnel because of the informal relationships developed with the individual who is having production problems; or (3) the manager's fear that the "Street" will not want to join the firm, the division, or the department if it is perceived that upheaval has occurred and the situation is deemed an unstable one. These reasons are worth examining briefly.

In the first instance, the fear of retaliation by managers or other personnel outside the situation is an especially important deterrent for managers to take personnel action in a securities firm. All around the manager there may be other professionals of sufficient informal or formal authority who can become involved in the personnel process and can either prevent or deter any action that may need to be taken. Not to be Machiavellian, this potential exists perhaps everywhere and in every organization. It may be pronounced in securities firms because of the many reasons others can use for retaining a professional. Because many professionals can be deemed to be relatively productive, and because the goals and objectives for most personnel are flexible, individually oriented, and can change in a short period of time, a case can be made for or against many employees in any given situation. Another reason is that strong relationships can develop between problem professionals and others who are either on the same managerial level as they are or on a higher one.

Some brief examples might suffice. A trader, who a trading

department manager believes is underproducing, can seek refuge with the division manager and can also develop supportive informal relationships with other traders who may perceive that they may someday be in a similar position if their production level is not what it should be because of market conditions and other situations out of their control. An account executive, whom a branch manager believes is not working to capacity, may have developed a relationship with a regional manager or another rather senior manager of the firm so that increased pressure on the account executive for productivity as an incentive may not have the effect that it should. In situations where the branch manager believes that the account executive should not be working at the firm, the possibility is left open for others to intercede on the account executive's behalf, especially if, for instance, it can be argued that the account executive is about to open some major accounts or services important ones.

In the investment banking area, a banking department head may have reason to ask an investment banker to leave the firm for contributing to the loss of one or two clients. Members of the firm's executive committee, however, might view the banker's presently existing relationships with other clients as critical to the firm's overall investment banking program and also may perceive that the banker's potential to develop a business with certain clients may be important to the department's long-run success, all of which would weigh heavily in the banker's favor. In other cases, the peers of the investment banker can suggest to the head of the banking department that the professional in question has been crucial to the success of their efforts with a number of clients and perhaps is on the verge of acquiring new business.

Involved in all these situations, to a greater or lesser degree, are questions of the relative worth of a particular employee based on contributions that are seen as being as qualitative in nature as they are quantitative, and also the support that individual has or can garner from others in the organization who have the potential to intercede on the employee's behalf. In most cases, managers do not take immediate action without consulting a number of others. This process, then, becomes a developmental one wherein other professionals can contribute along the way, thus extending the time required to make a final decision. In some places, the blade of the guillotine drops swiftly, long before anybody has been consulted or has even known that the blade was on its way down. In most situations, however, this is hardly the case, and in many, talks have already been held by the manager with the employee. Once alerted, any employee having any political sense at all can get a hearing with those whom the individual has associated with successfully over time. Yet, the important point here is that the points of access that can be developed and operationalized by a professional in a "what-if" situation can be many and effective and, in some cases, can lead the manager to wonder if the assessment about the employee is an accurate one or whether it is worth the loss of political mileage to turn the individual out of the firm if others can question the logic of that decision.

In some cases, the loss of personnel can be fast in the securities industry, perhaps quicker than any other industry in the world. Two-week notices of resignation hardly exist in securities firms, especially at the relatively high levels of employment. In the wake of an afternoon resignation from one securities firm, professionals have been known to be at the desks of other firms working with the same clients the following morning. If professionals have developed any personal associations of any depth with fellow employees at their old firm, and if those individuals are equally as employable, it is not beyond the realm of possibility that the professional will seek to take them to the new firm. Conversely, it is not unlikely that professionals will seek employment at firms where their colleagues have gone. The specter of this possibility, which is organizational upheaval, could ultimately redound to the disadvantage of managers whose departments or divisions are in such a state, perhaps as a result of their action taken to remove a particular employee. Not surprisingly, most managers at securities firms are loath to have this scenario land in their laps, and this results in managers prolonging action that might otherwise be taken.

Somewhat related to this situation is the possibility that other professionals will not join a firm or a department that they perceive to be in a state of disarray, thus supplying another deterrent for managers to take corrective personnel action. This has been a traditional fear of Wall Street management; in some instances, it is a real one, but in many others, it is simply perceived. It probably takes a real departmental, divisional, or firm personnel upheaval to deter professionals from joining a securities firm in the wake of such difficulties. If the compensation package is right, contracts, if any, are secured, management presents a united front to the prospective employee, and the candidate develops a relationship with senior management prior to joining the firm, little should deter personnel movement. Getting a small group of good people in the door of a firm in the aftermath of a major personnel problem is the first step that a firm or department may want to take to reestablish itself as a viable place for future employment.

Whether real or perceived, these are some of the hurdles that must be overcome by all managers in the securities industry when contemplating actions that will result in the discharging of employees, particularly those who occupy potentially important or productive positions in the organization. This conceptual view alone, however, does not deal with the issue of which managers in a securities firm are capable of, and have the authority to, make those kinds of decisions and which professionals are likely to bear the brunt of them. The following section deals with these issues.

THE POSITION OF MANAGER

Theoretically, individuals who hold the title "manager" are in a position to levy sanctions and provide rewards for those who are under their supervision; but these possibilities may not necessarily also include the unilateral power to dismiss the employees. Dealing out punishments and rewards may entail approval from other professionals above the manager in the organization's hierarchy. In most cases, such indications of approval or problems with an individual's work are not of such a momentous type that require detailed review by others. When a manager contemplates dismissing a professional, however, some discussion with others and their approval often does. Unlike the doling out of raises or bonuses or requesting employees to assume additional responsibilities, most of which entail senior management providing some kind of support, the unhappy task of letting someone go usually involves the input of a number of professionals.

Not all managers have equal formal authority and informal influence in major personnel matters. In a securities firm, some managers possess stronger authority than others in this area, so that two groups having different relative strengths emerge. Managers who seem to have a stronger formal authority in personnel situations include: branch managers and regional managers; heads of capital markets departments, such as those who manage government, corporate, equity, and municipal departments; heads of investment banking areas, such as those who manage corporate and public finance departments; and managers who are in charge of information services departments and product services divisions, among others. Some professional managers at securities firms have somewhat limited formal discretion in leveling the ultimate sanctions on recalcitrant or unproductive personnel but have strong potential informal input into the decision-making process because of their close working relationship with those individuals and the ability to monitor their activity. These include some heads of particular trading desks and certain institutional sales areas of larger securities departments, the managers of the various sections of the investment banking division within the corporate and public finance departments, senior officers within the information and product departments, and similar ranking professionals in the various other support departments of the firm, such as legal and compliance, administrative services, and so forth.

Not all the managers of a securities firm are mentioned in these two groups; if they had been the list would have run a number of pages. Those cited here are representative of managers who have either of these types of authority inherent in their roles. This dichotomous grouping shows that there are managers who can virtually take management problems into their own hands, perhaps with the input of others who rank well below them. It also isolates a group of managers who have the requisite abilities and required information about the progress and production of personnel under their supervision and who know perhaps more about those particular jobs than anybody else so as to be in a particularly potent position to recommend personnel decisions of either the most positive or the most drastic sort but who lack the formal authority to take unilateral action. The senior level managers to whom these managers report defer to them as those who are in the best position to provide this type of information about lower to midlevel personnel.

One of the most complex dismissal processes in the securities industry is the one where senior managers have to remove other managers, particularly in a situation where those managers with the stronger formal authority must take action against those whose authority is limited in scope, but informally potent in a particular area. (Equally as difficult is when a manager must do the same to a so-called "big producer.") When senior managers are involved in these kind of situations, they are subject to all the considerations discussed earlier, they impact the evaluative personnel process, and they sometimes prolong the time it takes to make a drastic personnel decision. When midlevel managers are the focus—however enormous their responsibilities are for the firm's capital or to its clients— discussions generally evolve into questions as to whether the manager is rehabilitative, transferable, useful in other situations, or willing to have someone else take over.

IN THE HANDS OF MANAGEMENT

The process of dismissing personnel in any setting, be it public or private, is a difficult one with which to deal. Sometimes it hurts the manager initially as much as it does the employee, although of those who have been on the receiving end, few would agree with this statement. More than that, it affects those professionals in and around the department or small business unit. The grapevine being what it is, personnel dismissals could end up affecting others within the firm, especially those who have known the individual either professionally or socially. For managers who have been with a particular organization for a long period of time and also who have been close colleagues of them, the whole situation is at best dismal and at worst extremely upsetting. In organizations of any type, however, be they profit or nonprofit, large or small, widely profitable or not so, the evaluative personnel process, which at times entails the dismissal of some in an effort to better the organization or a particular area, is a major function of management. It requires detailed personnel evaluations, progress analyses, and monitoring of the goals and objectives of all departments and business units within a company. In a securities firm, it is especially important because, for lack of a better description, so much is at stake in the capital markets. It is also a very difficult one in a securities firm because of the specialized nature of the jobs involved, the inherently complex process of personnel evaluations, the potential loss of other employees, and the uncertainty produced by such situations that could end up involving the input of other managers. It is indeed a corporate fact of life and a very important one in securities firms that needs to be handled with as much dexterity as almost any other corporate management decision.

PART 4

TOP MANAGEMENT AND STRATEGY

CHAPTER 18

THE SHAPING OF THE SECURITIES FIRM: THE CEO AND TOP MANAGEMENT

THE CEO

More than anyone else, the chief executive officer (CEO) of the securities firm—the number one professional in the management hierarchy—determines the firm's direction, its strategies, the allocation of its resources, and the members of the top management team. To be sure, studies of all types of chief executives abound in the literature on management, social science, and government. Indeed, the number one slot and the person who occupies it—whether governor, mayor, president, or chair of a private or public company, executive director of a government agency or nonprofit corporation, or even president of the United States—has received a lot of attention from writers, analysts, and readers alike. Most studies acknowledge and document well the pivotal role the chief executive plays within any organization. In government, very often the chief executive is chief legislator, chief of the political party within a given jurisdiction, chief administrator of government agencies, chief architect of the administration's policies, programs, and plans, and most important to some, chief government spokesperson to the public. In the private and public corporate arena, the chief executive's role assumes many of the same functions, in both style and substance, ranging from the ceremonial to the strategic. All chief executives perform their functions with varying levels of success and panache. The CEO of a securities firm has many of the same duties, assignments, roles, and responsibilities; but the nature of the firm and the industry serves up to the CEO, and even to the firm's top management group, some interesting, challenging, and in many ways, unusual managerial tasks for those at this "megamanagement" level.

The securities firm CEO, whether holding the additional title of chair or president, is the lightning rod for the firm's employees and many clients. In the securities firm, therefore, the CEO's involvement with the operations and activities of the specialized divisions, departments, and the big producers assumes a significance not usually apparent in many other companies. Indeed, the CEO of a securities firm is like other chief executives when looked upon as being all things to all people; the CEO not only must fit that description but also must be able to make good in all those roles for the firm to be mobilized as a cohesive business.

THE CEO AS PRODUCT RESOURCE CHIEF

Investment Banker or Product Originator

Few professionals ever think of the CEO of a securities firm as one who is deeply involved in the product origination process, but the CEO is, and sometimes very intimately. For instance, over recent years, corporate and public finance departments have used the firm's CEO on major presentations to large or continuing issuers and clients, and many issuers have seen the presence of the CEO at such gatherings as an indication of interest and firmwide support for them. This is especially important in the securities industry because of the need to risk the firm's capital to support an underwriting of the client's securities. When done in an underwriting of significant size, the CEO is sometimes made aware of the situation and provides either an implicit or explicit blessing on the activity. In addition, as seen through a follow-the-leader syndrome, firms that have not in the past toted the CEO along to presentations of major importance feel compelled to do so lest their firms be accused of not having the same level of interest in the client as firms that flaunt the presence of the CEO. Likewise, clients may believe that the less senior level support shown to them by the securities firm, the less important they are as a client to the firm, and as a result, that they should work with those firms showing the greatest interest.

Over time, the CEO has often developed more than an ephemeral relationship with a firm's public or corporate finance clients, which is important to the firm so that the clients' relationship to those servicing the accounts in the finance departments is transcended by the CEO's relationship to clients. This sometimes minimizes the clients' relationship to other professionals in the entire organization. To be sure, other senior executives of firms could assume this role of offering firmwide interest and support to clients of their finance departments, but none have the clout, prestige, and aura of the CEO. In the best of cases, no other professional in the securities firm does this job better.

Product Arbiter

In the product development process, the CEO of the securities firm, perhaps not unlike the chief executive's counterparts in other corporate organizations, assumes an offshoot of the role of senior product originator, namely that of product "arbiter." Although the CEO is hardly immersed in the product development process of the securities firms—a task usually left to product development specialists both within and outside specific product areas such as stocks, municipal bonds, real estate, and the like—the chief executive, in the final analysis, plays a critical role in determining firm support and resource allocations to products, whether in their incipient stages of development or well along in the product development process. The CEO gives the go-ahead for major product development activities, a decision based on an overall idea of where the customer market may be headed, the direction of the industry, the appeal of the product vis-à-vis its costs and the costs of other products in the securities marketplace, and realistically speaking, the faith the CEO has in those professionals who deliver some of this information. Although many others are involved in this process, in a world of less than limitless resources, the CEO is the product arbiter of last resort.

In the securities industry, however, CEOs face an increasingly challenging task in their role within the product arena. One reason, discussed throughout this text, is that the vast array of products developed and marketed by securities firms makes the product arbiter role a complicated one at best. Not only must an increasingly thin layer of resources, in capital and human forms, be spread across an ever-expanding number of products, but also product complexity makes resource allocation that much more difficult. There comes a point where the CEO becomes the product "spigot," turning the firm's resources either on or off. Moreover, with various specialized areas of the securities firms developing products of their own through derivatives of existing ones or by working with others within the firm on new products, a certain amount of competition develops in product arenas for funds, support, and even claims to resultant revenue. There are a whole host of competitors, each claiming that more support for their products will result in a better bottom line for their department, or related departments, and the firm. The problems inherent in the product arbiter role then become cloaked in subtle departmental and divisional competition for all types of firm support.

Capital Committer for Products

When the firm requires a major capital commitment for a particular product area in an effort to move with industry trends and apparent potential profit-making activities, the involvement of the CEO becomes an absolute necessity. In the securities firm, the CEO's role looms large because of the funds that must be allocated to a given product area and conversely away from others and because such situations often put capital at risk and thus expose the firm to potential losses that could come swiftly and in large amounts. Examples of new products needing huge capital infusions and with the potential to cause losses when used include merchant banking activities, wherein the firm injects its own capital into ventures, the underwriting, trading, and selling certain types of variable rate securities and other newly devised investment alternatives, including all types of complex securitized investment vehicles and other derivative securities.

Perhaps the most important aspect of the CEO's role as capital committer is seen when the role of product originator dovetails with the role of product arbiter. This situation occurs, for instance, when a securities firm embarks on a major effort to build up or enhance its corporate or public finance department. Large amounts of capital are usually involved in these cases, and one goal of the effort is essentially to develop more new issue products for the firm's sales force. It is critical to note, however, that this kind of effort rarely takes place in a resource allocation vacuum; more often than not, tremendous resources are provided to this activity at the expense of others—a scenario that must of necessity be supported and directed by the CEO.

In brief, it is especially important to note that some of these product-oriented roles of the CEO are also within the purview of the senior-most managers of the firm. Furthermore, these roles assume an underlying theme of strategic policy formulation and decision making on the part of both the CEO and top management. From a functional perspective, however, it is the CEO who is at center stage in all these product processes, and the chief executive's role in these cases bears heavily on the success of the firm in the product process.

THE CEO AS MARKETING MANAGER

Product Marketer

Few individuals conceive of the CEO as a marketing manager; rarely is the CEO involved to any significant extent in the product marketing process, and the CEO seldom spends much time touting the value of specific stocks, bonds, or other securities. In a number of senses, however, the CEO is the firm's chief marketer, of its products and of the firm itself. No other officers have within their official functions the wherewithal, both formally and informally, to act in this capacity. While the ultimate extent to which the CEO assumes active involvement in the role as the firm's number one marketer depends on the individual holding that office, the opportunities to maximize this role of the chief executive remain almost limitless.

Oftentimes there are a few investment vehicles that generally could provide investors better returns than those of other investments available in the marketplace. In other instances, the firm, through any of its product departments or its corporate or public finance divisions, may be making available a new, noteworthy, or unusual investment whose financial attributes make it particularly attractive to certain investors. Perhaps at other times particular market conditions result in turning certain securities into quite appealing products relative to other available alternatives. For instance, impending and likely changes in interest rates could cause conditions that will isolate specific investments as excellent ones for a specified group of investors. In any of these cases, and in other similar ones, the CEO brandishing pen and paper or operating through a firm-wide communications system, can call attention to these investments, which would focus the firm's professionals on them. Any product having the imprimatur of the firm's chieftain who has isolated it from the mass of available investment vehicles should, in a few words, receive a marketing lift. If the CEO continues this kind of activity in a measured way and is right on or close to the bull's eye, there is very little else that could compete with this kind of internal marketing clout as far as investment accuracy goes.

Firm Marketer

In yet another important way, the CEO is the securities firm's main marketer and chief developer of "esprit de corps." Put differently, the CEO markets the firm to its own employees, the very first group that must be sold on the firm, its capabilities, its potential, and its people. Although once again some chief executives perform this role much better than others, and in a few firms, senior managers other than the CEO have been given this task or have assumed it, it is one generally associated with the firm's number one manager. In the entrepreneurial setting of the securities firm, it is difficult but very critical.

Different CEOs, to be sure, have different personal styles. This is important to recognize because developing esprit de corps in an enthusiastic but believable way focuses attention on the CEO's personality and ability to appeal to diverse constituents—the firm's employees, particularly its professionals—who are developed in certain ways by their own entrepreneurial spirit, drives, and styles. They have their own inner gyroscopes focused on outdistancing their own successes, beating the market, and providing better service for their clients. Keeping that kind of momentum going, propping it up when it falters, or even getting it going in the first place is a herculean task, and that responsibility falls on the shoulders of the firm's chief executive more than anyone else.

In this role, the CEO of the securities firm faces structural and informational hurdles. In operationalizing the requests of personal persuasive power in an effort to establish rapport with the firm's professionals located around the globe, the problem of proximity often rears its ugly head. The CEO cannot be everywhere and know every employee, although one or two in the securities industry have visited most of their branch offices and do in fact have an uncanny ability to remember names of employees, their spouses and friends, and most important, their achievements on behalf of the firm or otherwise. This is a difficult way to generate enthusiasm, but it is an effective one. On the communications front, a few CEOs are adept at writing and regularly issue memoranda to the firm's employees about the firm's progress, its plans, its successes, and those of its employees. When this approach works, it works well; many employees actually look forward to these epistlelike statements, and some even keep them for reference. This communication implicitly says to employees that the senior person cares enough about them to take the time to inform them about what is going on. More broadly, it is a statement by the firm about its interest in its employees. Most of all, from an internal marketing standpoint, it seems to work.

The CEO, however, faces a challenge to this role as chief

marketer, which is endemic to the securities firm in many respects. This is posed by the firm's specialized nature and the expertise that must be developed within each given product area for the various functions housed under its roof. Hardly any chief executives have been involved in every product or function of a securities firm on their way up the corporate ladder. Fewer still have developed an intimate knowledge of a large number of them, but most CEOs have an excellent working knowledge of many product areas and have actually been experts in a few of them. It is not expected that every CEO be truly knowledgeable about every area, but the chief executive must be conversant with the vast majority of them, otherwise the possibility of a potentially ever-widening credibility gap remains a realistic one.

THE CEO AND THE CORPORATE PARENT

Complex Roles

The rash of takeovers of securities firms by major corporations in recent years, principally during the 1980s, has resulted in new and uncharted roles for the securities firm CEO—those of representative to, and employee of, the corporate parent and as representative of the corporate parent to the securities firm. For the first time in the lives of many securities firm CEOs, there is a boss to report to, either a single individual at the parent headquarters, or more often, a group of senior executives who are top management of the organization and of whom the securities firm CEO is one. Although the CEO works collegially with this group, the CEO subtly reports to them in different ways and to different individuals depending on the particular situation and the formal and informal structure established, which is apt to be modified over time. To some CEOs, this is a somewhat unnerving experience at first, and perhaps it should be. What this new relationship does, however, is to cast the CEO in a number of new, sometimes conflicting, often difficult to manage, and rather complex roles as a company head whose parent, in almost every case, has not had any experience in running a securities organization with all the daily risks and rewards that come along with a firm impacted, on a moment-to-moment basis, by the securities markets.

From the perspective of the acquiring parent, the securities firm is seen as an investment, principally with a view for the long term. Typically, however, this long-term view abruptly changes to a short-term orientation when the year-end figures roll in, which can be widely off the firm's projected mark because of the nature of the securities industry. Thus, the securities firm CEO is immediately cast in the role of defender of the firm if projections do not materialize as planned. From then on, both the chief executive of the securities firm and the parent company's management team must each adjust their financial and planning expectations; the former usually becomes more precise in the business of planning, while the latter develops some flexibility in having the securities firm meet corporatewide goals and objectives.

These changes in management expectations do not imply that the securities firm was lax or lacking in the traditional planning process of the larger corporate world or that the corporate world had a stricter and more controlled developmental and goal-laden orientation. It does suggest, however, that there is some meshing of organizational cogs that must initially take place if there are to be some synergetic opportunities for each company as a result of the new corporate combination, as both entities usually expected. It is then that the securities firm CEO and the parent both assure their management teams and employees that each firm would, in a number of ways, be helped by their association with the other; and the securities firm CEO becomes cast in the newly found role as representative of the parent company to the securities firm.

Implicit in this role, at least initially, are two messages that the securities firm CEO usually attempts to impart and that most employees wait anxiously to hear. In seemingly stark contrast to each other, the CEO announces that the parent intends to employ its assets to help the securities firm in any way possible; but owing in large part to the unusual nature of the securities business, the firm's risk policies and practices, and its compensation standards, parent company interference with the firm will be minimal. From a management standpoint, thus, the securities firm CEO is at once cast in the dual parental roles of provider and protector. Indeed, in a very real sense, the securities firm's employees come to see the CEO as such in the time thereafter.

Synergy as a Process

Detailed and enumerated expectations notwithstanding, much evaluation remains to be done on the extent to which the predicted synergies between securities firms and their acquiring companies materialized, and it is worth discussing here because of the importance the CEO plays in the process. This analysis has four basic dimensions: the expectations of the parent, the expectations of the securities firm, the results as seen by the parent, and the results as seen by the securities firm. The evaluation may be further fine-tuned to an analysis of how each expected the results would affect them, and how each expected the results would affect the other party, and, in the final evaluation, what actually happened, from an independent analyst's standpoint. Unfortunately, this entire process assumes a time horizon, and most analysts agree that the greatest impacts resulting from these new corporate combinations will occur years in the future.

A number of propositions are identifiable at this point in time, however. First, the highly touted and imminently expected synergies are, in fact, a slowly evolving process requiring planning, coordination, and a paradigmatic discovery, especially in the product sales field. It is unlikely that salespeople of each newly merged firm, who sell totally different financial or service products, will be able to sell effectively all types of products, such as securities, real estate, insurance, and credit card services. It is difficult enough to master an understanding of, and ability for, selling products within a single group. Efforts at joint marketing, however, can be successful even in a relatively short period of time. There are many other related kinds of synergies, some obvious and others less so, which have resulted from and will be the product of these megamergers. Exchanging customer lists, funneling corporate and institutional clients from one firm to the other to provide the client with one-stop services, and offering easy access to the public of similar products all housed under one corporate roof may be among the major benefits of newly merged firms.

The vast proportion of discernible corporate progress achieved through the mergers and takeovers of securities firms, however, has come largely and immediately in four forms:

1. The boosting of a securities firm's capital base through different forms of monetary infusions, or commitments from the parent company, if and when the need for additional funds arose.
2. Direct access by the parent through the securities firm to the world's capital markets, and a ready-made asset in the securities firm for use in the employment of the parent's strategic corporate objectives.
3. A new subsidiary for the parent company making it more diversified than before and providing it with a readily available customer base.
4. A forum to exchange ideas and interweave the business development plans of both companies' small business units.

The point here is that the success of a securities firm's relations with the corporate parent is determined by the firm's CEO more than any other professional.

THE CEO AS THE FIRM'S PUBLIC AMBASSADOR

One of the more unquantifiable roles of the securities firm CEO in terms of its effect on the organization's "bottom line," but one which certainly adds qualitative dimensions to how the firm is perceived by its clients and the public alike, is the CEO's role as the firm's ambassador to the public. This entails the ongoing development of the CEO's image, the publicity of the CEO's activities, and concurrently, the successes of the firm. For a securities firm, this aspect of the CEO's job and the perception created by the firm's senior manager have become peculiarly important over recent years. For a long time, the CEO and the securities firm itself were cloaked in an aura of secrecy owing to some extent to the confidentiality of the firm's business and the relatively small numbers of its employees, but really resulting largely from the fact the securities firms of yesteryear, and many up until the mid-1970s, were privately held. As securities firms merged with others and as firms were taken over by corporations that were usually unlike those of the securities firms themselves, the securities industry entered into an era of greatly increased public competition. The firms were also thrust into a corporate world accustomed to developing customer awareness of companies and their products through tremendous increases and advances in publicity and advertising. Because more than most companies securities firms were asset garnering machines, the firms had to sell image as well as product to all of their clients to a greater or lesser degree. Over time, the most likely symbol of the firm was its CEO; but until only very recently, few securities firms employed the CEO directly in advertising, unlike many industrial corporations nationwide. The creation and development of the CEO's image, which spilled over to that of the firm, was far more subtle. The CEO was used as a securities firm spokesperson or ambassador to the media and ultimately to the public.

This was an important new dimension of the CEO's job because it carried with it potential long-range effects on the development of the firm's client base and on garnering and keeping the very best professionals—the lifeblood of any securities firm. The clients of a securities firm, by their very nature, want to be associated with a firm they believe is and will continue to be a winner, one that is financially secure with adequate capital at its disposal, and one whose employees will provide the financial advice and products at least on a par with the best available from any other firm for their particular situation. Similarly, much of the way a securities firm motivates its professionals, as discussed earlier, is through the development of organizational ethos. This attracts clients, to be sure, but more important is that it helps keep professionals producing and attracts others.

In a great many cases, prospective new employees look to the CEO in making a decision to join the firm. A large percentage of potential big producers contemplating movement to a new firm want to and actually do spend time with the CEO. Very often these meetings are anything but perfunctory introductions. To new employees, the CEO's image, role, plans, and dialogue with them have a far greater impact on attracting top talent and keeping the best professionals at any organizational level than do those of CEOs in most other corporations. Indeed, to those within the securities firm and to the world outside it, the CEO is the firm's ambassador; but the role has real teeth in the securities industry.

THE CEO AND THE TOP MANAGEMENT TEAM

Who Is Top Management?

"The chief-executive job in every business (except perhaps the very smallest) cannot properly be organized as the job of one man," argues Peter Drucker. "It must be the job of a team of several men acting together."[1] The top management team in a securities firm is defined here as its executive committee—that small group of top managers who are part of the firm's much larger board of directors, but who supervise the departments and groups managed by other members of the board. The board of directors of most securities firms, or the firm's partners in some cases, can number up to 60 individuals, and at a few firms well above that total. Each manages a given department or area of the firm and the size of the board depends on the extent to which the firm's myriad departments are represented. Yet, key decisions appropriately involving both strategy and structure fall into the purview of the top management team or the executive committee, however they are defined.

In a securities firm, top management is composed of a handful of managers having broad control over major divisions within the firm, each of which is composed of any number of departments engaging in complicated and specialized activities. Notably represented in top management are the heads of the retail system (if any), and the investment banking, research, operations and administrative services, and capital markets departments, and also the CEO, president, chair of the board, or vice-chair, depending on whether these titles and responsibilities are separately delegated or are given to one or more individuals. In some firms, other professionals may be included in this inner circle, such as the firm's designated risk manager, the heads of international operations, the commodities department, the corporate and public finance departments, the information services area, or the firm's economist. Every firm's top management team has a slightly different configuration, depending on the firm's emphasis and activities and each manager's capabilities and responsibilities. Some firms even have a subgroup of the top management team patterned after the "office of the chair" established by some industrial companies over recent years.

The top management group, however, has two distinguishing features. First, it is an overwhelmingly diverse one, in terms of responsibility, expertise, and number of employees under each member's jurisdiction, all of which is compounded by the specialized nature of the departments each manager supervises. Secondly, it is run, structured, sanctioned, and promoted by the firm's CEO. Top management, as Drucker suggests, "is not a committee. It is a team. A team needs a captain. The captain is not the boss; he is the leader."[2] There is some controversy in management literature as to whether managers have the same innate qualities, developmental paths, and fundamental job structures as leaders, and if individuals can effectively be both. For the purposes of this discussion, however, the CEO is seen generally as the top management team's front-runner, connotations of the term "leader" notwithstanding.

Resource and Recognition Allocator

The CEO as top management team leader overseeing this group represented by such diverse and often subtly competing interests casts the CEO into a role not totally unique to corporate management but unusual in its breadth, depth, and dimension. Each division represented by those on the firm's top management staff has its own needs for capital, personnel, compensation, and benefits, but each division chief also wants some kudos, or more formally stated, high praise from the CEO. On the surface, these needs of division chiefs do not sound unusual. The securities firm's divisions and departments, while originally conceived of, and in the minds of many still thought of, as stand-alone profit centers, are very much entwined and interdependent, often far more than division chiefs and department heads would care to openly admit.

For instance, the capital markets group takes risks in trading and underwriting securities, but the retail group, by selling those securities, limits that risk. The investment banking departments, both corporate and public finance, create products for the firm's institutional and retail sales force; but perhaps without that sales force and the firm's capital base and trading capability, product creation via the banking avenue would be difficult. Additionally, the sales force markets products, but this activity would otherwise be limited without a capable research department. Trading, underwriting, and sales activities occur effectively on a moment-to-moment basis; but without an effective operations department and communications and information processing networks, these basic firm functions would have limited profitability and could result in significant losses. Even within each department of each division, such as municipals, corporates, governments, equities, commodities, and public and corporate finance, there are delicate balancing acts occurring among small business units that are really responsible for returning profit to the securities firm. The bottom line results from a convergence of forces that most professionals admit to understanding fully; but the firm's diversity of specialized interests causes centrifugal forces to vie for recognition in all forms. These forces are served up to division chiefs and placed on the top management table during the resource allocation and strategy development process. Complicating matters further is simply the specialized nature of each business unit, department, and division represented by each member of the firm's top management team. Each member is also in a way cast in the same role as the CEO when balancing the often competing claims for resources and recognition by those under each member's supervision.

Top Management Melder

Standing at the threshold of top management's diversity of interests and expectations located at the highest level of the securities firm is the CEO. As top management leader, the CEO is thus cast in the delicate role of building a top management consensus; the CEO must, in a few words, blend together the diverse constituencies represented by those in top management as well as top management itself. This role is operationalized during and through the resource allocation process. Interestingly insightful and indeed applicable is a comment by Drucker who suggests, "Members of the top management team need not like each other. They need not even respect each other. But they must not agitate against each other. In public, that is. . . ."[3] Implicit in this statement is the idea that the real give and take, the ultimate corporate compromises, battles, engagements, and mediating, are lodged within this small group of the firm's senior executives. To be sure, some of the development and structuring of major firm resource allocation procedures and decisions could and sometimes does extend to and take place within the broader confines of the entire board. The top management group should be the logical place for this; and within a securities firm, this concept is proportionately more significant, given the number and diversity of semiautonomous departments represented in that small microcosm of the firm itself.

Nonetheless, "the top-management task," observes Drucker, "requires systematic and intensive communications among members of the top-management team."[4] This dictum is certainly true. Yet, the specialized nature of the securities industry requires intense communication especially at the top management level across horizontal lines of corporate divisions, so that the proper firmwide decisions can be made and sent down the vertical chain of command to the divisional and departmental levels. Put differently, the prerogatives of decision making in a securities firm are at the department level, and department heads must provide the vertical glue to bind their small business units horizontally. Loose-fitting horizontally aligned business units in a securities firm do not communicate and coordinate by themselves. It is vertical pressure that makes this happen. However, department heads must also be mandated and motivated to do so by their divisional chiefs and representatives in the top management team.

As a result, the top management team must be a cohesive unit, must have a firmwide battle plan that transcends its own jurisdictional management responsibility, and must convey this downward through the organization. This entire situation creates the CEO's role as "melder" of the incredibly diverse interests within a securities firm, all represented in one form or another by the chief executive's top management team. To be sure, the perceived profit center orientation of the securities firm modified by departments and divisions that are actually rather dependent on each other (and should be increasingly so in the future to maximize a firm's profits in any given arena) makes the role of the CEO as "melder of last resort" a critical one indeed. Specialization complicates the successful development of this role, and the CEO must therefore ferret out all available information about the business units reporting to top management team members from them and others. Based partly on this information and partly on other data, the CEO and the top management team can then turn their attention to what is prehaps their most important role—that of developing firm strategy.

NOTES

1. Peter F. Drucker, *The Practice of Management* (New York: Harper & Row, 1986), p. 168.
2. Peter F. Drucker, *Management: Tasks, Responsibilities, Practice* (New York: Harper & Row, 1985), p. 622.
3. Drucker, *Management,* p. 622.
4. Ibid, p. 623.

See also:

"Going Public on Wall Street," *The New York Times,* January 1, 1986.

"The Perils of Being Near the Top: Why Brokerage Firm Management Can Be Dangerous to a Career," *Investment Dealer's Digest,* December 1, 1986.

"Stalled Synergy: Many Firms Back Off from Offering Arrays of Financial Services," *Wall Street Journal,* November 12, 1986.

CHAPTER 19

STRATEGY: THE FIRM'S MOST IMPORTANT PRODUCT

Peter Drucker's famous question, "What is our business and what should it be?"[1] forms the basis of issues relating to a firm's business strategy. This question, however, is actually a superordinate one that top management seeks to answer before, during, and after the more mundane, but no less important, strategy issues are developed. The question is above and beyond what some senior corporate managers, and many in the securities industry, view as the strategic dilemmas they face daily.

Corporate strategy, as defined generally by Donaldson and Lorsch is "the stream of decisions over time that reveal management's goals for the corporation and the means they choose to achieve."[2] The decision-making process may be framed, according to these writers, by "corporate leaders' desire to assure the survival of their company . . . [providing] the driving force for their initiatives and strategic choices."[3] Strategic decision making usually involves macroorganizational decisions made by top management that are expected to reap returns for the company within a projected environment of specific dimensions. Although these decisions are long range, they do, and perhaps must of necessity, have many incremental decisions within them that must be made in the context of the larger goal-oriented process. Consequently, strategic decision making for most organizations has involved a broad perspective of the company, what it does, and what it is expected to be doing in the future together with and supported by smaller departmental decisions and actions.

In the securities industry, strategic decisions involve a macroorganizational approach, such as one that moves a securities firm corporate ship into the future world of enormous capital-based organizations, trading large amounts of securities around the clock with on-line real-time data bases on which to make critical capital allocation decisions. Within the context of a securities firm with its vast number of specialized small business units each engaging in vastly differing activities and widely varying products, strategic decision making often also has a microorganizational focus that does not necessarily involve a large number of corporate departments or business units acting together. In these instances, strategic decision making assumes a departmental or divisional component of insulated activities. Consequently, in a securities firm, it is important to realize that what may be a strategic decision from top management's standpoint and from the standpoint of one or two departments and that may result in general firmwide benefits is not necessarily viewed as a major organizational change affecting all the firm's activities and the entire corporate compass, at least initially.

TYPES OF SECURITIES FIRM STRATEGIC DECISIONS

With many of a securities firm's strategic decisions being organized around departmental and divisional development, there are a number of generic types of strategic decisions in which top management of a securities firm normally becomes involved. For instance, some strategic decisions are technical in nature and involve an overhaul of a securities firm's communications and information processing systems. This usually requires that decisions be made about computer hardware and software purchases and the development of an entire department or division expected to evaluate, implement, or alter the way the securities firm processes information and disseminates it.

Another major type of strategic decision a securities firm may make could be of the product-oriented variety. This occurs when top management makes a conscious effort to put the firm's resources behind the development of a product or a series of related ones of such breadth and dimension that they are likely to change dramatically the product revenue stream generated by the firm. Sometimes this process involves the creation of a product that can be used to garner customer assets, or it may mean a product-related service. In the former case, an example would be an asset management account, and in the latter situation, a credit card service would be illustrative. In a larger sense, certain firms have developed new product-related services, which may really be separate businesses in and of themselves. These might include insurance or real estate activities.

Another type of strategic decision made by top management of a securities firm could involve using the firm's resources to back the development of a specific department or division likely to have some major impact on the firm's strategic path of growth. Most notably, securities firms have thrown substantial resources into the development of corporate finance departments over recent years. Top management has seen this as an ongoing effort to provide additional products to the firm's institutional and retail sales forces and also to garner fees and even some prestige by developing the firm's investment banking business.

Other strategic decisions sometimes have to do with a new business for the firm that may have spillover benefits to other activities in which the firm is presently involved, especially those that are sales related and could be used as part of a general package of financial services provided to the firm's retail or institutional customers. This could be the wholesale development from scratch, or even the direct purchase, of an operation that is not at the present time an activity in which the firm is engaged. For example, some securities firms have either purchased or developed investment research departments or mortgage banking activities, some of which have had unusual products or market niches.

Top management of the securities firm has also made strategic decisions relating to the capital or risk allocation process. Some of these decisions have been unanticipated because they were a reaction to market conditions or the origination of products by the firm itself. These have been situations where the firm has decided to allocate a certain proportion of its capital toward risk-related activities in specific securities areas. This has been a two-edged decision-making sword. On the one hand, the firm threw its resources behind a specific department or securities area. On the other hand, it took the use of capital from other areas and thus limited profits and losses that could have resulted in these departments. The entire process thus became a strategic decision-making one of the most fundamental sort. Similarly, major management changes are actually strategic decisions by top management to reorganize the firm's senior personnel to handle better the workload or provide direction and developmental opportunities for the firm's departments and divisions. It is also a way to develop senior managers.

Yet another top management strategic decision made at most Wall Street firms is whether or not, or the extent to which, the firm should develop its international securities business, including trading, underwriting, sales, and investment banking activities. Indeed, in early 1986, Samuel L. Hayes III, professor of investment banking at the Harvard Business School, said in *The New York Times* that "hardly a day passes now without one of Wall Street's giants opening a new office abroad, raiding top talent to beef up overseas operations or acquiring a foreign securities company." He noted further that "there is no historical precedent for this—there has never been a truly global business like this is becoming."[4] As a result, the decision to develop a securities firm's international operations in any way that the firm sees fit is an important, and perhaps sweeping, strategic decision of top management and should be viewed as such even though the decision often involves all types of important decisions within it that relate to different types of internationally related activities, such as the development of a specific kind of information and communications system or an investment banking presence. For instance, in developing the firm's international business, some securities houses have concentrated on excelling in trading around the clock in securities in which the firm has a distinct capability. Other securities firms have desired to develop an international merchant banking arm to their corporate finance departments. As a result, not only is the decision of top management to develop the firm's international operations an important type of strategic decision, but the way in which management goes about implementing that decision is also strategically significant.

There are probably a number of other types of strategic decisions. Without spending too much detail and time on the obvious, it is sufficient to say that strategic decisions in a securities firm often involve microorganizational plans and the use of departments and personnel to implement them. Often they are focused on and implemented by specialized business units within the firm, even though the effect of the strategic decisions is potentially far-reaching. In time, these decisions could affect some other departments and divisions within the firm or could incrementally move the firm along a path different from its original one or along one that top management believes to be of future opportunity. Ultimately then, these types of strategic decisions may in fact affect the mission and the business of the securities firm in the long run, although this may not necessarily happen.

STRATEGIC DECISIONS FOR DIFFERENT TYPES OF FIRMS

It goes without saying that different securities firms make different types of strategic decisions with different emphases and different effects. There are specific types of securities firms, however, that focus their strategic decisions along the lines of their types of businesses and thus must cope with the same general issues in their strategic decision-making process. For instance, institutional securities firms without large retail branch office systems have a much different group of strategic decisions to be implemented and strategic questions to be answered than those of other types of securities firms. These firms must concentrate on penetrating the institutional market, which must, of necessity, entail the development of a trading capability of the kind best suited for their institutional sales purposes as well as the development of investment banking departments, either corporate or public finance or both, which are successful at originating new issue underwritings, particularly as a senior manager.

There are many ancillary activities that help an institutional securities firm develop to its greatest potential.

These usually include such support functions as a highly visible and successful research effort, a closely followed chief economist, and many other services related to investment banking underwritings but not necessarily entailing the actual underwriting function.

There are other large securities firms and some of smaller size that have both institutional and retail sales capabilities, and these firms often vie for the same kinds of clients. A few of these firms have outdistanced the others in the institutional area, particularly in the investment banking arena, in their ability to originate underwritings. To some extent, the kinds of strategic decisions that must be made by the top management of these firms are generally of the same variety and often focus on the broad range of decisions enumerated in the previous section. In these firms, the strategic decision-making process is often one that is competitive within senior management ranks, as different areas of the firm represented by different managers all come to the strategic decision-making bargaining table compete for the firm's resources. Critical to the process at these securities firms is an ongoing review by management of exactly where the firm is putting the weight of its resources. Much vacillation and change in the allocation of resources within a short time frame often leads to results not necessarily as successful as would otherwise be the case.

Midsize securities firms often have the most difficult time in the strategic decision-making process, not only in isolating the kinds of strategic decisions top management must make, but also in answering the questions that the tough strategic dilemmas pose and in implementing the appropriate solutions. Usually, midsize securities firms have a fair number of retail branch offices and moderate-size institutional sales, trading, underwriting, investment banking, and research capabilities. Strategic decisions made by top management at these firms usually involve defining as best as possible the firm's market share in a specific area that management would like to penetrate, and then developing a plan to capture market share increases in that area or even creating a market niche in a particular product or service in which the firm is not presently involved. One of the more difficult hurdles to overcome by top management at these firms is the competition in all areas by the larger securities firms that have substantially developed institutional and retail components. These larger firms have usually engaged in a substantial amount of nationwide advertising and also have the revenue stream and capital necessary to place behind the development of different businesses and the trading and underwriting of securities. Midsize securities houses often run right into this wall of resistance in implementing strategic decisions to develop their firm's businesses. As a result, the strategic decision-making process is often one that is longer, more complicated, and more difficult to chart a course of action to implement. These concepts will be developed later in the next section on strategic decision making for the midsize securities firm.

WHO ELSE MAKES STRATEGIC DECISIONS?

Securities firms make important decisions through top management dictums for reasons relating to the possibility that the activities will be profitable, will be synergetic with the firm's existing operations, will provide value-added benefits, will result in some cost benefit to the securities firm, or will create a new activity for the firm even though the function is expected to be experimental or developmental in nature. For a long time, strategic decision making at securities firms was done largely through in-house processes and by top management. Over recent years, firms have begun to use outside management consultants to study their operations, organizational structure, market niche in specific businesses, and personnel qualifications. These consultants have suggested answers to these types of questions, and management of the securities firms has seemed to follow many of the suggestions that the consultants have made without too much argument, although there is no way to quantify this.

Isolating problems and possible activities in a securities firm about which strategic decisions must be made is both a top-down and a bottom up process. Although once relegated to the wood-panelled boardrooms of the firms themselves, the strategic decision-making suggestion box has been thrown wide open to outside individuals and others within the organization, who, even though they may occupy low to midlevel management ranks, have developed a fairly well-thought-out plan to solve either a particular need of the firm or to develop an activity that will fit within the securities firm's business menu or is likely to be a welcome addition to it. Much of this is the result of securities firms burgeoning in their number of employees and variety of activities, so that many senior managers now do not believe that they have a total lock on all available information and all potential profitable businesses that are even remotely securities related. This has added immeasurably to the entrepreneurial nature of the securities firm. Indeed, many professionals who now occupy important positions in securities firms' executive suites have arrived there only recently, but with the thrust of their ability toward developing a new business and generating enormous amounts of revenues. Most notably, this has occurred in the mortgage finance and trading areas, the mergers and acquisitions arenas, and the high-yield bond departments.

IMPLEMENTING STRATEGIC DECISIONS

For a securities firm, the implementation of strategic decisions inevitably evolves into a problem of managing organizational change, largely because most of these decisions result in a change in activities either within a department or small business unit or even on a macroscale for the securities firm as a whole. Often, but not necessarily, this draws on professionals whose work may either be related to the new activity or may be extremely helpful in its development. As a result, one of the most critical decisions involved in implementing strategic operations in a securities firm is putting the right people in charge of the new activity or the restructuring of an older one.

In any securities firm, the implementation of a strategic decision in the wake of its announcement must be handled by management in the best communicative form possible. Often such decisions come in a volcanic eruption replete with memos sent throughout the organization; and this is certainly one

appropriate way to handle the need for corporate communications in events like these. It is also important, however, to have
some ongoing communication process between management and
those affected in the wake of any such decision-making announcement. So that professionals not make incorrect assumptions about the reasons for strategic decisions, the way they
were implemented, and their expected results, management
should take a hands-on approach to communicating the hows
and whys of their strategic decision-making process.

EVALUATING STRATEGIC DECISIONS

Critical to the strategic decision-making process is the feedback
provided over time about the decisions and an evaluation made
about their effects. There are a number of questions that might
be asked about them at times of periodic review that are not
necessarily applicable to every type of strategic decision in a
securities firm. Management must make a valued judgment
about the decision's worth and whether or not the activity, if
there was one initiated, should be continued. In any event, some
questions include:

Was the activity resulting from the strategic decision effective?

Did it achieve the percentage of profit expected?

Did it produce an adequate rate of return, return on equity,
or return on investment?

Was it synergetic with the activities of the firm?

Did it provide significant diversification or provide value
added benefits to the firm or to a particular business unit
within the firm?

Did it achieve any of the goals sought, and to what extent
was this so?

All these questions are important ones in the strategic decision-making evaluation process, and there are certainly
others; but very often in a highly competitive atmosphere where
time is of the essence, many managers forgo a formal periodic

review of a decision or activity even if it is of a strategic orientation. Such activities often get buried within the corporate body politic, providing some professionals with the opportunity to champion the decisions as managers of the new bureaucracy and without the formal review procedures that might lead their own managers to render adverse verdicts. Without the review process, even modifying an activity along the same general lines of its formulation, but in a way so as to minimize any unanticipated problems that have occurred, is largely forgone in such an instance.

SUPERORDINATE STRATEGIC DECISIONS

Aside from the types of strategic decisions outlined earlier, in which a firm and its top management may become involved and which are likely to affect the firm's long-range growth and financial success, today's securities firm is presented with strategic decisions of a superordinate sort that often involve the future of the firm as a unique entity and in which top management at many firms has already begun work on. These involve the merger or sale of the firm itself. Decisions about this possibility could include the following options: buying a securities firm; merging with other securities firms; going public; selling stock of the securities firm to an outsider; selling the securities firm to a larger company; or even contracting its activities or extricating itself from a merger in which it had previously been involved. None of these are directly related to any department or small business unit within the firm, so that they are important strategic decisions.

Many analysts have come to realize that how these decisions are made is as much a function of whether or not they make financial or business sense as they are a result of the personal predispositions of the securities firm's top managers and sometimes the entire board of directors. It would not be fruitful, and perhaps it would almost be impossible, to detail all the reasons that such decisions are made at securities firms. These have been alluded to throughout this text and have much to do with the need of the firms for additional capital and the wish, in some cases, that the top managers and other professionals within the firm would not have their capital subject to risk. The reasons other companies become involved in the securities business can range anywhere from the need to diversify their businesses to a business interest in Wall Street. Divestiture and buy backs occur when the expectations of top management are not achieved. This is a broad conceptual framework about the decision-making processes of the most significant kind within the securities firm.

STRATEGIC DECISION MAKING FOR MIDSIZE SECURITIES FIRMS

Most securities firms in the industry today are not large in size and do not have the seemingly unlimited resources of the retail and institutional giants; few firms are even in that class. The vast majority of firms are small to midsize, have up to 50 offices, and have no highly visible corporate or public finance departments. These firms comprise the vast number of securities organizations in the industry, and as such, they have the most perplexing strategic decision-making problems because they operate among giants. Most of these firms are also not of the boutique variety with developed specialties in particular areas of finance, sales, or trading who survive in large part on revenues generated from their specialized types of activities. Strategic decisions for midsize firms have become the most important activity in which they can engage. These decisions generally involve creating a customer for their services, which are usually the same type as those which other firms provide to the same or similar customers; but their competition is those firms of a much larger size with greater amounts of capital, many more products, and a much larger share of the new issue origination business. What midsize firms actually try to do, and what may not be immediately apparent when compared against their larger counterparts in the industry, is to develop a definable customer base for their specific activities and differentiate these from the services provided by the much larger firms. The ability of midsize securities firms to do this will either insure their survivability in the future or will result in them succumbing to the tentacles of other larger firms or in their going out of business altogether.

There are no easy answers to any of the kinds of strategic decisions that midsize securities firms must make. The most that can be said for these questions is that while the answers differ from firm to firm and sometimes so do the specific questions, the larger issues remain generally the same. As a result, this section is divided into parts focusing on the major activities of these securities firms and raising the kinds of issues and questions for which there are no across-the-board answers, but with which management must wrestle on a daily basis. Just understanding what these questions are presents a smorgasbord of conceptual problems to be addressed by top management of midsize securities firms in an effort to develop them, make them more profitable, and insure their future survivability. To be sure, there are many small to midsize firms that, regardless of whether they activate a full-scale strategic decision-making process along the lines of the questions posed here, will survive long into the future because of the loyalty of their clientele or because they engage in certain types of businesses or provide specialized services with such expertise that they can compete against any securities firm in the industry. Nevertheless, the kinds of issues posed here are the ones that must be addressed, and, although there may be others, they represent an important sampling of what top management at midsize firms face each working day.

The Securities Sales System

The key questions of a strategic nature facing top management in a midsize securities firm and relating to the retail branch system may be divided into five categories. These include: the development of the account executives; the branch offices; products; marketing; and advertising.

Questions relating to the account executives include:

Should the firm hire big producers or try to develop their own?

Should the firm hire big producers in all areas or hire them in specific ones?

How should the firm increase the production of its own account executives?

Questions relating to the branch office system include:

Is it best to develop more branches in smaller cities where there is less competition from big firms?

Or should the firm develop strong regional identities and strengths?

Or should the firm wait for mergers of other firms and take advantage of their branch office fallout?

There are also important issues about product development that must be addressed by midsize securities firms. These include:

When does it become too costly for the firm to develop its own products?

How should the firm compete against its much larger competitors in the "assets under management" game?

When is it profitable for the firm to sell the products offered by other competing organizations without hurting its own image and client base?

Questions relating to marketing and market segmentation include:

Is there a market segment to attract that is not serviced by the large retail-oriented firms?

Or should the securities firm attack a certain segment of its competitors' market?

On the institutional side of the marketing effort, questions to be asked are:

What market segment should the firm seek?

What marketing strategies should it employ if it does not have a large amount of new issue products?

Advertising is an important issue facing midsize securities

firms, and the following questions are usually the ones most often asked:

Is creating an image for the midsize securities firm necessary?

How does the firm compete against the large firms in advertising?

When does advertising become too costly for the midsize firm?

Is it better for the firm to advertise regionally and create an image that way rather than employ full-scale nationwide advertising?

Is advertising based on products a worthwhile endeavor?

Or should a midsize securities firm virtually disregard the advertising business because of the competition in it?

Investment Banking and Investment Research

There are a number of issues that must be addressed if the midsize securities firm is going to make any strategic decisions about developing its investment banking and research departments. These include the following questions:

Is there a need for more new issue corporate and public finance products?

If so, how does the firm develop its corporate and public finance departments with other larger competing securities firms having a great proportion of the underwriting business?

How does the firm create a market niche in the corporate and public finance business?

How does the firm attract and hire corporate and public finance personnel?

Is it feasible for the firm to hire teams of well-established public and corporate finance professionals who have a market niche, or should the firm develop its own along a broader client base?

Is it worth developing a research effort along the lines of competing firms?

Is it best to develop a research effort that is market-niche oriented, and if so, how does the midsize firm do this?

Risking Capital and Merger Options

Strategic decisions of top management in a midsize securities firm regarding the risking of capital are very important, largely because there is usually not a great deal of capital to spread over the existing needs. Questions relating to capital and risk allocation priorities involve the following issues:

How does the small to midsize firm risk capital and maintain a syndicate presence and a good inventory in as many securities areas as possible?

How does the firm allocate capital to service midlevel institutional and retail clients?

When and how does the firm originate large deals and allocate capital to them, while still limiting the risk to itself?

These are just some of the issues that top management faces in risking the capital of small to midsize firms. To be sure, there are others; but beyond the capital allocation process, top management usually has a relatively risk-adverse posture, and this may conflict with decisions to develop an institutional presence and originate corporate and public finance new issues where the firm must risk increasingly larger amounts of capital as a senior or comanager.

In the seemingly endless evolution of securities firms, which is a process that is involving more and more mergers and takeovers, small to midsize firms usually become likely targets. They may not be adverse to being acquired, but some desire to maintain their identity, retain their present management structure, and receive enough compensation so that the entire process is worthwhile. These are not all the reasons that a midsize securities firm would agree to being acquired or to selling a portion of itself to a larger purchaser. However, they do represent important considerations that are often the stumbling blocks to successful mergers and takeovers of securities firms and other companies. Some of the major questions midsize securities firm management deals with on an ongoing basis in the merger or takeover option area are the following:

How to select, initiate, contract to, and successfully purchase other firms.

How to determine the best and most timely way to be acquired (partially or wholly) by a larger firm or other financial or corporate entity.

How to maintain the name and independence of the securities firm to the greatest extent possible.

How to discern an adequate financial rationale for being acquired.

Strategic decision making for midsize companies is particularly important in any industry, but it is especially so in the securities one. Because the industry is developing into one that is less homogeneous than it was many years ago and now has a number of financial giants doing a lion's share of the business, some of which are owned by much larger corporations or financial institutions, the small to midsize securities firms are being thrust into an increasingly competitive environment and, in many cases, do not have the resources to compete with the financial giants of today. Consequently, it is increasingly more important for these firms to develop an ongoing process of strategic decision making to achieve their optimum market niche in whatever businesses they select as the ones they either want to be in or believe are the ones in which they have some competitive edge. The larger strategic decisions, which usually involve developing their ongoing activities that often have been better developed by the major securities firms, are the kinds of decisions requiring careful forethought and analysis. For midsize securities firms, the entire strategic decision-making process of today and its relative success will foreshadow their future financial viability.

NOTES

1. Peter F. Drucker, *The Practice of Management* (New York: Harper & Row, 1986), p. 56.

2. Gordon Donaldson and Jay W. Lorsch, *Decision Making at the Top: The Shaping of Strategic Direction* (New York: Basic Books, 1983), p. 6. The authors state that their definition follows those of Kenneth K. Andrews, *The Concept of Corporate Strategy,* rev. ed. (Homewood, Ill.: Dow Jones-Irwin, 1980), pp. 18–21, and Henry Mintzberg, "Patterns in Strategy Formation," *Management Science* 24 (1978): 934–948.

3. Ibid., p. 9.

4. *The New York Times,* April 1, 1986.

CHAPTER 20

REORGANIZATION AS A MANAGEMENT TOOL

THE CONCEPT OF REORGANIZATION

One of the most unusually potent managerial tools for making change at a securities firm is the process of reorganization, which is essentially an in-house tactic employed for organizational development purposes often by top management and for strategic purposes. Any individual at any company who is faced with the prospect of a reorganization anticipates contending with an emotionally problematic and, in some cases, hair-raising experience. Questions such as, "Where do I fit in in this process?", "Who am I going to report to?", "How is it going to affect my income?", and "What is it going to do to our department?" are among the many issues that might come immediately to mind. The most significant question usually is, "Will it make any difference to the firm or to me as an individual?" Corporate reorganization of any dimension has been basically an organizational tool employed in wide-ranging forms, some of which result in job changes and restructuring at the very upper echelon of the organizations, but affecting most people's lives only marginally. Others have been so sweeping they overhauled and changed the organization dramatically.

As used in the securities firm, the reorganization process, employed at any level, assumes tremendous significance as one of the only management tools that can be effectively used to change the firm's nature and direction abruptly, largely through restructuring personnel responsibilities. What is important is that it can be made to seem totally reasonable from the perspective of individual promotion, better coordination, improved control, and better allocation of resources more directly toward client needs. To be sure, reorganization in the securities industry is often simply a "people mover," and, with little or no fanfare, the reorganization process can easily change a few reporting relationships so as to make departments work so much better than they have before that it is almost unlike reorganization in any other corporate business. It can also take place with a minimum of disruption.

When corporate restructuring happens in a securities firm, it usually does not result in the major kinds of alien relationships that occur in other corporations as a result of this process. This is so because most forms of reorganization are simply modifications of presently working relationships among securities firm business units within a department or division or, on a higher level, among division heads and their superiors. In the former situation, many of the small business units are interdependent and could already be working in close relative proximity with each other. In the latter situation, so little day-to-day control over departments and the small business units within them is exercised by those senior managers high within the securities firm's corporate hierarchy that changes at this level are more of a restructuring of relationships among the most senior staff to allocate firm resources better and provide broad-based direction from above for the departments and divisions. Viewed differently, reorganization in either case appears, and may actually be, a rational approach to dealing with what might be termed "people problems."

As a matter of fact, in corporate forms of organization such as securities firms with extreme degrees of functional specialization resulting in small business units and individual entrepreneurs having great autonomy, derived in part from a sort of perceived profit center atmosphere—from individual professionals to departments to divisions and to branches—reorganization may be the last, if not the only, major opportunity for organizational change. From a theoretical standpoint, organizational development, so important to the effective ongoing nature of corporate life, can be achieved reasonably and with some ease through reorganization at any level within the securities firm.

In their broadest form, corporate reorganizations have traditionally been focused on achieving efficiency, better reporting relationships, more cost-effective operations, and some improvement in the hierarchical structures of organizational life. To a somewhat lesser extent, but certainly in a great number of these cases, corporate restructurings or reorganizations have been designed to change the managers' respective responsibilities and thus place those with greater capabilities in the same positions. This has been an important aspect of corporate reorganization at most major companies.

In the securities industry, however, reorganizations are typically assuming more of the personnel-related function, designed to achieve better management or leadership at any organizational level. Indeed, at the securities firm, reorganizations now usually involve senior management's desire to put better and more knowledgeable people at the helm of departments and divisions. This is not to say that there has not been at least some accent on achieving efficiency and improving reporting relationships among other things, especially for many years when securities firms were much more compartmentalized and departmentalized, in large part, because of the profit center orientation of the firms that was altered when interdependence of the firm's functions began to result in mandates for better coordinative mechanisms. The slowly evolving dual nature of reorganization in securities firms, resulting from the need to restructure departments for all the traditional reasons as well as for the purpose of putting the best people in charge can be described through examples in the investment banking, capital markets, and products divisions.

INVESTMENT BANKING: CORPORATE AND PUBLIC FINANCE

Traditionally, the corporate finance and public finance departments at securities firms were seen and managed as separate organizational units, each having its own manager and usually reporting to different individuals. In some instances, there may have been an overall head of investment banking who supervised both corporate finance and public finance; but even in these cases, these departments were operated somewhat independently of one another. Perhaps the only area of the finance effort where there was some mixing of personnel through involvement on deals and the contacting and developing of clients was in the industrial development revenue bond and pollution control area before the Tax Reform Act of 1986. Securities issued in these forms came to market through governments or public agencies that served as conduits for the issues, the security for which were payments made either through leases, loans, or installment sales agreements by corporations.

In the wake of the Tax Reform Act of 1986, many firms on Wall Street reorganized their investment banking efforts by more closely aligning the corporate finance and public finance departments, either in whole or in part. The early moves in this direction came from coordinating the mortgage finance effort in the corporate finance department with the housing finance area of the public finance department to achieve better coordination and control of these activities, with a view to garnering clients which could issue either taxable or tax-exempt securities. Reorganization also occurred here because both finance departments had been in touch with developers involved in taxable and tax-exempt housing and mortgage financings.

Another area of investment banking departments that has seen a number of reorganizations at securities firms over recent years is the health care area. Once there was a notable division in the way securities firms sought health care business. The corporate finance departments had the mandate to develop their health care departments by working with corporate health care companies that issued taxable securities, while the public finance department sought health care business from public agencies and hospitals issuing tax-exempt securities through authorities or local governments of general jurisdiction. Because of the Tax Reform Act of 1986 as well as the changing nature of the health care industry, some securities firms restructured their health care efforts to accommodate a more wide-ranging group of activities under one organizational roof to service the changing needs of all health care issuers who have accomplished the issuance of securities in both tax-exempt and taxable modes.

At the departmental level, reorganization in the corporate and public finance departments has been fast and fierce in the last couple of years. Most notable has been the restructuring that has occurred in public finance departments at most securities houses. The ongoing public needs for increased governmental services of all basic types has spawned the development within the public finance departments of so-called infrastructure groups to assume new business efforts for transportation, water, education, wastewater, and other related revenue bond programs.

Although these reorganizations within the structure of the investment banking departments have been the immediate result of a developing need to service clients in different ways than before, either because of new tax legislation or the changing financial needs of the clients themselves, they have had, at their core, the need to place better people in charge. Reorganizations in all the above examples have been accomplished to shore up weak departments or develop others, thus allowing the best managers to take charge and restructuring the jobs of the ones whose departments or groups have not been accomplishing at the desired level of success.

CAPITAL MARKETS

In the capital markets arena, which principally covers equities, municipals, corporates, governments and mortgage-backed securities, and the trading, underwriting, and sales activity related to these product areas, there seems to be a number of new reporting relationships that have been accomplished by a reorganization effort in one form or another. At the higher management levels, the corporate and government bond areas sometimes have been subsumed under one manager who supervises all taxable fixed-income securities, as opposed to all the fixed-income areas reporting to a single individual who supervises taxable and tax-exempt fixed-income securities or even to the head of the capital markets group.

Even within any one of these product areas and their derivatives, such as corporate bond trading and the high-yield corporate bond desk respectively, there are a number of organizational options for different reporting relationships. The corporate bond area may be headed by a single individual who supervises the general corporate bond department as well as the newer high-yield bond area, or it could be split into two separate groups with a manager for each, and each manager reporting separately and directly to another higher level supervisor in the taxable fixed-income area or in the fixed-income securities department generally. There are also a number of possibilities for reporting relationships within the government and equity product areas. Once again, while restructurings and reorganization in the capital markets area are cloaked in a better coordinative way of doing business, the underlying rationale for the new structure may be, in the final analysis, a "people decision" because better management is seen to be one of the few significant ways to develop the specialized product areas and the small business units within the securities firm.

THE PRODUCTS DIVISION
AND SUPPORT AREAS

In the products division of the firm, which includes the marketing, origination, and service departments, there are myriad possible reporting relationships. Many firms, to be sure, have tried a number of these approaches; and as the quest continues to fill and meet customers' needs over the years ahead, many other reporting relationships will be tried and reorganizations will occur. Nevertheless, reorganizations in these areas are also implemented to put the best people in charge of the various product services departments, namely, those professionals who can handle the largest responsibility with the greatest expertise and vision, both of which are especially important for the management of the complex and diversified product areas in a securities firm.

MANAGEMENT AND REORGANIZATION

In short, the reorganization process in a securities firm serves up to managers an efficient way to provide for client needs better, to improve efficiency and coordination, and perhaps most important, to put the best people in charge. Reorganization can be fast and fierce in a securities firm, with a minimum amount of disruption, largely because, when explained properly, it can easily be legitimized because of the interdependency of the small business units, and in some cases, departments and divisions, and the resultant need for better organizational coordinative mechanisms. With little confusion and strain, reorganization can be used again when new management is brought up from inside or in from outside. Reorganization in the securities firm is thus perhaps one of the most important prerogatives of upper management and one of the most useful ones.

PART 5

RECRUITMENT AND PERSONNEL DEVELOPMENT

CHAPTER 21

THE FIRST STRIPES OF INVESTMENT BANKING: ABILITIES, DEVELOPMENT, AND TRAINING

ANALYSTS, SUMMER ASSOCIATES, AND ASSOCIATES

Perhaps the most sought after entry-level employment job in all of corporate America is one in investment banking at securities firms, in corporate finance, public finance, or securities sales and trading. The traditional conception of entry-level investment banking jobs is that they are available for graduate business school students after they finish their degree; interviewing takes place during their fourth term in business school, which occurs, for most students, during the spring of their second year. This is so for students seeking full-time associate-level jobs in investment banking, but entry into the field at that level can also come after employment by other firms whose business is either related or unrelated to investment banking and thus somewhat after an individual's business school experience. These, however, are not the only avenues open to young professionals seeking employment in the traditional areas of Wall Street's securities firms.

Since the mid-1970s, some firms have developed programs for those without advanced degrees. These are open to qualified candidates who hold only an undergraduate degree. An agreement is usually reached by the firm and the new employees that their term of employment will be for approximately two years, and then they will leave the firm, presumably to attend graduate business school. Many securities firms have also developed somewhat extensive summer programs for students who are between their first and second years in business school, so that this offers another opportunity for individuals to secure employment at a securities firm before they can be selected for full-time entry-level positions in one of the more traditional areas reserved for business school graduates.

Despite all these formal programs for students seeking employment in the investment banking field, surprisingly little is known about the activities occupying the early career years. Much of what goes on and the process of hiring individuals has been, like most other activities within investment banking firms, restricted to a word-of-mouth system. Perhaps most importantly, there is really no material available at the present time to show, in a relative amount of detail, what is expected of corporate finance and public finance associates during their training period as well as what should be their goals for development as investment bankers. Put differently, although these are some of the most sought after positions for highly capable, competitive, and entrepreneurial business school graduates and others, most of those seeking this kind of employment have only a vague knowledge of what is expected of them and what the positions involve.

THE THREE JOBS AND THEIR PURPOSES

All three entry-level positions—analyst, summer associate, and associate—have many things in common, such as the kinds of individuals who seek out these potential employment possibilities as well as what must be learned in the jobs and the kinds of activities that must be pursued. Firms have decidedly different views of what these jobs mean and how they monitor the activities and relative success of the individuals who hold these positions. The jobs, by their very nature, are as important to the firm and its professionals in the investment banking and capital markets areas as they are to the employees themselves. This stems in large part from the progressive nature of jobs as seen from the firm's perspective, and also as viewed through the eyes of senior professionals at other firms who may have the occasion to review resumés of individuals who have successfully completed a term of employment at one of their competitors in any one of these three positions. This is not to say that these positions are in any way pyramidal and that the success a new professional achieves in one necessarily correlates to success in another or can realistically be translated into an "edge" for a job in subsequent years. For all professionals involved in the investment banking business, or in any other business for that matter, employees bring two tangible attributes to the employment bargaining table—themselves and their track records.

The Position of Analyst

Of the three entry-level investment banking positions, the one of analyst is least understood and least publicized. A number of years ago, a few investment banking firms started programs whereby qualified recent undergraduate degree recipients could get a position at a securities firm, usually in the investment banking division. From the firm's standpoint, this was seen as a way to garner attention from students and schools long before the process of interviewing the M.B.A. graduates began. It was also a chance to monitor the progress of certain students who the investment banking firm believed might become potential candidates for full-time positions after business school and who also might be the industry's leaders in the years ahead. The positions were originally designed so that the analyst would spend two years at the firm and then go on to business school. In some ways, therefore, the positions were created to meet the requirements of many business schools that viewed formal business experience in the aftermath of receiving an undergraduate degree as an important aspect of an individual's application to their M.B.A. programs.

Many applicants believed that if some of the most sought after jobs for M.B.A.s were at investment banking firms, then it might be appropriate to receive their pre-business school training at those firms because, they might, as a result, have a better chance of getting into business schools and also of gaining employment at the investment banking firms after business school.

This is not illogical, but much of its logic depends on the success a given individual had in all of these endeavors. In any case, a host of Wall Street firms followed the leadership of the few who had established the analyst programs, and many firms today actively recruit analysts from the nation's undergraduate institutions.

The job of analyst is a somewhat amorphous one, partly because most analysts do not have any formal business-related experience or perhaps even course work and because much of the work involved in the investment banking area is learned through on-the-job training. This process is complicated by the fact that the analyst's position is limited in time at the firm, usually restricted to about two years. The job itself can be a progressive one over the two years analysts spend at the firms, and the degree of progression is very often dependent on their own abilities and the extent to which the full-time senior banking professionals and even the associates allow them to assume greater responsibility over time. Much of the work is in and of itself a learning experience, but a great deal of it involves the preparation of proposals and presentations for clients and potential ones and could involve some time-consuming administrative tasks. It can also require the preparation of detailed financial analyses for specific financing alternatives for a client and perhaps even a certain amount of client contact and new business work with associates in the department and senior banking professionals.

The Summer Associate Position

The summer associate position is generally viewed by securities firms and summer associates alike as the precursor to a full-time job in investment banking, either at the firm in which the summer associate was employed or at another securities firm. Because of this fact, the position of summer associate is usually a better publicized one, and some firms hiring associates full time in the investment banking departments through on-campus or off-campus interviews combine their interviewing process for summer associates with the one they do for full-time associates, usually during the spring semester or fourth term of students at the business schools. Competition for these positions is keen because they are generally considered a first step into investment banking, can help accustom the summer associate to work at these firms, and add an important element to their resumés for the time when they interview for full-time associate positions. In addition, over recent years most Wall Street firms in New York have established a collegial association whereby summer associates can visit each other's firms on a formal or informal basis and meet with personnel there. Very often there are collective meetings, lectures, and informal gatherings, all of which seem to spark some competition for the summer associates among the securities firms themselves. For those involved in the process, it is an interesting one, but it must be kept in mind that there are far fewer students who are able to receive offers for positions as summer associates than there are who ultimately receive offers for full-time associate positions later on in their business school experience.

Because most summer associates have a substantial amount of business school course work under their belts, they can usually become involved more easily in the corporate or public finance work typical of the investment banking arena than can analysts. Although there is not much formal training for summer associates beyond some basic work in relevant areas for individuals who may be involved in projects necessitating a specific type of knowledge, much attention is paid to summer associates at the securities firms. After a month or so, it is not unlikely that the full-time investment banking professionals would assign tasks requiring a moderate amount of responsibility and finance knowledge to these individuals who would be working under their direct supervision. In an unusual way, the summer associate program allows summer associates and full-time professionals to check each other out. All of this could, but does not necessarily, provide common ground for establishing relationships in the future, largely because most summer associates seem to end up being employed by a securities firm, if they choose to be. Whether or not the firm is the one at which they worked over the summer, they may be working with the people they have met during the summer on financings where they have clients in common or may be competing against them.

In short, the summer associate position is a good one for the associates as well as the firms employing them. It provides an opportunity for summer associates to get used to the firms and for the firms to get used to them; it offers a kind of common ground whereby summer associates can meet their counterparts at other firms and exchange information about the firms and the kinds of jobs available; it is an opportunity for summer associates to see if they really want to go into investment banking on a full-time basis after business school, or if the risks and hardships are simply not worth the rewards to them; and it also provides an opportunity for full-time professionals at the firms to monitor the work of the summer associates and to continue their relationship with the schools from which the summer associates were hired.

The Position of Associate

The position of an associate in an investment banking firm represents the very first open-ended full-time position designated for those individuals who would like to pursue a career in investment banking, whether in corporate or public finance or in securities sales or trading, and who have passed the necessary hurdles including the competitive process of interviewing, and in almost all cases, have received an M.B.A. or some other applicable advanced degree. The designation of the title "associate" is usually one conferred and held for a few years depending on the firm and the number of ranks it has under the vice president level. Some firms have only the ranks of associate and vice president, and others have the ranks of associate, assistant vice president (or associate vice president and sometimes both), and then the rank of vice president. In any event, the progression of associates up through those ranks or the relative success they have during the time when they are associates may be totally dependent on them as individuals vis-à-vis the department in which they are employed. There are really no set rules in this process. Somewhere during the time that these newly minted graduates are working at the associate level, they usually develop some type of specialty or area of expertise or interest and gravitate to that area through their own self-propulsion or through a formal or informal mandate by management. In most firms, associates are exposed to a number of senior people and a number of different areas within their investment banking departments during the first few years of employment. Some associates specialize immediately on joining their firm because they have expressed either a specific direction or have done related work in the field and are uninterested in becoming involved in any other banking area, and the firm agrees that it would probably be unnecessary or not useful for them to do so. These situations, however, are more the exception than the rule, and most associates are given a broad exposure to all the banking areas in the department in which they work and spend a good portion of their time developing the technical, and even social, skills necessary to become fully competent in investment banking or in securities sales and trading, if they are employed there.

The position of associate is as much a professional developmental one as it is one of a social indoctrination into the firm and its ways—the social mores, do's and don'ts, ups and downs, general processes, and personalities in the very specialized and competitive world of investment banking. As a result, many individuals who have gone through this stage generally agree that it is a formative one, both professionally and socially, and it is one to which different individuals adapt and are adept at in widely varying degrees. Although difficult to describe, the associate stage is also laden with expectations of how, what, and why things should be done in a certain way as viewed by both the clients and the senior professionals in the securities firm, and it takes a fair amount of mental gymnastics and adaptability, after many experiences, to learn the ways of the world in the field of investment banking. It is not possible to describe here all that could go on and all that needs to be learned and developed during the first few years of an individual's career as an investment banker. It might be useful, however, to discuss a conceptual framework of what is necessary in general to develop for professional and individual purposes in both corporate and public finance, and then to suggest what might be considered the various levels of development in those areas.

THE REQUISITE CAPABILITIES OF AN
INVESTMENT BANKER

Individuals entering the field of investment banking, and even those who have been in it for a couple of years, often have questions about the capabilities they must develop in order to succeed in the business and also about the levels of development to be passed in order to reach some degree of professional proficiency in the field, a concept that has usually not been explained well to them if it has been explained at all. Having an understanding of the requisite capabilities of an investment banker and the levels of development is important because, without a true understanding of them, most professionals will never develop fully as investment bankers.

As a result, each working day a new employee should have some knowledge of what an investment banker is and does and also what is required to achieve those ends. This is important because, conceptually speaking, investment banking or finance departments are only as good as their people, and their people are only as good, in relative terms, as the degree to which each has progressed through what might be considered the seven levels of an investment banker's development, and how well each has become adept at the required capabilities. Some of this material and these concepts are usually first exposed to the new investment banker through the firm's training programs, but this exposure is just the tip of the iceberg in terms of the need of investment bankers to work on their own capabilities and monitor their own development. All of this usually takes a few years.

There are basically five capabilities a new investment banker must develop to be successful in the field. These are delineated below, and although they may vary from firm to firm and department to department in both conception and design, they basically represent some very important capabilities in which investment bankers must have a firm grounding for them to be successful in the field. They are not the be-all and the end-all of investment banking, and many bankers have achieved notable success without being experts in some of these areas, while others have developed an expertise in areas beyond the scope of these five capabilities. As a theoretical framework for thinking about the field of investment banking, however, they offer some good benchmarks or guideposts bankers can use to monitor their progress. At the very least, a discussion of these should answer many basic questions about what new investment bankers are supposed to learn and what capabilities they should develop.

Technical Abilities

The early years of experience for investment bankers in a corporate finance department stress the development of the banker's professional and analytical capabilities through applications of more theoretical concepts in corporate finance to practical business situations. This process helps bridge the gap between the business school curriculum and the application of those principles to real world situations. Most of the analytical work has to do with equity, debt, and variations of these securities as applied to corporate decision making. Bankers must develop a fluency with financial statements and financial ratios as applied to particular industry groups of companies and specific companies themselves. Investment bankers are often asked to make comparisons of companies along the lines of financial characteristics so that industry trends can be discerned and comparative advantages and disadvantages of corporate strategy can be illuminated. Investment bankers are also required to develop a working knowledge of the cost of capital concepts and the comparative financial advantages of using different types of financial instruments for specific companies. This is a particularly important tool today because of the burgeoning number of different market-related debt and equity mechanisms that can be used to lower the cost of capital for those accessing the financial marketplace. Some of this work involves so-called "spreadsheet" analysis, and this has become a preoccupation of new investment bankers.

For investment bankers who begin specializing in particular industries early in their careers, and for others who desire to gain a broader understanding of different industries for their intellectual curiosity and also with the idea that they may have to specialize in a particular industry later on in their careers, a certain proportion of their time should be spent on studying some broad corporate banking issues. These include attempting to understand what makes particular industries tick, what the important aspects of strategic decision making at the corporate level are within certain industries, what the opportunities as well as the problems for a company within those industries are, and what the future holds for companies in specific industries as seen from a macroeconomic and financial environmental perspective. Some of this analysis has global dimensions, but for new investment bankers, it is particularly important to develop a wide-ranging knowledge of a number of industries so that they might apply concepts and tools from corporations in one industry to those in another and also show clients a breadth of understanding about corporations nationwide and worldwide. Also, the creation of new types of securities over recent years through the collateralization or securitization of different kinds of investment vehicles has created a new market of which the investment banker must develop an understanding and knowledge. Bankers must become familiar with asset and mortgage-backed securities, leasing arrangements, and all kinds of securitized investment vehicles. An in-depth understanding is not necessary, but a fluency with the concepts involved in each and a general overview of their marketplace is important in grasping the essence of these new financial concepts in the corporate world.

The professional and analytical capabilities that must be developed by investment bankers entering the field of public finance is somewhat different from those required in the corporate finance arena. Public finance professionals do not really deal with companies that have the ability to issue stocks and all different types of investment vehicles. Government entities with which public finance bankers deal usually issue only debt or short-term investment vehicles as well as some new securities options for particular projects, either new or existing ones. Consequently, public finance investment bankers must develop a knowledge of project-type financial arrangements, including their financial viability, which usually entails understanding the security, credit, feasibility, cash flow, and other types of revenue bond analytical tools. This requires a working knowledge of all types of revenue bonds and the concepts involved in making the securities issued by these entities ratable, sellable, and purchasable. For most public finance investment bankers, this follows an understanding of general obligation bond issuers and an economic and financial analysis of them. All of this is usually a precursor to the specialization in particular revenue bond areas by public finance investment bankers. The knowledge thus acquired provides the investment banker with the foundation on which to impart financial advice.

Understanding the Structural Finance Framework

An investment banker must also develop an understanding of the regulatory framework and documentary parameters in which securities are issued. Bankers in the corporate finance area must be schooled in due diligence procedures as well as the legal requirements for securities offerings which include federal and state laws, NASD (National Association of Securities Dealers) and NYSE (New York Stock Exchange) regulations, and SEC (Securities and Exchange Commission) requirements, among others. They must develop a capability to write and understand term sheets, indentures, subordination agreements, contracts, leases, and loans, and to explain the debt and equity structure of companies. Some of this work entails the commitment to memory of regularized procedures, but other tasks involve applying the banker's own creativity to explain a company's finances to investors and others through the documents required in securities offerings.

The public finance investment banking business places an unusual emphasis on the documentary foundations of a bond issue, and therefore a thorough grounding in understanding, developing, writing, and explaining the documents behind a public finance underwriting is particularly important in this area. Much of the negotiated public finance investment banking business is, for lack of a better description, indenture driven, and the document work required for such municipal bond offerings, which include summaries of all the material as part of the foresection of the official statement, are the backbone of the municipal bond industry. These documents may include: the indentures of trust, loan agreements, lease agreements, other types of contracts, bond resolutions, supplemental resolutions, and bond purchase agreements. Most issuers have the ability to, and indeed do, use many of these documents as part of their financing program, especially in the revenue bond area. The documents can be extremely complex and also run hundreds of pages, so that writing and understanding them requires an expertise developed over time, but it is critical to the field of public finance.

Investment bankers in this area must also understand the regulatory framework in which they operate. Much of this today is rooted in federal and state laws, requirements by some regulatory agencies, the Municipal Securities Rulemaking Board, and recent strictures laid down by the Tax Reform Act of 1986. Nevertheless, the emphasis here is on the documentary foundations of the public finance business; and it is worth noting that, although the kinds of documents are generally the same for most revenue bond issuers, the particulars involved for each type of revenue bond may vary widely. As a result, while some of this knowledge may be transferable from one revenue bond category to another, most investment bankers must develop a working knowledge of each area's documents separately.

Computer-Related Knowledge

Most individuals entering the field of investment banking have been exposed to the use of the computer, specifically the personal computer, and the software used on this computer has appliations for finance concepts and models. It has been found, however, that exposure to these hardware and software tools does not necessarily translate into a user's ability to apply them to work in an investment banking firm. As a result, most new investment bankers spend a good amount of their time developing a computer capability that directly pertains to the kinds of work they must do. Some investment bankers end up developing such a keen interest or unusual ability to do this type of work that they remain within the computer group of their investment banking department for years. This may not sound like a goal to which all new investment bankers should, would, or could aspire, but it does underscore the importance of computer-related work for today's financings in the investment banking world. Indeed, much business is either won or lost by investment banking departments because of their expertise, or lack of it, in the computer-related financing areas.

Computer work in the corporate finance business usually involves the development and application of financing techniques. This includes measuring the relative value of different financial alternatives and their cost of capital, including present value analyses under a variety of circumstances. Computer software tools can be applied to spreadsheet analysis and to the comparative evaluations that must be made of company financials when different accounting concepts are involved. Sophisticated computer work can be done to predict changes in a company's financial ratios with the projected use of different financing vehicles. Much of the corporate finance computer-related work, however, involves the cost analysis of different financial options with a series of built-in assumptions, any of which can change over time, and under different scenarios, and the computer models can spew forth various results on a comparative basis.

Public finance computer work can range from the production debt service schedules to such complicated analyses as crossover refundings. The complexity of the work is reinforced by the fact that most long-term municipal bond issues come to market with serial and term maturities, and there are a seemingly endless potential number of structuring possibilities, all of which must be designed to curry the interest of investors, while the issuer must be capable of making the required amounts of debt service payments to comply with provisions in the bond indenture. Particular types of bond issues often have extremely complex cash flows that require high-level computer expertise, and some investment bankers specialize in these kinds of areas. In today's investment banking world, a knowledge of the computer and its application to corporate and public finance work is a necessity.

Knowledge of New Financing Vehicles

The volcanic surge of newly created financing mechanisms used by corporations and governments has resulted in the need of investment bankers to be thoroughly conversant with these financing alternatives. Very often, as noted earlier, the appropriate application of them to issuing entities in particular circumstances could mean the difference between getting the business or not. In most competitive situations in today's investment banking world, an understanding of most of them, together with an unusual, and perhaps a somewhat proprietary, new financing concept, only allows you into the competitive arena. After that, the issuer, be it a corporation or a government, makes the final decision of who will be its investment bankers and what financing techniques will be employed. In any event, investment bankers in both corporate and public finance must have a working knowledge of these financing techniques, alternatives, and mechanisms.

In the corporate finance arena, the more notable and recent ones employed include interest rate swaps, hedging techniques, the use of futures and options, and money multiplier securities. There are a whole host of other types of mechanisms, and they seem to be growing by the day, so that the enumeration of them here could become an exercise in futility. The point, however, is that they have become an important part of the investment banking marketplace, and more than that, they are an especially significant new business tool.

In public finance investment banking, there has also been a tremendous growth in what might be called "market-related debt mechanisms." These include variable rate securities, put option bonds, zero coupon bonds, interest rate swaps, hedging techniques, and other investment vehicles, which could be grafted onto the traditional means of issuing bonds in the municipal industry through serial and term maturities. Many municipal bond issues have used liquidity or credit enhancements as part of their security mechanisms, providing the issuer with all types of options and alternatives from which to choose. This also provides investment bankers with a financial alternative forum from which to give issuers advice tailored to their own situation. Here too, just as in the corporate finance arena, market-related debt mechanisms, some proprietary in nature and others not, have been used successfully as new business tools in public finance over recent years. Indeed, investment banking in general has gotten far away from the more traditional types of securities offerings that came to market in similar form and were called "plain vanilla" financings.

Social Abilities

Perhaps more than anything else, the investment banking business is a people business, and the client–investment banker relationship may be as much a personal one as it is a professional one. Investment bankers, like physicians, are individuals to whom companies or governments turn when they are in need of health advice, financial or otherwise. Although many corporations and governments have built up in-house staffs to assume a small amount of this responsibility, usually held to be within the purview of the investment banker's mandate, the vast proportion of financial advice and capital markets-related information is handled for companies and governments by investment bankers. It is these individuals who, aside from being in daily contact with the securities markets and thus having an unusually large amount of information about the financial marketplace, provide for the long-term financial health of companies and governments. No other individuals and very few professionals are in a position to do so. Investment bankers' constant contact with the markets, the rating agencies, similar issuers, and a bevy of ideas and financing possibilities make these bankers uniquely important commodities to corporations and governments alike. Like physicians, however, there are some doctors to whom, despite their wide-ranging knowledge and expertise in their specific fields, we do not turn for some reason, however qualitative and difficult to describe. Conversely, there are others to whom we gravitate, whom we trust, and with whom we would like to deal for the rest of our lives, their notoriety notwithstanding.

As a result, the social abilities of an investment banker, however broadly defined, must be developed if they are to be as successful as possible. There are probably a number of these traits that are definable and necessary to foster for any individual in an advisory situation. There are other particularly important ones in the world of investment banking, as there probably are in many other fields or professions. Yet, they seem to be especially vital to the successful development of investment bankers, as much for what they do for the client as for what they say about those who have been able to develop these traits.

As a number one priority, investment bankers must develop an ability to cultivate both respect and trust. Investment bankers must engender respect, for their own professional capabilities and for what they are as human beings. Equally important, investment bankers must be trusted colleagues of their clients and must be individuals whom the client can trust with the very survival of their company or government. To clients, these two traits represent the confidence they have in their investment bankers, and this underscores the confidentiality in business dealings that must necessarily flow from these types of relationships. It is not easy for any individual to develop the abilities to be respected and be trusted, but in investment banking, they are usually critical to the long-run success of a banker.

Like any people-oriented business, the field of investment banking requires that its professionals do a substantial amount of speaking to clients in a variety of circumstances. Sometimes this involves giving formal addresses to boards of directors of companies or groups of corporate leaders. In other instances, it may be necessary for investment bankers to give presentations in competition with bankers from other firms to managers of corporations or officials of governments or revenue authorities. Sometimes bankers must become involved as speakers or panelists in company or industrywide functions or at association meetings of government officials. It goes without saying, therefore, that most investment bankers must be good public speakers, whatever their method of doing so and whatever the forum.

More than that, however, there is another type of speaking in which investment bankers must develop a proficiency, although it is not usually thought of in the same vein or in the same frame of reference as public speaking. This type of communication involves private speaking or the ability to communicate effectively with another individual on a one-to-one basis. This may sound trite because each of us everyday communicates to others in one-on-one relationships. When an individual is in an advisory capacity, however, such as the one in which an investment banker is, the ability to convey one's thought, opinions, advice, and even personality in a thoroughly acceptable and understandable way assumes a significance that runs far beyond the nonchalant relationships we usually have with other colleagues or professionals. To carry this discussion one step further, it is very often not only what somebody says that is so important or makes the difference between continuing a relationship with that individual or cutting it off, but also how one says it that could assume much greater importance immediately and over time.

Another trait that investment bankers must develop is somewhat related to this. It is a sense of what clients are not saying when they are speaking. This is not easy to do, but if individuals are to become truly successful in almost any profession, especially in the field of investment banking, it is important to develop. Perhaps this comes through an understanding of body language, voice intonation, the ability to delicately probe individuals about what they are saying or what was meant without transgressing a boundary of thought or words created by individuals where they do not want others to trespass. Perhaps an important part of this ability is the development of an individual's native or innate intuition. As many will suggest, intuition is a function of experience and other perceptible factors that come into play during a communicative experience with another individual. Suffice it to say that understanding what clients may not be saying is the culmination of a developmental process both for the banker and for the client–banker relationship.

Not every investment banker will be able to become totally proficient in all these five areas. Nor may it be necessary that they do so. Different individuals will gravitate to different areas and develop varying levels of proficiency. Others will "stick to their knitting" and become extremely successful in just one of these areas. Let there be no mistake, however, without a strong grounding in all five capabilities, an individual's success as an investment banker will be limited.

THE LEVELS OF DEVELOPMENT

There are really no defined levels of development in the process of individuals becoming successful investment bankers. There are no set job descriptions that coincide with different ranks, nor are there specified jobs into which investment bankers can normally fit, either when they are within a given organization or are hired into a different one from the outside. Nevertheless, there seem to be approximately seven distinct groups of investment banking skills which, while not necessarily hierarchically based, do have a measure of ordinal ranking to them.

    1. *Proposal Writing.* The most basic investment banking function and the one usually assigned to new bankers is the writing of proposals for potential clients and for existing ones when either new financing alternatives are being suggested or when clients are intending to interview a number of firms in an effort to review their relationships with them or begin using them as advisors or underwriters. Some of this work involves putting together "boiler-plate" material for the presentation booklet, which in some cases can run hundreds of pages. A certain percentage of the work also involves the development and supervision of the presentation of financial advice. Usually a few associates work on a single proposal under the direction of perhaps a senior associate or a vice president. In some cases, the proposal work is actually for an individual who is in the general category of managing director or close to it and is the one who usually signs the letter on the proposal. Working on these proposals can certainly be tedious, and when done under time constraints, which is usually the case, can result in an exhausting effort at best. What this type of work does do for new investment bankers is provide them with a broad view of the firm and what the investment banking department believes is important to present to the client. It also gets the investment banker involved in the development of financial recommenda-

tions. This forms the basis of the investment banker's development in the area of providing professional banking advice to clients.

2. *Computer Work.* As an offshoot of an investment banker's work on the more general aspects of the proposal comes work in the computer-related area of providing financial recommendations. This does not necessarily mean that the investment banker transfers to the computer group if there is one. It does mean that the investment banker becomes accustomed to generating the kind of numbers and other computer-based material to support the financial recommendations or alternatives that are ultimately presented to the client or potential one. This is a step up from proposal writing and begins to involve the new investment banker in the "nitty gritty" of providing professional investment banking services.

3. *Comanager Deal Processing.* This next level of development puts the investment banker in contact with the client. In this particular role, the investment banker is a comanager on an upcoming financing and helps oversee the development of the documents with the senior manager, lawyers, and other comanagers. The role is not as large as that of the senior manager, but it does provide the banker with an overview of the entire securities issuing process, from setting up a schedule, to allocating responsibilities, to receiving feedback on documents and major issues, to providing the client with market-related data on a consistent basis, to working with a large number of parties involved in the deal, to establishing a successful working relationship with the senior manager and the company or government. In most instances, the investment banker assigned to a deal as a comanager is the firm's contact point until the pricing of the deal, and sometimes during it, from the standpoint of relations with the company or government. In this capacity, the investment banker works closely with the firm's underwriting department and those of the transaction's other managers.

4. *Senior Manager Deal Processing.* As a senior manager on a financing, the investment banker is in a much sought-after role. Not only is the senior manager the investment banker or firm to which client looks for financial advice but is also the one whom the client expects to provide most market-related information pertinent to the deal. The senior manager is also, with the advice and consent of the client, the court of last resort for the scheduling and timing of the issue, structuring of it, and the pricing strategy; is the point of contact for all deal-related questions; and is thus the apex of the decision-making process about the issue itself. In the role of senior manager, the investment banker gets a chance to participate in the entire deal-making process from a position of substantial responsibility, making it the next level of development for an investment banker.

    5. *Providing Basic Financial Advice.* Some consider the ability to provide clients with basic, sound financial advice as the next level of an investment banker's development, while others consider it to be on a par with the ability of a banker to be a manager of any financing. Providing financial advice to issuers, either on an on-the-spot basis or after a short period of time allowed to the investment banker to formulate some opinions, is not necessarily a capability of every investment banker who can manage any financing, although more often than not, it is. There are, however, some investment bankers in every department who are the type of individuals with the intellectual capacity and professional experience to provide sound financial advice and financing alternatives on a consistent basis to clients of the department and potential ones, either directly or through other investment bankers within the department who are in more contact with the clients themselves. This is not necessarily an area to which every investment banker gravitates, nor is it an ability every investment banker will ultimately develop. Many bankers can do this fairly well, however.

    6. *Providing Creative Financial Advice.* Few individuals in an investment banking department, be it corporate or public finance, have the capability of providing clients with truly creative financial advice, largely because such advice comes along once in a very long while. Some investment banking departments do have one or two individuals who have this capability and do it on an ongoing basis, thus acting as their department's standard bearers. These professionals are given the most difficult financial problems to solve, and they usually work with the department's largest and most important clients. Very often they are intimately involved in the details of difficult financings, whether they be market related or concerned with the issuer's credit rating. These bankers may have all backgrounds and abilities, ranging from mathematical to conceptual to legal or even to accounting or engineering. Whatever the case, they represent an unusual group in the investment banking arena; and while not many investment bankers can successfully reach this level of achievement, it is certainly important for all of them to understand the thought processes and financial suggestions provided by this type of individual.

7. *The New Business Professional.* Very few investment bankers in any department are real new business professionals or "rain makers." If that were the case, every banker would be bringing in deals, and there would be no one to work on them, process them, or try to get new ones. To some extent, every investment banker is in fact involved in the new business activities of a department, to a greater or lesser degree. Only few investment bankers, however, can bring clients to the firm on a consistent basis. In many ways, all six levels of development mentioned above lead naturally to this one. This, however, is a theoretical statement only. For some reason, certain individuals have an ability to bring in new business, while others simply do not. Of those who can, each has developed a different level of expertise in different areas, so that there are really no set abilities an individual must have to do this, aside from the obvious, which requires the banker to be professionally astute and socially adept.

THE INVESTMENT BANKING TRAINING PROGRAMS

Training programs at investment banks differ widely from one another. Some training programs are large and structured, while others are small because of the size of the class of new investment bankers and are of a short duration. In these instances, most of the training is done on a one-to-one basis, with investment bankers working with the new recruits. Most training programs have classes that bridge the gap between business school and the working world of the securities industry both in style and substance. In one form or another, analysts and associates alike must develop a working knowledge of financial concepts and the extent to which they are applied in corporate and public finance. In addition, they must have some exposure to the sales, trading, and underwriting departments of their respective capital markets divisions. (Training for summer associates is much abbreviated and usually encompasses some of the same material presented in the regular associate training classes.) The following discussion therefore provides a description of the kinds of concepts presented in most training programs for corporate and public finance investment banking analysts and associates.

The Analyst Training Programs

It is generally assumed that when individuals join an investment banking department as analysts, they are relatively unfamiliar with the basic financial concepts employed in either the public or corporate finance business. Most analysts are hired directly out of college, and as a result, only a few have had significant courses in finance or business, although some have undoubtedly had some exposure to these areas. Because analysts will usually be with the investment banking firm for approximately two years, the firm often sees fit to provide a relatively comprehensive but short training program for these individuals. Very often, this training program is piggy-backed onto the one designed for associates, so that analysts start the training program slightly ahead of the associates. When the associates begin their program, analysts may join for a small portion of it, although this varies from firm to firm. In some firms, the corporate finance and public finance analysts are lumped together for the initial stages of the training program. Later on, they are separated and given some hands-on experience in the areas in which each would be working. This results in corporate finance and public finance analysts having some exposure to the concepts and financial tools required of each other, but this is seen as a positive rather than a negative feature of the programs. This is so largely because corporate and public finance investment bankers do work on financings together, whether they are of the project type or in specific revenue bond areas where the underlying credit may be a company or the entire deal itself may be a taxable one. These kinds of relationships support the trend on Wall Street to develop closer working relationships between the corporate and public finance departments in investment banking.

There are some basic corporate finance concepts to which the analyst must be exposed, and it is worth listing a few of them to provide a flavor of the kind of material that must be digested in the early stages of an investment banker's career. Classes or group discussions for analysts may include the following topics: corporate financial reporting, including balance sheets, income statements, and resultant financial ratios; bond mathematics; the time value of money; present value securities analysis; financial forecasting; pro forma financial statements; and spreadsheets. Special additional classes are given to corporate finance analysts in basic computer work, including graphing and the use of software programs applicable to the corporate finance business.

Analysts in the public finance department usually participate in the corporate finance analysts' training program, but they also have their own training activities more applicable to the municipal bond business. Public finance analysts are given a broad exposure to municipal budgeting and the analysis of state and local financial statements. Emphasis is placed on the economic and financial underpinnings of state and municipal credits before tackling the different types of revenue bond issuers that usually come to market on a negotiated basis and thus require the expertise of public finance investment bankers. Analysts are then expected to develop a broad understanding of the different kinds of revenue bonds, such as those issued for public power, housing, hospitals, water and wastewater, and transportation purposes. Each has its own intricacies and unusual characteristics, and each requires a special understanding of the competitive milieu in which the project is operated, as well as the kinds of engineering and financial feasibility studies that form the basis of the project's development. Furthermore, the analyst must become familiar with the different financial ratios used in public finance investment banking and how each applies to the different types of revenue bonds. These include the debt service coverage ratio, the debt service safety margin, the debt ratio, the net take-down, the operating ratio, and the interest coverage ratio. Analysts are also expected to become accustomed to working with the computer and be able to use it to develop debt service schedules and some basic refunding analyses. Both corporate and public analysts are also given some exposure to trading, underwriting, and sales activities, both institutional and retail, in order to acquaint them better with the market-related aspects of the corporate and public finance business.

The Associate Training Programs

The training program for associates in investment banking at securities firms can be a rigorous one, and in some firms, can last for three to six months or more. The basis for the training program is usually a month or two of regularized classroom work. At some firms, this classroom situation can last longer, and in others, it can last equally as long but not necessarily on an eight- to ten-hour a day basis. Once again the corporate and public finance associates usually train together, and after a while, they then break up into their respective groups and work on follow-up activities separately with their own corporate and public finance departments. During this process, associates are usually required to take the necessary regulatory examinations so that they can be fully active participants in the activities of the securities firm. In addition, both corporate and public finance associates spend a significant amount of time on the trading, underwriting, and sales desks of their departments, and sometimes, for introductory purposes, work with the somewhat related capital markets departments, such as government bonds, and other areas in which their banking departments are not wholly involved.

 Classroom work for corporate finance associates attempts to bridge the gap between the type of knowledge acquired in business school and the application of this educational experience to the practical skills required to tackle investment banking problems in the real financial world. Among the topics covered in the corporate finance investment banking training program are:

securities offerings; due diligence procedures; the marketing of the firm and the department; a detailed analysis of the pricing of a securities issue; and explanations of how to work with investors of all types. More conceptual training program topics that can be applied to providing companies with financial advice include developing business, financial strategy, creating wealth for shareholders, evaluating returns on equity and earnings per share of companies under various economic and financial scenarios vis-à-vis the company's business strategy. Associates are also given some broad exposure to the various kinds of financial instruments that they may have occasion to discuss or use. These include collateralized securities, money market instruments, convertible securities, and an array of different types of instruments, which could be issued by corporations and other entities.

The training program also covers all types of new financing vehicles in some depth because of the need of investment bankers to become conversant with these instruments as part of their new business efforts. Moreover, associates are exposed to information on the broad industry groups with which investment bankers have occasion to work. These groups of companies include utilities, financial institutions, emerging growth companies, service-oriented corporations, other nonindustrial companies, and corporations with a broader international business. Finally, associates spend a significant portion of their time developing an advanced computer capability, which helps them apply the concepts learned in the training program to manufactured and real-life examples so as to better prepare them for the time when they will be requested to do this type of work for clients and potential ones.

The kind of training provided investment bankers in the public finance area really does not bridge the gap between the knowledge they acquired in school and the application of that education to problems and issues of government entities seeking to issue securities in the capital markets. This is the case largely because there is really no gap to fill; at the present time, there are hardly any courses in public finance investment banking at any school in the country. To be sure, some schools, particularly those that offer master's degrees in public administration, do provide some course work relevant to the public finance field. Some business schools also have sections or portions of their investment banking courses dealing with the municipal securities market. These graduate curricula, together with others in the economics, political science, and the public policy area disciplines do have a few courses relating to the kinds of activities in which government officials become involved when their needs center on the raising of funds through the issuance of municipal securities. Nevertheless, there is hardly a single course given at any school that deals totally with the investment banking field as it relates to public finance and municipal bonds. Consequently, the type of training required of individuals who are at the entry level in the field of public finance at securities firms requires a sort of bootstrap approach to skill development and knowledge acquisition in this area.

As a result, the type of training that must be provided to new investment bankers in the public finance area must be at once conceptually sophisticated and also understandable and practical. If the material is presented in a classroom setting, most firms divide the sections along the lines of the different categories of municipal bonds in the marketplace, such as general obligation bonds, including state and local credits, and the various types of revenue bonds including housing, public power, transportation, and other types of securities. The new investment banker is given the opportunity to review and study official statements representing these types of bond issues, and a substantial amount of time is spent by the senior staff in helping the associates understand the conceptual aspects and practical considerations in successfully bringing a bond issue of each type to market.

The development of new financial vehicles in the municipal bond market has led public finance training programs to allocate a substantial amount of time to exposing associates to those brought to market over recent years. In addition, credit enhancements and municipal bond insurance have been important elements of many financings for issuers who employ these tools in order to receive a higher rating and thus lower their interest costs, so that training programs have set aside a certain amount of time to explain the use of these instruments to associates.

Finally, because municipal bond issues require relatively heavy documentation, a substantial amount of time is spent going over what is required in the documents of each type of bond issue. Also, in the case of corporate finance associates, public finance trainees spend perhaps two to three months working with the computer on all types of functions related to public finance work.

The Firm's Interest

Training new employees at an investment banking firm is a complex process, but for new employees and for the firms themselves, it is a most important activity for professionals at the firm. Many consider new recruits as the life blood of the investment banking effort at securities firms, and many firms do not seek senior people from competitors, but rather prefer to "grow their own." Consequently, most firms spend a tremendous amount of time working with new employees at all levels in the investment banking area. Rather than think of this time spent as a period of lost opportunity costs to the firm, most senior investment banking professionals believe it to be an increasingly important part of their overall professional activities.

CHAPTER 22

HOW TO INTERVIEW WITH AN INVESTMENT BANK

The question of how to interview itself is a classic one for those seeking employment anywhere at any time. Certainly there have been enough articles and books written about the subject to fill the library of any individual truly interested in this technique many believe to be more of an art than a science. Interviewing at an investment banking firm, however, is notable for two other important reasons. The first is the small number of individuals ultimately securing an offer among all who are interested and have been interviewed. Investment banking firms have been known to interview literally hundreds of candidates from the nation's top business schools and select only a small group to whom they will finally give offers of employment. Secondly, interviewing at an investment bank is in fact noticeably different from interviewing at other corporate entities and nonprofit institutions. This is not to say that those who are successful at the latter may not be successful at the former, or vice versa, but the individuals who are ultimately selected by the investment banking firms are often somewhat different from those who are not. The process itself is also usually different; it is longer, more involved, certainly highly competitive, and designed to isolate those who will be successful. The people selected will hopefully not only be able to develop the intellectual talents to set them apart from others nationwide in perhaps the most competitive business in the world but also will be able to cultivate the social abilities with which to garner clients and, most importantly, to keep them. Very broadly speaking, these are the kinds of characteristics, both individual and professional, most employees seek. But the nature of the investment banking business, in corporate finance, in public finance, and in sales and trading, is such that it caters to only a certain individual, and ultimately, it is that type of individual who will be successful in the field and even enjoy the business.

There are basically two types of jobs considered to be available for entry-level employment in an investment bank. One is in the investment banking firm's finance departments, either in corporate finance or in public finance; the other is in securities sales or trading. Most investment banking firms have separate interviewing processes for corporate and public finance, and many solicit those interested in sales or trading positions at the same time and through the same process. Even though some interviewees will ultimately go into a firm's sales or trading departments, the initial contacts are usually made through the firm's public or corporate finance departments. These areas usually have larger ongoing recruiting programs than the sales and trading areas, and firms often find it easier to recruit through established programs in finance than to recruit separately for sales and trading positions, although certain firms have well-established dual recruiting processes in both finance and sales and trading.

Once individuals have reached the stage of interviewing at an investment bank, obviously little can be done to change their scholastic history and previous employment record. There are, however, a number of ways the interviewees can improve their chances of being among the few selected for the extension of an employment offer. Rather than discuss these in terms of do's and don'ts, ten do's are emphasized. They represent a composite picture of what many believe are important characteristics investment banking firms look for in potential employees at the entry level, whether in corporate finance, public finance, sales, or trading, although there are some differences among these. The attributes delineated here, to be sure, are not intended to be all inclusive, and certainly not to be representative of any particular investment banking firm or any individual interviewer or candidate. They are only intended to be helpful comments and suggestions so that those who are being interviewed can put their best foot forward during what many consider to be a long and arduous process, and perhaps the most important one of their lives up to that date. These characteristics are divided into ten discrete areas.

1. *Direction.*   Perhaps one of the most important characteristics an interviewee must exhibit when seeking employment in an investment bank is to show a sincere interest in the investment banking business and that the direction of their career points towards investment banking for the foreseeable future. Some interviewees have gone far in the interviewing process to show that their background, education, work experience, and overall interest point to investment banking, and as a result, they have built up directional momentum towards investment banking as a career. This type of self-proclaimed direction is not a prerequisite, but it does help in the interviewing process. This is not to say that those individuals seeking employment have to show, beyond a shadow of a doubt, that they decided on investment banking as a career at birth. Indeed, some of the most appealing interview candidates, and some of the most successful investment bankers, have had interests and previous work experiences totally alien to the investment banking business. As a matter of fact, there are many fields through which individuals can acquire personality attributes, different skills, other interests, and even technical knowledge that are not in any way related to the securities industry but useful for work in it. Government service, consulting experience, accounting work, and engineering employment are some notable examples.

Nevertheless, the reason a candidate should show at least some strong degree of direction towards investment banking as a career is that it provides those ultimately making the selection of these candidates with two important elements to the process that have long-term benefits. The first is that those with the greater degree of direction toward the business are less likely to leave it and thus cost the firm that has employed them tremendous expenses in training them and lost opportunities during the recruit's early years, which were required to help the new banker develop successfully. Second, those individuals with a sincere interest in any business are more likely to put forth as much effort as possible to achieve success in the business, ultimately resulting in additional efforts on behalf of the investment banking firm employing them. In any event, those individuals interviewing for entry-level investment banking positions should certainly attempt to show some kind of sincere interest, desire, and direction toward investment banking as a career, as other individuals would show when interviewing in different types of businesses.

2. *Controlled Aggression.* It is no secret that in the competitive business environment of today most, if not all, employers seek aggressive individuals as future employees so that their firm is able to meet that competitive challenge. With competition in the securities industry as perhaps the fiercest in the business world, it is not surprising that securities firms also have developed a keen interest in seeking and hiring aggressive professionals. Aggressiveness, however, can be a two-edged sword. In their zeal to show this competitive drive, many applicants have in fact oversold their aggressiveness in the interview setting, and this has, not surprisingly, worked to their disadvantage.

Aggressiveness, to be sure, can turn people on, but it can turn people off equally as quickly. Many clients have found the aggressiveness of institutions and individuals who service them to be more than they can handle on a long-term basis. As a result, some clients have turned their cheek to continually aggressive behavior on the part of those with whom they are expected to work. Similarly, and on a more personal basis, there is only so much aggression an interviewer can take in a given interview situation before the interviewer wants to leave. Consequently, one of the key abilities for interviewees with investment banking firms to develop is the wherewithal not only to show the interviewer that they are determined, competitive, and aggressive enough to compete in the toughest of arenas, but also that they have developed the capability to control their aggression, and thus make their behavior palatable to clients over the long haul.

3. *Sense of Humor.* Perhaps the most unsung personality trait interviewers look for in many business areas is a sense of humor. At best, those individuals with a sense of humor probably do not take themselves so seriously that they alienate others around them, and very often, this can prevent a difficult situation within the office or with clients from deteriorating into a serious conflict. At worst, those without at least some sense of humor may be, for lack of a better description, simply boring. To carry this rule one step further, no interviewer wants to be bored. Interviewers have said that they could not even make the candidate smile. This is not to say that interviewees should have a monologue ready for the interview or that banking professionals go around cracking jokes during the pricing sessions of deals or perform slapstick stunts during document sessions. Those may be descriptions of individuals who some consider to have a certain type of sense of humor, but this kind of activity is not likely to be appreciated in an investment bank.

Nonetheless, the investment banking business, like many others, is a people business. One of the most important personality characteristics of individuals that quite often makes them likable, understandable, and like "real people" is a sense of humor. Interestingly, one of the most important traits men and women look for in potential dates or partners is a sense of humor. If a sense of humor is so very important in those kinds of relationships, there is no reason why it should not be equally as important with those, and to those, individuals with whom people work throughout the day.

4. *Nonargumentative.* One of the more important reasons why some individuals are not given job offers at investment banks is that they wind up unexpectedly in a modest argument with the interviewer. Quite often, the interviews at an investment banking firm are of such a long duration and of such depth that the conversation leads to political matters, public policy questions, corporate financing alternatives, political economy, or even world affairs and international politics. With interviewers in the proverbial driver's seat, very often questions are posed to the candidates that not only have no right or wrong answer, but that could also have answers not likely to jibe with the position or beliefs of the interviewer. As the conversation moves forward, divergent views become even more pronounced and therein lies the potential for problems.

It is very important that interviewees handle this situation delicately, deftly, and with a degree of sophistication and understanding as to what the dynamics of the situation and the particulars of the topic under discussion are and how they might be interpreted by the interviewer. In some ways, this mental and verbal agility required of candidates means that they must have acquired a sixth sense about reading people and must have developed an ability to deal with these situations. This is not to say that interviewees should remain passive, agree with the interviewer, and in effect, become "yes people." This strategy is likely to boomerang. What it does require, however, is that interviewees present their case in a subtly persuasive manner, perhaps even posing ideas as questions to the interviewer to elicit the interviewer's opinion.

What these difficult situations show is whether or not individuals being interviewed have the ability to make their points delicately and in a inoffensive manner to another individual who has a different opinion or position. In effect, then, these situations point up candidates' ability to sell advice successfully or at least make a position understandable to one who does not share that point of view or belief. These skills are very important in a service-oriented people business such as investment banking and, in many cases, the ability of those individuals seeking positions in investment banks to perform well under these circumstances is shown either inadvertently or by design through the interview process.

5. *Enthusiasm.* One of the personality characteristics that helps secure employment in many fields, but especially in investment banking, is the enthusiasm for the job that the candidate exhibits during the interviewing process. Interviewers and clients alike appreciate an enthusiastic individual. Enthusiasm is especially important in investment banking because the field is a service-dominated business where people-to-people relations are critical and are often the tie that binds clients to firms. Enthusiasm spreads and is shared, whether it be for a client, a client's ideas, a client's plans for programs, or even for a banker's firm, and the firm's financial advice. Individuals who are enthusiastic are often those who are willing to go that extra mile in terms of work output that is often required on a daily basis, and in very difficult situations, such as those typified by many in the investment banking business. Being enthusiastic, however, does not mean that an individual should be so bubbly

that it grates on even the closest colleagues. Carrying enthusiasm to that degree is neither useful nor appropriate.

6. *Loyalty.*   One of the least talked about individual characteristics that has gone far in helping candidates secure jobs in investment banking, and the lack of which has resulted in individuals not receiving offers, is the ability of potential employees to exhibit and exude loyalty to those for whom they have worked. Sometimes candidates exude loyalty overtly and in other cases show loyalty in more subtle ways. The first reaction most interviewers have to seemingly disloyal candidates is to query whether they will be disloyal to the interviewer once hired. The second reaction is to question whether the candidates will be disloyal to the firm or to the firm's client. These questions may be obvious concerns to both interviewers and readers. Nonetheless, interviewees still have a tendency to make somewhat negative comments about people, situations, or institutions with which they have been affiliated.

7. *Respect.*   A corollary to loyalty and another individual characteristic that must be exhibited by interviewees is respect for the interviewer and the interviewer's firm. It is hard to imagine that some candidates do not exude at least a modest amount of respect, but oftentimes, this is the case. The lack of respect comes through in very subtle ways—sometimes through a passing glance, a roll of the eyes, or some other type of body language. Exuding respect certainly does not mean that candidates should sit up in their chairs like puppy dogs awaiting their owner's beck and call. It does mean, however, that interviewees must at least acknowledge that they got into their present position through the firm's recognition of their merit, and that the firm the interviewer represents should be given respect.

No interviewers will like people who do not show respect for the interviewers and their firm. The ability to show respect is very important in the investment banking arena because clients expect it, colleagues require it, and the milieu in which the investment bankers work demands it. In an industry where a glance or a subtle gesture can be acted on, dispensed with, or have a number of significant meanings, the ability to exude or exhibit respect assumes great significance.

8. *Knowledge.*   The more typical series of questions that has been asked for years by interviewers requires candidates to show at least some knowledge of the industry, the firm, and the specialty area for which the candidates seek employment. These types of questions have not changed over the years, and they certainly have not been altered in any significant way for today's candidates in the investment banking business. What is important, however, is that information about the investment banking industry, particular firms, and specialty areas within investment banking firms is, and has always been, not easy to come by. The fact that many investment banking firms have gone public over recent years may alter this situation, but information about the business in general, what actually goes on, and what is expected of new recruits is likely to remain available in large part only through word of mouth. Garnering such information, however, does not therefore necessarily require some clandestine operation on the part of those interested in investment banking as a career. Still, getting this kind of information does require at least a little research, and the ability to do this kind of work as seen through the interview process is some kind of indication that candidates have some direction, a knowledge of the industry and the job for which they are seeking employment, and the desire and direction to seek out this type of material.

For the interview, this type of information also forms a common ground for discussion between the interviewers and the candidates. It gives candidates the opportunity to ask questions about the industry and the firm beyond requesting information of a rudimentary nature. It also provides interviewers with a springboard from which to launch discussions about the industry, the activities of the firm, and the interviewers' departments, as a means to probe more deeply into the candidates' interests and discern, to the extent possible, whether interviewees will be successful at investment banking once hired. At the very least, a knowledge of the investment banking business is required to achieve a modest degree of success in the interviewing process.

9. *Strengths and Weaknesses.* Another classic interview question is one that requires candidates to discuss their strengths and weaknesses in whatever form they so choose. On the strength side, the classic answers range anywhere from discussions about academic achievements, personal successes, leadership qualities, and other positive attributes. Weaknesses are more difficult to describe, largely because many people do not believe that they have any highly significant ones, and also because candidates are trying to show their best side during any interview process. Nonetheless, the classic answer to the question that seeks to elicit a description about candidates' weaknesses is one that describes certain personality weaknesses that could also be interpreted as strengths, such as determination, asking too much of oneself, being an overachiever, being highly critical of oneself and one's peers work, and other similar guises. When interviewing for an investment bank, it is important that candidates stress leadership, the ability to analyze problems, some achievements, notable high goals and standards, and the ability and desire to spend long hours at work. These types of qualities can be used for the strengths and weaknesses side of the question if structured properly.

10. *Be a Winner.* An offshoot of the strengths and weaknesses question and one characteristic candidates must in some way show interviewers is that, somewhere along the line, they have been "winners." There is no specific activity in which candidates must have succeeded, and there is no particular way that candidates must show that they have achieved a kind of undisputed success. Yet, it is up to candidates to convey to interviewers that success and winning have been and will be in the candidates' cards. Interviewers want individuals who have been at the top in their class, have been extremely successful at work, and perhaps have achieved notable successes in other fields of endeavor, whether those be athletics, music, or art. It is not expected that everybody achieve success in everything. It is hoped, however, that the experience of success has had the effect of making candidates expect it of themselves in the future. Investment banking is a fiercely competitive field, and those doing the interviewing like to see and expect to hire candidates who have made success a way of life.

CHAPTER 23

FIRST-RATE TALENTS AND TRAITS OF SECURITIES FIRM MANAGERS

Perhaps the most critical question facing corporations today is how they can develop better managers. Indeed, if the answer to this interrogative was well known, there would be very little need for the proliferation of books and treatises on the subject of management in all its various forms. Subsumed within this question are such issues as the kinds of personality traits that must be developed to better enhance managers' ability to deal with problems and make appropriate decisions and also the types of technical know-how managers must have to insure that their directives are well founded, and thus that their department moves along in the appropriate fashion, with its goals paralleling those of the corporation. Consequently, managers today must have the ability to select the right kind of people for their management positions—those who are and will be first-rate managers in the future. A professional who is an excellent manager has certain innate qualities that aid in the process of management development, and developing of managers is just that—as much as process as it is a matter of selecting those who have this kind of potential. In short, management success is achieved when the appropriate individual with the right inherent qualities is provided with a developmental forum on and through which the process of management development may be appropriately activated and insured.

In a microsense, the entire process of management development is certainly different for each industry, each firm, and each particular job within any company, but there are certain management strictures applicable to a good many situations. For a manager in the securities industry, four important qualities have been isolated to be developed and acted on to minimize what may be a large proportion of the major management problems occurring within securities firms. There are doubtless other qualities and characteristics managers within these firms must have and should develop; but the ones selected seem to be those that can help alleviate many personnel problems within securities organizations. These, therefore, are a representative sample of what may be the minimum standards securities firm managers should develop to maintain continuous success within their departments or divisions, and also to prevent any conflicts from mushrooming out of their managerial control. The following are the four important managerial strictures, with their associated problems.

1. *More than any other single management dictum in the securities industry, managers must show their employees that they know who is and who is not producing or who is or is not a producer.*   In the securities industry, there is nothing that impairs managers' credibility more than their inability to recognize or show their employees who is an active member of the department's revenue-producing team. Interestingly, the lack of ability of managers to show awareness of the quality of employees impugns their credibility among the nonproducers. It implies to all that the managers do not truly understand the area under their supervision, have employees who are their favorites, or are protecting themselves by recognizing the achievements of midlevel producers or nonproducers far out of proportion to any contribution that they may be making. In a similar way, by not giving the appropriate recognition to the big producers of a department, managers stifle enthusiasm and esprit de corps among the very best people within their given area. There is potentially nothing more disastrous to a department in the securities firm than factionalism resulting from inadequate or inappropriate recognition of individual achievement.

Typically, these kinds of problems occur in the management of departments within a capital markets division of a securities firm or within an investment banking area. Sometimes they happen in product support or service departments and other similar divisions. In some instances, inadequate recognition assumes significance in the institutional sales arena, in cases where the salespeople are given remuneration not on a quantitative commission basis, but rather based on more qualitative methods, usually involving a salary plus bonus compensation plan. Within the branches of a securities firm or in other areas where compensation is totally based on a quantitative system such as pure sales commission programs, managers are left less room to either show appreciation of those employees who are producers or to build up the achievements of those who are not: the commission-based remunerative system does most of the recognition for managers of those types of departments or branches. Nevertheless, managers can promote, in a number of ways, those who are true producers and also show concern for those who are not. In any case, perhaps the single most important thing managers in the securities firm must do on a continuing basis is to promote, support, and encourage the real producers under their jurisdiction, and show others that they fully recognize both who is and who is not producing.

2. *As a corollary to number one, the second most important managerial edict in the securities industry is that the manager must, and must be known to, actually reward those who are the producers.* This process represents one of the securities industry's true management statements, whether or not it means much to those who receive better compensation and higher accolades. In almost all cases, however, it certainly does mean something and represents an important way of developing esprit de corps within any given department or organization, as a method to promote and inspire better individual performance in the highly entrepreneurial atmosphere of a securities firm.

Rewards dispensed at the discretion of management, as noted earlier, most notably come in the form of bonuses that have qualitative and quantitative aspects to the amount ultimately provided. Severe management problems have arisen at virtually every securities firm when management rewarded producers compensation in amounts that were close to the amounts paid to individuals who were not as productive. In these significant instances, it was not the actual amount of compensation that was provided that caused concern and problems, but rather it was the relative amount that did. In many such cases, management's inability to, or laxity in, rewarding producers significantly more in compensation than those who were not producers resulted in the producers leaving for greener pastures. Stated succinctly, management in the securities firm cannot keep or hire top people unless those professionals are rewarded on a markedly and proportionately better basis than those who are not as successful.

3. *Securities firm managers must understand those areas under their supervision.*   It is generally agreed that one of the most complex problems of securities firm management resulting from specialization is the situation wherein a strong manager of specialized areas is promoted up through the ranks of a securities firm and at each subsequent level, the manager winds up supervising unfamiliar areas. Managers may reach relatively high levels within the firms and may be in control of a number of departments or divisions, some with which they are partly unfamiliar and others of which they have only a modest amount of knowledge. This situation has, time and time again, led to management problems of the first order within securities firms, although this is not a necessary result. Indeed, problem situations have occurred because competent professionals under the jurisdiction of the newly promoted managers who are unfamiliar with the specialized areas within their domain have sought to control, direct, and often even discuss the edicts and advice of their superior. In these cases, perhaps there has been good reason for the specialists to assert authority based on the in-depth knowledge they have of the field relative to that of their manager. Nobody doubts that this is a possibility, and in some cases, may in fact be necessary at times. Even in the best cases, however, these types of situations lead to a subtle and ongoing erosion of the manager's authority, if the process goes unchecked.

The development of these types of management difficulties is not only a likely event within the structure of a securities firm, but it is also one that is somewhat difficult to circumvent. As managers succeed in given areas over the long haul, they develop a certain amount of knowledge about specialized areas that are somewhat related to their own and with which they have, over time, come in contact and of which they have developed a moderate mastery. After they begin working with other employees in these related specialty areas, an acceptance of the managers and perhaps even a degree of camaraderie between the managers and others in the related departments ultimately occur. When new managers are needed for those related areas, such as when senior management seeks to improve coordination between those areas or even desires to develop further related areas, the managers with a modest knowledge of those areas, but who have been accepted by employees in the related areas and have shown success in their home specialty, are often the choice to head such departments. Over time, similar situations occur that may result in the movement of these managers up the securities firm hierarchy and the subsumption under their jurisdiction of new specialty areas, until it becomes rather difficult for the managers to have even a total knowledge of all the specialized areas of the firm within their domain. Additionally, the movement of managers up the corporate hierarchy does not necessarily have to assume such a slow and incremental path. Many managers are catapulted into the firm's senior hierarchy with little opportunity to come in contact with the areas under their jurisdiction and supervision. From a management standpoint, this situation is even more serious in most cases than the previous ones described.

In any event, installing or promoting managers to supervise any department in a corporation, especially one of the technical and specialized areas of a securities firm, who may have only a modest knowledge of the area is, for lack of a better expression, an accident waiting to occur. It is not good for morale; it certainly does not help in situations where the rewarding of producers is especially important; and in a risk-taking department such as an underwriting and trading area, it has the potential of resulting in losses, which could at times be substantial. The same scenarios are true in investment banking areas and branch office systems. Major administrative, managerial, and compliance problems could result in areas managed by those only somewhat familiar with the complicated and difficult position of branch manager.

Nevertheless, the promotion and appointment of managers

to positions that oversee areas unfamiliar to them is certainly not a new one in both the corporate and securities industry milieu. It does happen and will continue to do so because of the specialized nature of the securities industry, its firms, and its myriad technical departments and operations. Thus, many managers end up overseeing areas about which they have only moderate knowledge. One way around the problem, although one that will not ameliorate each and every situation, is to make sure that managers have a certain amount of on-line, real-time experience with and within an area they will ultimately be appointed to oversee. The amount of time required will vary from situation to situation, but simply thinking in these terms should result in some change in the way managers are developed within the securities industry. This is difficult to accomplish for senior managers overseeing many areas.

4. *Finally, managers in securities firms must be unqualifyingly excellent at interpersonal relations.* This may be obvious, but it is critical here. This is so for a number of important interrelated reasons. In the securities industry, most significant management positions require that managers supervise a number of semiautonomous and somewhat interdependent business units that require strong horizontal relationships to achieve maximum success in each given area, and for the entire group of units as a whole. These small business units that managers oversee, each having its own manager or head, do not necessarily cooperate, work together, and have the same agreed on goals in mind all of the time. These types of departmental amalgams simply do not result in "one for all and all for one" situations, regardless of how attentive the managers of the small business units are to the overall departmental goals.

What is required, however, is constant attention from the department's overall manager to the communication and cooperative efforts of the small business units the manager supervises. Notable examples of this are situations involving managers of the municipal, corporate, government, and equity departments in the capital markets area, each of whom supervises a division composed largely of trading, underwriting, sales, and support small business units. The point here is that the single most important way to maximize the potential benefits to the firm from a division composed of small departments is to have those individuals who manage the departments and the division as a whole be first-rate communicators and top-notch in the area of interpersonal relations.

In a corporate structure with specialized small business units requiring good communication among them in a horizontal fashion, such as those in a securities firm, it is also difficult to air management, personnel, and personal concerns to others across horizontal structural lines—that is, from one small business unit to another. Total departmental or organizational concerns are very often perceived differently by different professionals within each small business unit. Even managers of the small business units have difficulty making their concerns known to one another. In cases such as these, it is easier for managers who oversee all of the small business units to act as mediating forces and make certain that all those involved in managing the small business units understand each other, the goals of the department, and the objectives of the firm.

In these instances, where the problems inherent in horizontal communication come center stage in the management difficulties of the department, it is the vertical relationships of the managers of the small business units with the department or division manager that aid in communications. The overall manager, then, must be well schooled in interpersonal relations so that the managers of the small business units who report to the overall manager feel comfortable in airing their concerns and the concerns of others, and the manager, in turn, has the opportunity to work with them on molding departmental or divisional policy and procedures to develop a more cohesive, cooperative, and coordinative effort.

PART 6

THE SECURITIES FIRM IN THE FUTURE

CHAPTER 24

MACROMANAGEMENT ISSUES

STABILITY OF PERSONNEL

If hiring the right professionals and managers is crucial to the success of securities firms, retaining them is equally so. At the same time, personnel upheaval on a continuing basis does little to create a team atmosphere, does less for maintaining consistency in goals and objectives, and surely cannot do much for a firm's financial success over the long haul. Personnel stability is also critical to securities firms for other reasons. The specialized small business unit nature of the firms and the relations that often must be developed between and among units for them to prosper makes stable personnel relations proportionately more significant than would otherwise be the case. It is also expensive to replace top securities firm professionals; and if the process is a long one, there are either tremendous lost opportunities or potential financial problems resulting from other, and perhaps less capable, individuals filling in for the job during the employment search process. More than anything else, however, professionals are attracted to departments and firms with a history of personnel stability, and at the very least, do not seek situations where this is not so.

EXPANDING AND CONTRACTING FIRM OPERATIONS

It is well known that Wall Street securities firms have tended to overexpand their operations during prosperous times and abruptly contract them when the industry hits the financial doldrums. Management has been continually reminded of these facts in the nation's press and by professionals within and outside the firms. Any further harping on this may be tantamount to hitting a thumbtack with a sledgehammer, but it is nonetheless worth mentioning here.

Major factors contributing to the continuing problems of securities firm growth and development are, in large part, a function of the volatile nature of the world's financial markets, which make precise planning strategies difficult for the firms to institute. Management should nevertheless adopt a flexible program of controlled growth with the requisite sensitivity analyses and contingency plans that, when implemented, could go far in preventing overexpansion or deep cuts during times that previously resulted in either.

SETTING GOALS AND OBJECTIVES

Even though it may be hard to believe, the most perplexing and indeed classic problem facing securities firms, their departments, divisions, and branch offices, is the establishment and monitoring of goals and objectives. This difficulty, not unknown to major corporate entities, is particularly problematic for securities firms for a number of reasons, all resulting from attributes inherent to the securities markets and the organizational structure of the firms themselves. Surely the long-range goals of increasing profitability, establishing a greater market share, creating new products, or successfully developing new client relationships are measurable and achievable. However, setting short-term objectives as a way to reach those goals and establishing benchmarks to monitor the progress of an organizational unit is a much harder task given the nature of securities firms. Nevertheless, management's success in this area will be perhaps the most significant factor in the future financial stability and profitability of securities firms over the years ahead, and the relative success of this effort will be directly dependent on the quality of management.

There are a number of environmental characteristics endemic to the securities industry that make the establishment of goals and objectives for their departments and divisions a somewhat illusive task. The first problem, more inherent in the securities markets than in the firms, has been the cyclical nature of the stock market as well as the volatility of the bond markets over recent years. These situations do not help provide a steady revenue stream for the firms, but rather one that can be extremely variable even over short periods of time. This also makes it difficult for firms and departments to develop accurate budgets and to assess the reasons why they have or have not been met. Indeed, managers at securities firms simply do not have reliable crystal balls.

Conceptual problems relating to a firm's internal accounting procedures also create substantial hurdles to the creation of objectives and to their achievement. Under some accounting systems, certain departments receive credit for revenues generated to a greater or lesser extent than should normally be the case, and expenses are attributed to some departments when they should not be or should be more evenly distributed. This usually occurs in securities-related activities. Some revenues and expense allocation methods have the resultant effect of obscuring differences in the true net revenue streams for each area and, if weighted in favor of one or the other, often result in concern and disincentive for those individuals within the department who believe that they are assuming an unnecessary expense burden of the transaction or are not receiving adequate credit for the generation of revenues. Even when securities firms are evolving from a profit center mode to a firmwide profit one, concern by department or branch managers in the bottom line is difficult to obliterate. The point here is that unless and until firms adopt strict accounting standards for revenue and expense items together with benchmarks for revenues of business units that are achievable and acceptable, it will be very difficult for any department or any branch to establish goals for the long term, let alone set objectives.

Another element inherent to the securities firm that is often the cause of cyclical earnings is the risk involved in trading and underwriting securities. Generally speaking, even if a trading department's profit objectives are achieved over the short run, one loss could wipe out the entire year's profit. Conversely, in trading situations that have resulted in moderate losses for the entire year, a single trading transaction could successfully result in a profit of such dimensions so as to put the department back into the black. Most of these situations are understandable and explainable. It is more difficult, however, to assess the impact of moderate market-related net income increases or decreases over long periods of time as measured against specific trading objectives. In such cases, it is difficult to assess the extent to which income has been achieved as a result of the efforts of the firm's personnel or the activity in the securities markets, and controlling for all the income-producing variables associated with risk-taking activity is equally complex.

Additionally, expanding a department, branch, or even an investment banking division with high-cost injections of personnel impacts the bottom line over the short term. This, together with expenses for information systems, support personnel, and overhead, are heavy costs in the securities industry and impact management's ability to measure and quantify a department's achievement of objectives. Also, the ability of branches to set goals for development and profits has not been without problems. Few firms have developed a branch strategy for monitoring each branch's success over specified time periods. There have been few concepts of what a branch office should look like in its stages of development, so that branch managers use various scenarios to explain the financial position of their offices. For instance, a manager may be in the early stages of developing the branch, which may mean hiring a number of account executives and moving to new quarters, thus reducing branch revenues for the short term. In some cases, the branch may have lost top producers, or in others, it may have hired top producers who have not produced the level of revenues anticipated. In other situations, the manager may have recently hired a number of good producers who specialize in a particular investment area, but who may not be active revenue generators because of market conditions. In any event, and in most situations, there has not been a carefully plotted way of measuring a branch office development, although profitability has been an essential, stated goal.

These problems taken together with the facts that departments, branches, and divisions are in different stages of development and often have greatly varying goals and objectives for which their management can adequately make cases points to potential problems in monitoring and achieving them. This is compounded by market vagaries, accounting difficulties, holdovers of the profit center atmosphere within a firm's move to corporatewide profit goals, the difficulties inherent in expanding risk-taking departments, and the tremendous costs of systems development. As a result, there are no two units of any securities firm in the same stages of development or with the same bottom-line goals or with the same methods of achieving them. Departments and divisions, sales forces, trading desks, and finance departments are also at different developmental levels, in terms of servicing existing clients and creating a larger client base. All of this is complicated by different methods of accounting for revenues and expenses and the variations in net profits generated from different activities, which may seem legitimate for a given department or branch at a point in time but are not generally comparable across the board.

As a result, perhaps the most important tasks of the future securities firm manager are twofold. One is the monitoring of profit goals and objectives, especially in volatile financial markets, and the other is receiving a solid return on the investments a firm has made in expanding into new product areas and client services, while maintaining firmwide profitability and organizational control. These are management tasks of the first order.

THE BOTTOM LINE: SMALL BUSINESS UNIT MANAGEMENT

In a volume of this size covering an industry of such complex dimensions, it is difficult to pull a thread of commonality through the entire effort that would produce a single most important management dictum standing above all others as the most significant one on which the firm's top managers should concentrate. The wide-ranging and complicated nature of securities firm jobs, products, and services reinforces this thesis.

Securities firms, to be sure, are actually composed of many specialized departments and divisions, each of which has within it any number of small business units performing specialized, though sometimes interdependent functions, some of which also depend on the cooperation of, or coordination with, other organizational entities located outside the department or division in which the small business unit is situated. One of the great hallmarks bestowed by management on these small business units and their professionals is a striking degree of autonomy to risk the firm's capital, seek and develop clients, originate and market products and services, and generally engage in the development of an entrepreneurial business, however defined and in whatever form permitted.

Each small business unit, whether it be a branch office, a corporate bond-trading desk, a utility group in a corporate finance department, a municipal institutional sales department, or a mortgage-backed securities trading desk, carries with it all the organizational and business-related problems and possibilities of corporate entities of a much larger scale. The achievements and successes of each, are, more often than not, a function of the quality of its management. Whether problems exist in hiring the best professionals, motivating them effectively, compensating them appropriately, retaining them over time, establishing and adhering to goals and objectives, or working with other units, the success of each small business unit is often a function of the quality and expertise of its manager. The extreme degree of small business unit specialization and the expertise required of its professionals also makes its managers the critical determinants of the firm's future success. It is therefore up to top management to assure that each manager of every small business unit is the very best and most knowledgeable professional that the firm can hire. The financial success of any securities firm will be determined by the quality of those who manage its small business units, provided that the firm also has a quality upper-management group.

HORIZONTAL AND VERTICAL INTEGRATION

The specialized small business units of securities firms are also grouped under umbrellalike structures of departments and divisions. More than many perceive, these organizational entities are rather dependent on others whose work entails some interaction with, or support provided by, them. As a result, it is critical to the success of securities firms, and other organizations akin to them, that small business units or departments and divisions be closely aligned from a horizontal coordinative and communicative standpoint. Without this managerial dimension, it is possible that interdependent though relatively autonomous business units will, at the least, function with less than optimum success, or at the worst, operate at cross-purposes with one another. Many potential problems can be circumvented by placing the right professionals—the most knowledgeable experts—in charge of the firm's small business units; but that alone is not enough. To be sure, coordination, cooperation, and communication, all with a view towards department and firm-wide goals and objectives will not occur by horizontal managerial pressure alone, especially when this effort is exerted on highly specialized, decentralized, and autonomous small business units that often think they could and should have their own profit-making agenda.

Consequently, key to the success of securities firms is a management structure that is integrated on a horizontal basis so as to achieve a coherent and coordinative cross-divisional or departmental strategy, while at the same time, vertical pressure is applied downward by senior management on the managers of the small business units and departments so that they cooperate as fully as possible. This vertical pressure from middle- and upper-level management is critical in suppressing the centrifugal organizational forces likely to pull the small business units out of their coordinative orbits with one another. Indeed, congregated groups of small business unit managers located on roughly the same organizational plane as each other still require vertical pressure from managers above to keep horizontal coordination ongoing. It is this dual approach to the management of securities firms that is likely to result in their future success, however measured.

INSIDER TRADING

Perhaps in the minds of many individuals, so-called "insider trading" is an important management problem at securities firms. In reality, however, it is generally considered to involve the transgressing of laws and regulations by a small fraction of the total number of professionals in the industry and is therefore as much an individual difficulty as it is a problem facing the industry.

Without detailing in "legalese" all that is involved in insider trading, most industry professionals and writers perceive it to be the use of confidential information for personal gain, in broad terms. When an individual engages in this practice, many psychologists and psychiatrists familiar with the subject suggest that the motivation could be greed, the desire to outdo one's peers, or some problem stemming from an individual's childhood experiences or upbringing. The purposeful breaking of laws and regulations usually occurs for all of these reasons, among others, and therefore it is difficult for any industry to prevent.

Nevertheless, securities firms will undoubtedly take measures to limit the potential for abuses in this area. Among them will probably be restrictions on the access to information and those who have it, as well as educative programs for employees about what is and is not allowable activity in all areas related to information use. Many have also called for a more precise definition of exactly what constitutes insider trading, and whatever comes of this effort will be factored into management actions in this area. In any event, the problems relating to insider trading will certainly occupy an important part of securities firm concerns in the future.

TOMORROW'S MANAGER

Tomorrow's manager in the securities industry will have to be an expert in two senses. The securities firm manager of the future will have to be both a professional manager and an acknowledged expert in a number of specialized areas, especially if the way of the world in the financial services industry is likely to revolve around the successful integration of small business units and departments, which may be interdependent. "Making it by faking it" or "management by stirring the pot" is past history on Wall Street, as it is elsewhere—the stakes are too great, the competition is too keen, the technology is too encompassing, the pace is too fast, and the patience of knowledgeable professionals is wearing too thin. If a firm is not achieving, it is falling behind, with the resultant problems gurgling slowly in its wake. If times does not pass such a securities firm by, its competitors will.

The classic questions of who are the experts and whether putting big producers in charge with the hope that they will become good managers actually begs the questions themselves. Certainly many big producers are experts and in fact can be good or even great managers. As managers and under certain circumstances, they may even go on producing revenues in an on-line capacity to the extent allowed or even produce to a greater extent as a result of their new responsibilities. Those who have not been the best and do not understand generally the subtleties of getting business and the intricacies of client development, or specifically the delicacy of trading large positions, or who do not have the innate abilities required to garner investment banking clients successfully and to be successful in securities sales probably cannot lead those who do, on to be better. Indeed, those who can often do and those who have done so, probably can do more and should be provided the opportunity to do so. This is especially important in an industry, such as the securities one, that has tended to leave the best producers to their own devices and the most knowledgeable experts to their own thoughts and business plans. If there is one single concept that should become strikingly clear in the management of a securities firm, it is that greater concentration should be paid to those who are the very best at what they do if the organization is to move forward with those individuals as its standard bearers. Organizational need, common sense, and good management demand it. The most knowledgeable experts and the biggest producers, under the right conditions and with the appropriate incentives, also require it, and their peers and top management should appreciate it.

Tomorrow's securities firm manager therefore should be an expert professional to the greatest extent possible. A department or a division in a securities firm can only be as good as those professionals leading it. A professional's level of competence and an organization's consequent profitability are a function of the quality of its management. The nature of the securities industry and its firms makes this statement especially true.

NOTES

For additional information, see also:

Joseph Auerbach and Samuel L. Hayes III, *Investment Banking and Diligence: What Price Deregulation?* (Boston: Harvard Business School Press, 1986).

Samuel L. Hayes III, ed., *Wall Street and Regulation* (Boston: Harvard Business School Press, 1987).

CHAPTER 25

THE FINANCIAL SERVICES INDUSTRY: TODAY AND TOMORROW

For many years, the financial services industry was a segmented one. Basically limited to a substantial group of companies within the broadly defined category of nonindustrial corporations, the industry was represented by a number of corporations that did the vast proportion of their business in discrete areas of financial services. These companies engaged in the business of insurance, commercial as well as savings and loan banking, investment management, securities activities, various financial or credit services, and some were involved in a combination of a few of these activities. The fact that almost all of these companies engaged in one particular kind of financial service business was the result of the legal structure in which they operated as well as their natural inclinations during the first 50 years of the twentieth century, when the financial services business took a stronghold within the U.S. economy.

From a legal standpoint, both federal and state laws served to restrict the kinds of financial businesses in which companies were permitted to engage. The most important law regulating the activities of most major financial service organizations is the Glass-Steagall Banking Reform Act of 1933, which, in effect, separated commercial banks from nonbank dealers in the kinds of activities each could do, principally prohibiting commercial banks from the underwriting of most securities. There are a number of other federal laws, regulatory strictures, and court decisions that have served to reinforce the prohibitions against companies engaging in a vast array of financial service activities all housed under a single corporate roof. Equally important in regulating the activities of financial service companies have been the laws enacted by states through their ability to regulate intrastate insurance and banking activities to a relatively large degree.

Contemporaneous with the development of the financial service business along structured legal lines was the inclination of companies over many years to remain in the business in which they were successful and felt comfortable with, more commonly called the "stick to the knitting" syndrome. Indeed, the wholesale development of the U.S. industrial experience did not have, in its early years, the conglomerate business enterprise as its flagship corporation. Mergers and takeovers of companies whose businesses were either partly or totally dissimilar in nature were products of a more recent experience. When mass merchandisers and various other companies were emerging as the United States' largest purveyors of goods and services, it was unlikely that their senior executives thoughtfully considered an entry into Wall Street through any type of business relationship with another company. When insurance salespeople were selling life insurance and health and accident policies door to door, little consideration was given to the thought that they could also be selling credit card services, stocks, and bonds. When many corporations, both industrial and financial, accrued enough cash under management to need the services of professional advisors, few believed a securities firm business was a logical adjunct to their own capabilities. If the laws did not restrict these companies, then their own perception of the world around them did. The wholesale cross-fertilization of the financial service business was an idea that would be developed on a very large scale sometime in the mid- to late 1970s.

WHERE ARE WE NOW?

Even a cursory review of the activities now engaged in by major companies offering financial services would lead one to the conclusion that the financial service world of yesteryear, where each organization provided a specific type of service, is an era long since gone. The demarcation of corporations along the lines of the kinds of financial services they offered has given way to a world where customers can now receive all types of financial services from a single corporate entity. These changes, as obvious and major as they may appear, still have run up against the legal structural impediments of years ago. Progress in the financial service field, if it can be seen as such, has been the result of the seemingly natural business tendency of corporations to develop additional businesses within the legally allowable limits and also through mergers and takeovers, although few companies have nurtured financial service businesses as a result of in-house growth.

Thus, the vast proportion of major developments in the field of financial services has been the result of two important trends. The first is a function of securities firms, which were previously privately held, going public, leaving themselves open to buy outs, in whole or in part, by other corporate entities. Public securities firms have also either sold interests or their entire companies to outsiders over recent years. Both these developments were virtually unthinkable on a large scale until recently. A second major development that has served to turn the financial service business into a more homogeneous corporate form has been the penchant of banks to offer a wide variety of financial services that were once almost totally in the purview of credit card companies and securities firms.

If one were to construct a corporate typology that would represent the ways that corporations have become involved in different aspects of the financial service business, the configuration would have a number of parts. Among the major ones are cases in which corporations have bought securities firms; insurance companies have purchased securities organizations; diversified financial companies have bought securities firms; securities firms have established some banking services; banks have created financial service arms with a variety of financial products; corporate conglomerates have purchased financial service organizations; and most recently and perhaps most importantly, foreign companies, and usually securities firms, have purchased interests in U.S. securities organizations. All of these developments have occurred within legally permitted structures, although some required approvals. They all show, however, a desire of both parties to each transaction to provide a broader range of financial services to their customer base.

WHY HAS THIS OCCURRED?

Discovering in hindsight why corporations became involved in new businesses, some related to those that they presently do and some unrelated to them, is not only difficult but also, many argue, is not useful; it does not change what is or what will be, or the success that a company has had in the new business long after the strategic decision was made. Yet, this type of analysis does have some important aspects to it, even when the reasons for a corporate decision remain illusive or when the reason is the result of a convergence of forces, none of which can be pinpointed as the single most important one. What this kind of analysis does do, however, is provide a basis on which to assess the success of that corporate mission, in practical and conceptual terms, and a foundation or data base that can be used to measure the potential for success of similar decisions, all made within the broad context of corporate strategic policy.

At first glance, it might be arguable that the desire and the move of corporations to develop broader based financial service businesses results from a penchant for larger profits garnered through rapidly growing businesses by merging or acquiring of companies for costs that would be far less than the projected net revenue stream ultimately generated. This rationale sounds obvious enough, but it is one that is too all encompassing and may be somewhat off the mark in the financial service business.

Most new financial service corporate combinations that have come about in an effort to develop a diversity of these services have resulted partly from what many think has been the perceived belief of the senior-most management of these firms that these combinations will have some marked amount of synergy between them. Synergy in the financial services business can come in three different forms. The first is financial synergy. This is when the whole range of financial services was expected to be offered through combinations of securities firms, insurance companies, and other diversified financial service corporations. The second form, corporate synergy, is a much broader concept and encompasses the belief that a new financial service unit, as part of a larger corporate entity, will aid in the achievement of some type of "one-stop investment shopping," either at certain locally based outlets for the corporation's own goods and services or through direct client offers made by salespeople of both firms in their daily businesses. The third type of financial service synergy is the result of diversification by a company into a financial service business, either through development or acquisition, which is related to the company's present main business line. This has occurred when investment management firms have combined with insurance companies, or when banking institutions have embarked on major programs to provide financial advice to individuals, corporations, governments, or other institutions. This is investment synergy.

The movement by certain companies to a broader based financial service business has also resulted from three other important trends that are somewhat more difficult to place within the context of business strategy but are no less important than the reasons related to it, and are perhaps more so in certain instances. The first is that most financial organizations anticipate that there will be major changes in the laws governing the way they do business. This expectation has had a very long history, and some industry observers believe that it dates back to the day after the enactment of the Glass-Steagall Act. Others believe that, even in spite of a number of setbacks for those who would like to see major regulatory changes, the winds of change are in the air, and they will occur in the near future. Some argue that real change has already resulted because different financial service corporations have established separate corporate subsidiaries that have been legally held to be legitimite, but which, on their face, seem to contravene the intent of existing laws and regulations.

The second reason for the changing nature of the financial services industry, and a more unquantifiable one, is that companies have sought alliances with financial service organizations because of the expectation that their present lines of business will not be that profitable in the future. This rationale is much harder to discern on an across-the-board basis, but it is probably applicable to certain firms in specific situations.

Thirdly, perhaps the least quantifiable aspect of a company's movement to broaden its financial services business, such as to become involved in or with a securities firm, may be the desire by some of its top executives to get a foothold on Wall Street. For many corporate chieftains, Wall Street still holds some allure, and the fact that their desire to become involved in it can be cloaked in a rational approach to develop their company's financial service business may prove to be too attractive from both a business and personal standpoint to forgo.

THE PRAGMATIC ISSUES

The movement by companies to offer a broader range of financial services and products and also to engage in the financial service-related activities they were previously prohibited from developing leaves still unanswered some practical questions about the viability of providing such services. Not all of these questions are applicable to every financial service organization, and a few of them may be asked of almost every corporation providing any type of financial service. The purpose is that they can be asked of any company interested in developing a wider variety of financial services and also of those companies that have recently succeeded in developing either new financial services or some type of association with a company that did.

In any event, five significant questions can be raised about the new era of financial services in which companies are now competing. The first question is: Is one-stop financial shopping a realistic possibility? For this to be so, consumers would have to believe that they are getting a better deal in all their financial needs from a single source or a single corporate entity. Individuals would have to sever some relationships that they have developed with other financial institutions and with the employees who have been servicing their accounts. Consumers would also have to believe that it is better to have all their assets in one place and deal with one source for all their needs as opposed to having some comfort in a diversity of dealings with different companies. Conversely, individuals might feel greater comfort in having their assets tended to by different companies so that if one institution had financial difficulties, their assets in the others would be safe. Also, in the past, satisfaction for customers may have been in the knowledge that they were able to compare the cost and benefits of the financial services offered by one institution with those provided by another or that special requests would be granted from one institution when they might have been denied by another.

Finally, and perhaps most important, in individuals' dealing with a few financial companies may be their belief that a blemished record with one financial institution may not necessarily carry over to another, or that mistakes made by a financial institution in their account would not affect their other accounts at other financial institutions. For instance, if all of an individual's transactions were handled by a single company, a problem with one account may actually affect the status of the others. In short, if customers choose one-stop financial shopping as a convenient alternative to dealings with a number of different financial institutions, they would have to alter their beliefs about what does or does not make them personally comfortable in dealing with different financial service institutions.

The second question might be whether or not salespeople who sell financial products of a particular type are capable of selling financial products of another. For example, are securities salespeople capable of selling financial products offered by banks and insurance companies? Perhaps even more important than this issue, but related to it, is the question of whether it is a profitable activity for those who sell one type of financial product to become involved in selling another. There are no easy answers to these questions, and most depend on the types of products salespeople must sell and the extent to which they are expected to develop an expertise in all the products of a group they are supposed to market. Some industry analysts have backed off from the supposition that salespeople can sell many types of financial products effectively.

Furthermore, some would agree that it is probably not an efficient use of company resources to begin a process that would involve the wholesale training of salespeople to sell new products totally unrelated to the ones they understand and market, such as training insurance salespeople to sell stocks, bonds, options, or futures. This is not to say that some professionals would not be capable of selling two distinctly different groups of products or that it may not be useful for them to do so. On a large scale, most people believe that the effective product marketing forays for different financial products has occurred through joint marketing efforts of different groups of professionals selling companion products and also for selected products whose characteristics and likely customers are similar. For the immediate future, however, the jury is still out on this issue, and it may be that as new salespeople are trained and cross-trained in totally different product areas whose customers may have similar needs and characteristics, there may come a day when a substantial proportion of salespeople are capable of selling products unlike each other in a totally effective way.

The third question and one of the key issues still being raised in financial service organizations that have been merged into others is: How transferable are the customer lists? This question does not imply that customer lists should be sent from one salesperson to another or from one organization to another, so that each company and every professional can use them indiscriminately. What is implicit in the question, however, is the issue of the extent to which one company can effectively market the services or products of a subsidiary or companion company to the other's customers. Much of this issue hinges on the extent to which the customers of one company are similar to those of the other, so that the products of one would fit clients whose financial needs have been effectively serviced by products of another. Such a concept would necessarily entail a customer base of one company that is similar to that of the other.

Yet, for most financial service organizations, customers run the gamut of demographic, economic, and financial characteristics, so that in theory, customers of one company who use its products are likely to be able to use the products of another company. If not, in instances where there are clear differences in customer characteristics, albeit with some overlap, there might be the possibility of modifying the products of each company to cater to the different client bases of each; but that issue runs far beyond the question at hand. Most firms are in the process of trying different methods of developing and solidifying client bases of newly acquired or merged financial services companies. How this is done in the future and the extent to which it is successful are questions that still remain open.

The fourth question may very well be: Can a corporate full-service firm be successful? This type of company offers all kinds of customers a number of important financial products and other services. They might include brokerage or banking-type services, real estate work, insurance services and products, credit card services, and perhaps even manufactured goods. This question is an even more difficult one to answer. The extent to which an individual or a family will patronize a company and make use of all these various services, many of which run far beyond the financial product variety but are nonetheless supposed to be important in luring clients to the company fold, is a question that will be answered in time. For the moment, there are as many proponents of this concept as there are detractors. Yet, the fact is that many people believe it is feasible to attract enough steady customers to make each service profitable by itself and have, as its impact, a geometrically increased investment return for the corporate parent who owns the companies providing these services or offering them through its subsidiaries. The concept here is much like one-stop financial shopping, although it is a larger one, and as a result, must be cloaked in an aura of impeccable company responsibility and responsiveness to customer needs.

The fifth question might be: Is the offering of a broader range of financial products and services a profitable endeavor? At first, this might seem to be the most easily answered and the most important question, but answers are not easy to come by when the issue is profitability. Also, it may not be the most important question because there may be other benefits that come to a company from offering an additional financial product or service and that may be not profitable. On the profit side of the issue, there are all kinds of ways to measure whether a product or service is profitable. Net income that the new product generates is certainly a most important way. A product's help in getting clients through the company door, developing relationships with them, and having them make use of other company products are equally important to developing an overall profitable business. In addition, when isolated with its own profit line, a new financial product, group of products, or service may indeed be profitable but may not be profitable enough. They might not offer the parent company a high enough return on investment, return on income, or return on equity. While those returns may not be high enough for a particular company, they may indeed be as high as another company might hope to achieve. Moreover, one or two of these measures might meet company standards and one or two may not, so that management is presented with a decision about whether it should retain the product or service, modify it, or supplement it in ways that would result in higher profit margins in areas not meeting expectations or standards.

Finally, profitability may not be that important. A marginal return on a company's investment from the development of a new product or group of products or the takeover of a different type of financial service organization may provide profits of an unquantifiable nature. Management may believe that these new financial services or that the company itself is an important advertising tool, or that it changes the company's image to attract additional clients or provide management with a new pool of talent with broader visions and better capabilities. The product or service also may not be a moneymaker, and this is the concept behind "loss leader" marketing. There are probably a host of other unquantifiable ways management can perceive that a new financial service or product, or number of them, could ultimately be profitable for their company. It is also not impossible that management can use any of these reasons as a rationale just to keep a product, service, or a company under its corporate wing, for reasons of a more personal nature, but in the name of potential long-range profitability.

THE CONCEPTUAL ISSUES

There are four major conceptual issues for companies seeking to broaden the base of their financial service business or that have done so. The first question is a broad one and concerns two aspects of the firm's business strategy. The first question is: Can financial service organizations of a large scale offer something to customers that is markedly different from the services provided by its competitors? This is an important business strategy-related issue because it seems that the trend in some major financial service organizations toward the development of a multitude of financial service businesses and myriad products pits major companies against one another in their effort to secure new customers and further develop relationships with present clients in a market serviced by most of the companies and in very similar ways. This problem raises yet another issue related to the competitive strategy of financial service organizations and to the ability of these companies to define market share. Most major financial service organizations offer their products to a diverse market of customers, but it is very difficult, and is sometimes impossible, to define the extent to which a company has garnered a quantitatively defined market share of the customer base within a particular product or service business or from the standpoint of the whole array of services offered by the company as compared to those provided by other competitors. Feedback from customers about certain products is also somewhat difficult to receive.

As a result, making adjustments to products and services and developing others to tap a definable but as yet unreached client base is comparatively more difficult than it is for companies engaged in marketing more tangible products and whose services are provided to a quantitatively definable and characteristically identifiable client market. These issues raise problems for the development of business strategy on the part of financial service organizations, because if quantifying market share and receiving feedback about products are difficult, the firm then would also encounter problems developing a strategy around an objective that seeks to maximize market share or establish a market niche. This is especially problematic for companies that offer a very broad array of services, many of which are similar to those provided by their competitors.

A second conceptual issue, one somewhat related to the effectiveness of a financial service organization's business strategy, concerns the extent to which each company involved in the merger or takeover of another financial service organization has benefited as a result of the process. In instances where new corporate combinations have occurred, both parties have expected that benefits, presumably economic or financial, would ultimately accrue as a result of the new association. Some of these have been achieved and others were not anticipated. In almost every case, however, one organization or the other has benefited more from the new corporate combination. This assessment is helpful in developing a strategic game plan for both companies and should also serve as a blueprint for acquiring or developing additional financial services or products. Where this conclusion is applicable, securities firms have usually been involved with mergers or takeovers by or of other corporations, both financial service-oriented or otherwise.

Somewhat related to this is the third question of whether, in the merger or takeover of financial service organizations structure has preceded strategy, so that developing synergies from these new corporate combinations has been a decidedly difficult chore. Alfred Chandler propounded the proposition that structure of a business enterprise must of necessity follow strategy: that a company's strategy must first be developed so that the structure to carry out that strategy can then effectively be formulated.[1] When financial service institutions have sought partners to develop their businesses further, they have been presented with a structured business enterprise to merge with or to take over, and to develop within their present organizational structure. In these instances, the strategic synergetic opportunities have been vague initially, but certainly seemed doable and worthwhile. Without changing the organizational structure of each company, the development of a strategy to penetrate each company's companion markets and develop better products as a way to achieve a synergy has been a difficult task, although not an impossible one. The problematic aspect of it has been a result of the fact that management has been presented with two or more organizational structures that have been difficult to alter, so that strategy had to be woven into the structure rather than its more appropriate fit as a precursor to the development of a company's structure. In its quest to broaden its base of financial products and services, some merged financial service firms have seemingly turned Chandler's argument around and have made difficult a process that would otherwise not necessarily be so.

The last important conceptual issue facing firms that have embarked on a program to develop a major financial service business has less to do with the firms themselves than it does with the clients. What effect has the wholesale development of the financial service business had on the customer? Is anybody really better off as a result of the plethora of financial products in the marketplace today? Are more financial alternatives available at cheaper rates and in more understandable forms for customers? Or is the customer faced with a rather complex set of circumstances and products, from which to develop an individualized financial plan? From the standpoint of society, is it possible that individuals and others are better informed and more comfortable that the world of financial services and products has been offered, with a degree of complexity, to all those who are interested? Can financial service organizations be all things to all people? Ultimately, these are some of the conceptual questions that must be answered affirmatively if the financial service organizations of today are going to exist in the same form tomorrow. In the final analysis, the decision will be made by the customer, as it always is.

WHAT WILL THE FORESEEABLE FUTURE BRING?

Major changes in the way the financial services business is structured resulting from the breakdown of legal and regulatory barriers may or may not be a likely event in the very near future. Yet, enough evaluative material is presently on the plate of most corporations that offer financial services to force them into some assessment as to the nature, direction, and future of their business as it presently stands, whether or not major structural changes are likely as a result of any legal action. Some firms, for instance, have reached the point of divesting some of their financial services empire or have decided to allow others to buy portions of it. Another likely but obverse scenario is one that would lead other investors to buy into the financial services business in a large way. In the long run, however, top management is going to have to justify, on a fairly quantitative basis, the rationale and reasons behind continuing in the financial services business to any extent. And it is unlikely that this decision will be made in the near future for most firms.

THE SECURITIES INDUSTRY
AT THE CROSSROADS

Securities firms originate, market, and sell financial products, and presumably, they always will. The better they are at this, all other things remaining equal, the more profitable they will be. The firms also provide services of the financial variety to individuals and institutional investors, corporations, governments, and even competitors through trading securities with them and joining them in securities underwritings, so that the widest market possible is penetrated for the client and the underwriting risk is shared.

Throughout this book, the product orientation of the securities firm and the improvement of its product marketing and delivery services has been emphasized as a key to its future success. The securities firm, to be sure, is to a large extent a product-oriented machine and should be managed and analyzed largely as such.

Yet, viewed from a broader perspective, as noted earlier, securities firms are service organizations and are classified by many in those terms. In handling the investments of individuals and helping both institutional and individual clients to invest properly and wisely, these firms provide a service, and it is an important one. Through the firm's research capabilities and its trading and underwriting activities that often place the firm's capital at risk, securities firms offer clients service of an unusual variety when compared to those extended by other corporations and most other service companies. With the merger and takeover of many securities firms, and the extension in the lines of business of most of them, the industry has been catapulted into providing to its traditional clients and many new ones, services that were offered previously by companies specializing in those activities. Most notable among these are real estate, insurance, and credit card services.

In addition, and as a sort of capstone to this vast array of investments, securities firms have been offering a full line of financial planning services for many segments of their client base. This pattern of product and service development has helped metamorphose a once product-oriented industry that never fully viewed and treated itself as such, into a service industry, deeply imbedded with myriad service-oriented products available for its customers. Yet, the firms had no real history of the practices slated to make the very best use of the inherently great opportunities offered to its clients through its diversified and, in some cases, stunningly attractive array of services.

In a manner of speaking, the securities firm of tomorrow will have to sharply hone its product origination, marketing, and delivery skills with a focus on, first and last, better fitting product and customer. It will have to do so with the mind set of a mature service orientation, because ultimately many products that the firms are providing customers are of a service nature. The better the securities firms do this, by whatever means available, the more successful they will be as time marches on. To be sure, this sounds simple enough; but for an industry and its managers traditionally bent on achieving results, and perhaps rightly so, it involves a philosophical restructuring of their beliefs translated into precise managerial action. Paying lip service alone to this management edict will not pay a firm's bills.

The whole essence of this approach is a very old one indeed, propounded by Peter Drucker and others. It involves, logically enough, focusing first on the customer, developing the customer, servicing the customer, and creating other customers, at the same time as keeping a managerially watchful eye on the industry's environment with a strategic view towards the future of the business. In a sense, it stands the securities industry's own argument for existence on its head. It is not what the securities industry should do to keep itself going, but rather what it must do for its customers that will allow it to flourish. All other managerial dictums are just commentary on this general theme.

The securities industry, its firms, and its professionals will undoubtedly develop, to a greater or lesser degree, along these managerial lines. Products will be provided, customers will be serviced, and competition will continue. Some years from now, in the wake of the wholesale evolution of the securities industry, management experts and financial analysts alike will review the progress of the firms and the industry that stands at the crossroads of the world's capital markets. Perhaps there will be more reasoning and more reflecting. There will certainly be more writing and restructuring. The ultimate goal, however, will always remain the same—customer service through unremittingly exacting management direction and client focus. No matter how globally the capital markets evolve, no matter how complex securities products are, and no matter how complicated and diverse client needs become, management dictums for success really never change much, they just get a little better with time.

NOTES

1. Alfred D. Chandler, Jr., *Strategy and Structure: Chapters in the History of American Industrial Enterprise* (Boston: M.I.T. Press, 1962), pp. 1–17.

SELECTED BIBLIOGRAPHY

Andrews, Kenneth K. *The Concept of Corporate Strategy*. Rev. ed. Homewood, Ill.: Dow Jones-Irwin, 1980.

Auletta, Ken. *Greed and Glory on Wall Street: The Fall of the House of Lehman*. New York: Random House, 1986.

Barnard, Chester I. *The Functions of the Chief Executive*. Cambridge, Mass.: Harvard University Press, 1968.

Bloch, Ernest. *Inside Investment Banking*. Homewood, Ill.: Dow Jones-Irwin, 1986.

Carrington, Tim. *The Year They Sold Wall Street: The Inside Story of the Shearson/American Express Merger, and How It Changed Wall Street Forever*. Boston: Houghton Mifflin, 1985.

Chandler, Alfred D., Jr. *Strategy and Structure: Chapters in the History of American Industrial Enterprise*. Boston: M.I.T. Press, 1962.

———. *The Visible Hand: The Managerial Revolution in American Business*. The Belknap Press, 1977.

Collins, Eliza G. C., ed. *Executive Success: Making It in Management*. New York: John Wiley & Sons 1983.

Culbert, Samuel A., and McDonough, John J. *Radical Management: Power Politics and the Pursuit of Trust*. New York: The Free Press, 1985.

Deal, Terrence E., and Kennedy, Allen A. *Corporate Cultures: The Rites and Rituals of Corporate Life*. Boston: Addison-Wesley, 1982.

Donaldson, Gordon, and Lorsch, Jay W. *Decision Making at the Top: The Shaping of Strategic Direction*. New York: Basic Books, 1983.

Donnelly, James H., Jr., Berry, Leonard L., and Thompson, Thomas W. *Marketing Financial Services: A Strategic Vision*. Homewood, Ill.: Dow Jones-Irwin, 1985.

Drucker, Peter F. *Managing for Results*. New York: Harper & Row, 1986.

———. *Management: Tasks, Responsibilities, Practices*. New York: Harper & Row, 1985.

————. *The Practice of Management.* New York: Harper & Row, 1986.

French, Wendell L., Bell, Cecil H., Jr., and Zawachi, Robert A. *Organization Development: Theory, Practice, and Research.* Plano, Texas: Business Publications, 1983.

Goffman, Erving. *The Presentation of Self in Everyday Life.* New York: Doubleday, 1959.

Harvard Business Review on Management, Vol. 1, Classic Advice on Aspects of Organizational Life. New York: Harper & Row, 1985.

Harvard Business Review on Human Relations, Vol. 3, Classic Advice on Handling the Manager's Job. New York: Harper & Row, 1986.

Harvard Business Review on Human Relations, Vol. 4, Classic Advice on Leadership. New York: Harper & Row, 1986.

Hayes, Samuel L., III, Spence, A. Michael, and Marks, David Van Praag. *Competition in the Investment Banking Industry.* Cambridge, Mass.: Harvard University Press, 1983.

Heller, Robert. *The Naked Manager: Games Executives Play.* New York: McGraw-Hill, 1985.

Hofer, Charles W., and Schendel, Dan. *Strategy Formulation: Analytical Concepts.* St. Paul, Minn.: West Publishing Co., 1978.

Homans, George C. *The Human Group.* New York: Harcourt, Brace & World, 1950.

Hrebiniak, Laurence G., and Joyce, Williams F. *Implementing Strategy.* New York: Macmillan, 1984.

Kantor, Rosabeth Moss. *The Change Masters: Innovation and Entrepreneurship in the American Corporation.* New York: Simon & Schuster, 1983.

Kotter, John P. "Power, Dependence, and Effective Management." *Harvard Business Review* (July–August 1977), pp. 125–136.

————. "Power, Success, and Organizational Effectiveness." *Organizational Dynamics* (Winter 1978), pp. 27–40.

————. *The General Managers.* New York: The Free Press, 1982.

————. *Power and Influence: Beyond Formal Authority.* New York: The Free Press, 1985.

Lasswell, Harold. *Politics: Who Gets What, When, How.* New York: McGraw-Hill, 1936.

Lawler, Edward E., III. *Pay and Organizational Effectiveness: A Psychological View.* New York: McGraw-Hill, 1971.

Lawrence, Paul R., and Lorsch, Jay W. "New Management Job: The Integrator." *Harvard Business Review* (November–December 1967), pp. 142–151.

————. *Organization and Environment: Managing Differentiation and Integration.* Cambridge, Mass.: Harvard Business School Press, 1986.

Leavitt, Harold J., Pondy, Louis R., and Boje, David M. *Readings in Managerial Psychology*. Chicago: The University of Chicago Press, 1980.

Likert, Renis. *New Patterns of Management*. New York: McGraw-Hill, 1961.

Lucas, Henry C., Jr. *Coping with Computers: A Manager's Guide to Controlling Information Processing*. New York: The Free Press, 1982.

McClelland, David. "The Two Faces of Power." *Journal of International Affairs* 24, no. 1 (1970): 29–47.

———, and Burnham, David. "Power Is the Great Motivator." *Harvard Business Review* (March–April 1976), pp. 100–110.

McGregor, Douglas. *The Professional Manager*. New York: McGraw-Hill, 1967.

———. *The Human Side of Management*. New York: McGraw-Hill, 1985.

Maslow, A. H. "A Theory of Human Motivation." *Psychological Review* 50 (1943): 370–396.

Mintzberg, Henry. *The Nature of Managerial Work*. New York: Harper & Row, 1973.

———. "The Manager's Job: Folklore and Fact." *Harvard Business Review* (July–August 1975), pp. 49–61.

Moebs, G. Michael, and Moebs, Eva. *Pricing Financial Services*. Homewood, Ill.: Dow Jones-Irwin, 1986.

Odione, George S. *Management Decisions by Objectives*. Englewood Cliffs, N.J: Prentice-Hall, 1969.

Ouchi, William G. *Theory Z: How American Business Can Meet the Japanese Challenge*. New York: Avon Books, 1981.

Pascale, Richard Tanner, and Athos, Anthony G. *The Art of Japanese Management: Applications for American Executives*. New York: Warner Books, 1981.

Peters, Thomas J., and Waterman, Robert H., Jr. *In Search of Excellence: Lessons from America's Best Run Companies*. New York: Warner Books, 1982.

Peters, Tom, and Austin, Nancy. *A Passion for Excellence: The Leadership Difference*. New York: Random House, 1985.

Pfeffer, Jeffrey. *Power in Organizations*. Marshfield, Mass.: Pitman Publishing, 1981.

Porter, Michael E. *Competitive Strategy: Techniques for Analyzing Industries and Competitors*. New York: The Free Press, 1980.

———. *Competitive Advantage: Creating and Sustaining Superior Performance*. New York: The Free Press, 1985.

Pugh, D. S., ed. *Organization Theory.* New York: Penguin Books, 1984.

Rohrer, Hibler, and Replogle, Inc. (Staff of). *The Managerial Challenge: A Psychological Approach to the Changing World of Management.* New York: New American Library, 1981.

Rothstein, Nancy, and Little, James, eds. *The Handbook of Financial Futures: A Guide for Investors and Professional Financial Managers.* New York: McGraw-Hill, 1984.

Rumelt, Richard P. *Strategy, Structure, and Economic Performance.* Cambridge, Mass.: Harvard Business School Press, 1986.

Salancik, Gerald R., and Pfeffer, Jeffrey. "Who Gets Power—and How They Hold on to It: A Strategic-Contingency Model of Power." *Organizational Dynamics* 5 (1977): 3–21.

Sayles, Leonard R. *Managerial Behavior: Administration in Complex Organizations.* New York: McGraw-Hill, 1964.

Schein, Virginia E. "Political Strategies for Implementing Organizational Change." *Group and Organization Studies* 2 (1977): 42–48.

Sobel, Robert. *Inside Wall Street.* New York: W. W. Norton, 1982.

Tichy, Noel M. *Managing Strategic Change: Technical, Political, and Cultural Dynamics.* New York: John Wiley & Sons, 1983.

Tregoe, Benjamin B., and Zimmerman, John W. *Top Management Strategy: What It Is and How to Make It Work.* New York: Simon & Schuster, 1980.

Vroom, Victor H. *Work and Motivation.* New York: John Wiley & Sons, 1984.

————, and Deci, Edward L., eds. *Management and Motivation.* New York: Penguin Books, 1983.

Wallace, Marc J., Jr., and Fay, Charles H. *Compensation Theory and Practice.* Boston: Kent Publishing Company, 1983.

Weiss, David M. *After the Trade Is Made: Processing Securities Transactions.* New York: New York Institute of Finance, 1986.

Whyte, William H., Jr. *The Organization Man.* New York: Simon & Schuster, 1956.

Zaleznick, Abraham. *The Human Dilemma of Leadership.* New York: Harper & Row, 1966.

INDEX